SAINT / OEDIPUS

SAINT / OEDIPUS

Psychocritical Approaches to Flaubert's Art

William J. Berg, Michel Grimaud,
and George Moskos

with an essay by JEAN-PAUL SARTRE
and a new translation of Flaubert's
Saint Julian by MICHEL GRIMAUD

CORNELL UNIVERSITY PRESS

Ithaca and London

CORNELL UNIVERSITY PRESS GRATEFULLY ACKNOWLEDGES
A GRANT FROM THE ANDREW W. MELLON FOUNDATION
THAT AIDED IN BRINGING THIS BOOK TO PUBLICATION.

First published 1982 by Cornell University Press.
Published in the United Kingdom by Cornell University Press Ltd.,
Ely House, 37 Dover Street, London W1X 4HQ.

International Standard Book Number 0-8014-1383-4
Library of Congress Catalog Card Number 81-17441
Printed in the United States of America
Librarians: Library of Congress cataloging information
appears on the last page of the book.

The paper in this book is acid-free, and meets the guidelines
for permanence and durability of the Committee on Production
Guidelines for Book Longevity of the Council on Library Resources.

Contents

6   Contents

Preface

The psycho*critical* method, as the word implies, lays heavier emphasis on literary criticism than do traditional "psychological" or "psychoanalytic" approaches. Rather than plunge immediately into abstract concepts or "hunt out" symbols in order to establish the validity of a given theory, psychocriticism uses the text as a constant point of departure, reference, and return, and considers textual elucidation as its primary objective. Although the psychocritic focuses initially on fine details, their obvious sense or intrinsic content is seen to be less important than the relationships constructed by their interplay with other elements of the text. Literary meaning is created by the connection, conjunction, and confrontation of various textual features, and the first task of the psychocritic is to uncover similarities (of words or images), discrepancies (contradictions or gaps), and other associational mechanisms within the text. According to Charles Mauron, "such an operation demands a mental effort comparable to that of free association—that is, the suspension of our critical judgment, but it is united with an effort of singular vigilance allowing us, in the process, to grasp certain coincidences which, normally, would go unnoticed or be

7

rejected."[1] Clusters of such "coincidences" point to significant segments and areas of the text, which are superimposed to reveal recurrent patterns and configurations. The text thus appears as a network of isomorphic data, a matrix of potential meanings, which we must "process" or "work through" in order to discover major groupings and, indeed, the overall structure of the text. Like any structuralist approach, the psychocritical "teaches the predominance of the system over the elements, and aims to define the structure of the system through the relationships among the elements."[2] It is at this point, where it will serve to summarize and crystallize rather than to bias the analysis, that a psychological approach can be brought to bear on the inquiry. The validity of that approach can be assessed by its capacity to account for the entirety of the data and to "fit" the whole of the text, including the intrinsic meanings, the overt content, and the manifest plot structure. This fit can also be examined in relation to the author's life and to other of his or her texts, but only as a final step in the psychocritical process.

These principles explain most of the unique features of this book: the experimental format, the relationship of the contributors to each other, the focus on Flaubert's *Saint Julian,* and the inclusion of a new translation of the text.

The Introduction to this book points out the recurrent patterns yielded by *Saint Julian* without undue imposition and interpretation by the critic. Many of these patterns have previously gone unnoticed, while others have long puzzled major Flaubert critics such as Benjamin F. Bart, Victor Brombert, and Jean-Paul Sartre. The Introduction then poses questions concerning the overall relationship among these patterns as well as

1. "Psychocriticism," trans. Barbara Blackbourn, *Sub-Stance,* no. 3 (1972), p. 54. Charles Mauron was the first to use the term "psychocriticism" and indeed to stress the fundamental role of textual analysis in the psychoanalytic approach to literature. In this respect our book is greatly indebted to him. However, Mauron's approach is primarily intertextual and targets the *author*'s psychology or that of his "corpus," while the approaches represented in this book, with the exception of Sartre's, focus on the individual text and the psychological impact of literary entities, such as *narrator* and *character,* on the *reader.* For a list of works by Mauron and a partial list of critical studies on him, see our Reader's Guide, section 11.

2. Emile Benveniste, *Problems in General Linguistics,* trans. Mary E. Meek (Coral Gables, Fla., 1971), p. 83.

their possible psychological significance and, following Freud's counsel, stresses the need for "more than a single interpretation."[3] Chapters 1 through 3, written by William J. Berg, George Moskos, and Michel Grimaud in direct collaboration and in response to the problems posed in the Introduction, represent individual readings of the story from different psychological frameworks. Chapter 1 examines specific aspects of *Saint Julian*—distance, fragmentation, duplication, reversal, and the narrator's presence—in relation to standard Freudian concepts such as repression, regression, condensation, and displacement. Chapter 2 elucidates the legend from a Jungian perspective, stressing such notions as individuation, the ego and the self, myth, and the collective unconscious. Chapter 3 relates various features of the Flaubert story—absence, denial of affect, avoidance of bodily contact, and the use of discourse—to the reading process, highlighting developments in contemporary psychoanalysis. Extensive reference to Jean-Paul Sartre's *L'Idiot de la famille*, a twenty-eight-hundred-page psychobiography of Flaubert's early years, led the authors to include here, in Chapter 4, pages which deal directly with *Saint Julian*. Sartre considers complementary psychological concepts such as ritual murder, incest, somatic compliance, reconciliation, and salvation, and his study adds the dimension of the *author*'s psychology to those of *narrator*, *character*, *text*, and *reader* which characterize the other chapters. Finally, the Conclusion sets our findings for *Saint Julian* and our continuous discussion of art in general into the context of Flaubert's other works and that of recent developments in psychoanalysis, such as those of Heinz Kohut and the Chicago school. Therefore, while this book does have a sharp focus, since it concentrates on one story by one author from one general type of approach, it also incorporates the various hypothetical "subjects" of analysis—author, narrator, character, text, and reader—from several psychological points of view—Freudian, Jungian, Kohutian, Sartrean. As with any book, problems of selection and length obliged us to exclude extensive reference to other psychoanalytic theorists. Notably

3. From *The Standard Edition of the Complete Psychological Works of Sigmund Freud*, trans. James Strachey et al., ed. James Strachey, 24 vols. (London, 1953–74), vol. IV (*Interpretation of Dreams*), p. 266.

absent, particularly in a book dealing with a French text, is the approach of Jacques Lacan, which has achieved a remarkable following in present-day France. Our emphasis on a diversity of theoretical assumptions and the primacy of concrete textual analysis led us to exclude Lacan, whose concepts are based on those of Freud and whose contributions to literary studies have been principally on the level of theory rather than of literary analysis. Moreover, we feel that the principles of psychocriticism, set forth and applied in this book, could serve as a framework for any psychological approach to textual analysis.

The diversity of our theoretical assumptions along with the primacy of concrete textual analysis in the psychocritical method explain the need to focus on a single work; but why *Saint Julian*? Why the curious coupling of Saint (Julian) with Oedipus (Rex) in the title of the book? And why include a new translation of the Flaubert story?

The myth of Saint Julian the Hospitaler (or Hospitator), adapted by Flaubert in 1877 but probably nurtured from as early as 1835, when Flaubert was only fourteen, has such unmistakable parallels with the Oedipus myth that even the most cautious critics have acknowledged them. Julian, like Oedipus, commits a ritual parricide which had been predicted; and the narrator of the Flaubert tale goes so far as to suggest that the murder may be the result of a hidden urge on Julian's part—" 'Still, supposing I wanted to?...' " (I, 72)[4]—which has caused several critics to speak of an "Oedipus complex" in the Flaubert story. If the Oedipal parallel, whether by myth or by complex, has provided an interesting perspective from which to judge *Saint Julian*, Flaubert's version of the tale develops dimensions which enrich our understanding of the Oedipus myth, particularly in the functioning of the displacements of Julian's desires and in his subsequent sainthood. These might be seen as a resolution of the Oedipus complex or, in another framework, as a redemption premised on Julian's struggle for individuation. In fact, while

4. All references to *The Legend of Saint Julian the Hospitaler* are based on the English version of the story included in this book. The roman numeral (I, II, or III) designates the *section* of the story, the arabic numeral the *paragraph*, where the quotation appears.

Oedipal notions constitute an important starting point and focal point for our book, in much the same way as does the *Saint Julian* text, discussion is by no means limited to this topic and ranges from repression, regression, and reconciliation to love, rage, and denial of affect, while passing through many major psychological questions along the way. Indeed, we are ultimately less interested in the general form of the Oedipus "complex" than in its particular modes of elaboration within a given literary text and an individual human mind. The psychocritical approach contends that this elaboration often occurs on the most concrete level of the text, emerging through the forms of expression as much as through the content; details such as punctuation and paragraphing can signal significant segments of the text and suggest relationships with other textual elements. Michel Grimaud's new translation of *Saint Julian* retains features of the original French story eliminated in all previous attempts at rendering the text into English. Furthermore, the numbering of the text by paragraph constitutes an internal reference system that is accurate and highly accessible to the reader.

The locus of this project lies in an area situated between psychology and literary criticism, between science and the humanities. The authors were not content with brief incursions into this zone, but have attempted to explore it and contribute to its eventual demarcation and mapping. It seemed to us that these tasks required data which were accurate and exhaustive as well as instruments which were precise and readily utilizable. These principles led us to include a new translation of *Saint Julian* and a comprehensive reader's guide to psychoanalysis; we cite extensively from these sources, define terms and describe techniques from both literary criticism and psychoanalysis. It is our hope that this book will facilitate access to the area between these fields, encourage exchange across their boundaries, and thus contribute to the interdisciplinary movement that provided the initial impetus for this project.

WILLIAM J. BERG

Madison, Wisconsin

Recurrent Patterns in Flaubert's *Saint Julian*

William J. Berg

••

A comparison of Flaubert's *The Legend of Saint Julian the Hospitaler* with the sources of the legend from which he is known to have borrowed—the stained-glass window of the Rouen cathedral, E.-H. Langlois' lengthy description of that window in his *Essai historique et descriptif sur la peinture sur verre*... (1832), and Jacques de Voragine's *La Légende dorée*, a thirteenth-century collection of saints' lives—reveals that Flaubert made substantial alterations and additions to the story. Nowhere is Julian's obsession with hunting and killing animals emphasized and dramatized to the extent which we find in Flaubert's version of the story.[1] The insistence on dreams, visions, and hallucinations

---

1. Another possible source, which does mention hunting, is a Bibliothèque Nationale manuscript referred to as the "Prose Tale" by its proponents—Sheila M. Smith, "Les Sources de 'La Légende de Saint Julien l'Hospitalier' de Gustave Flaubert," M.A. thesis (Manchester University, 1944); Eugène Vinaver, "Flaubert and the Legend of Saint Julian," *Bulletin of the John Rylands Library* (Manchester),

would seem to be entirely of Flaubert's invention. In all earlier versions of the legend Julian's wife accompanies him into exile, whereas Flaubert insists heavily, in this and in other episodes, on the saint's solitude. Julian's personal feelings and obsessions, which constitute the important psychological dimension of Flaubert's story, are completely absent in the versions he is known to have consulted and are only hinted at in the other possible sources.[2] Victor Brombert finds that "perhaps the most significant departure from the sources is Flaubert's insistence on Julien's family situation,"[3] while Benjamin F. Bart notes that "Flaubert made numerous additions to his medieval sources: the

---

36 (1953), pp. 228–244; and Colin Duckworth, ed., *Trois contes* (London, 1959). They base their argument on the connection in the Tale between Julian's cruelty to animals and his subsequent fate, which plays a major role in Flaubert's version of the legend. In a more recent reassessment of the question of sources, Alan W. Raitt ("The Composition of Flaubert's 'Saint Julien l'Hospitalier,'" *French Studies*, 19 [1965], 358–372) discounts this theory and embraces the notion, previously advanced by Jean Giraud ("La Genèse d'un chef-d'oeuvre: 'La Légende de Saint Julien l'Hospitalier,'" *Revue d'histoire littéraire de la France*, Jan.–March, 1919, pp. 87–93) and René Jasinski ("Sur le 'Saint Julien l'Hospitalier' de Flaubert," *Revue d'histoire de la philosophie*, April 15, 1935, pp. 156–172), that Flaubert may have read a modern adaptation of the tale by G. F. G. Lecointre-Dupont, "La Légende de Saint Julien le Pauvre, d'après un manuscrit de la Bibliothèque d'Alençon," in the *Mémoires de la Société des Antiquaires de l'Ouest* (Poitiers) for the year 1838, pp. 190–210. In neither case can the source be documented conclusively; in neither case would the source be more than a point of departure; and in no case can the suggestion or identification of a source furnish a response to the essential question: why was the author attracted to the source? Such a response can be best approached, however, by concentrating on Flaubert's own additions, which constitute his personal reactions to the legend; that is why the question of sources is not irrelevant and why I have decided to document Flaubert's deviations from earlier versions of the legend. For a definitive treatment of the question of sources, see Benjamin F. Bart and Robert F. Cook, *The Legendary Sources of Flaubert's "Saint Julien"* (Toronto, 1977).

2. Both Smith and Duckworth speak of the "psychological intensification" in Flaubert's tale, and even Raitt can agree with them on this point: "The fact that Miss Smith and Dr. Duckworth may be wrong about the version of the prose tale which Flaubert read in no way detracts from the validity of their conclusions about the alterations which he made in the original legend, especially in Julian's psychology" ("The Composition of Flaubert's 'Saint Julien,'" p. 272, n. 74).

3. *The Novels of Flaubert* (Princeton, 1966), p. 222. Note that the French spelling, Julien, appears in many of the quotations cited in this book, although in our own texts we have preferred to use the·English spelling, Julian.

scenes of Julien's childhood, the story of his wanderings, and in particular the accounts of Julien's two hunts."[4]

Certainly, as Bart suggests, the bulk and the most vivid of Flaubert's additions to the legend are dramatized in the three extended scenes that terminate each section of the story—the placement, like the use of dramatization, serving to signal their importance. In the first of these scenes, beginning with "One winter morning" (I, 50)[5] and running to the end of Part I (I, 84), Julian's massacre of various animals, particularly the stag who predicts that he will kill his father and mother, is dramatized. The second scene, beginning with "One evening in the month of August" (II, 27) and ending with the end of Part II (II, 85), depicts Julian's monumental failure in attempting to duplicate the slaughter of animals as well as his eventual (and predicted) killing of his parents in their stead.[6] In the third scene, beginning with "One night as he slept" (III, 22) and continuing to the end of the third and final part of the story (III, 57), Julian, having become a boatman in the service of others, embraces a leper who transforms himself into Christ and carries Julian to heaven.[7]

By deriving the characteristics common to these three scenes, the recurrent words, images, and patterns that bind them together, we can get a better idea of the overall structure of the story and its psychological significance for Flaubert.

Dreams

The atmosphere of all three scenes suggests a *dream*, vision, or hallucination. Flaubert accomplishes this effect in large part

4. "Psyche into Myth: Humanity and Animality in Flaubert's *Saint-Julien*," *Kentucky Romance Quarterly*, 20 (1973), 317.

5. All references to *The Legend of Saint Julian the Hospitaler*, in this chapter and in the following ones, are based on the English version of the story included in this book. The Roman numeral (I, II, or III) indicates the *section* of the story, the Arabic numeral the *paragraph*, where the quotation appears.

6. According to Duckworth, "there is no detailed description of the murder scene in any previous version" (*Trois contes*, p. 209).

7. In no source, verified or proposed, does Julian ascend directly to heaven with the leper (see Duckworth, *Trois contes*, p. 59).

through the rhythm of the scenes.[8] He also situates the events in the twilight zones of "morning... before daybreak" (I, 50), "evening" (II, 27), and "night" (III, 22) and further obscures them with doses of "haze" (I, 55 and 81), "fog" (I, 56 and III, 37), "shadows" (II, 27 and 53), and "darkness" (II, 54, 58, 73 and III, 29), which render the decor less precise, the perception of objects and events less certain. The improbable nature of the events described—the multitude of animals massacred in Part I, their complete invulnerability in Part II—particularly evident in Flaubert's additions to the original story matter, makes them seem more like hallucinations than like "real" scenes. In each of the three scenes there are also direct references to the uncertainty of Julian's perception, which tends to render their "reality" somewhat suspect: "He was hunting in some indeterminate land, for an indefinite time, solely because of his very existence, everything fulfilling itself with the ease which one experiences in dreams" (I, 56); "imagining he could see" (II, 53); "he imagined seeing" (II, 76); "he imagined hearing someone call him" (III, 22). Finally, the number of dreams and hallucinations which Flaubert identifies as such in the rest of the story affects the reader's evaluation of the three major scenes as well, particularly when there is an obvious *similarity*, as between the following, highly significant paragraph and the entire first scene:

> Sometimes, in a dream, he fancied himself like our father Adam in the midst of Paradise, among all the beasts; by extending his arm, he made them die; or else, they filed past, by pairs, in order of size, from the elephants and the lions to the ermines and the ducks, as on the day they entered Noah's ark. From the darkness of a cave, he aimed unerring javelins at them; others would appear; there was no end to it; and he awakened, wild-eyed. [II, 20]

---

8. Brombert (*The Novels of Flaubert*, p. 220) has noted that "a temporal unreality achieved through the rapid succession of tableaux such as occurs commonly in dreams is one of the characteristic features of this tale," which parallels Sartre's remark that "the story itself, in its rhythm, retains certain qualities of a nightmare: things appear and disappear suddenly, in the nick of time.... The massacres are dreams" (see Chapter 4, p. 193, of this book). Duckworth (*Trois contes*, p. 200) notes that "this dream-like sequence is entirely of Flaubert's invention."

In other instances it is the *contiguity* of a dream reference to a major scene which compels the reader to associate them, as is the case with the series of hallucinations directly preceding the third scene. When the narrator states, for instance, that "each night, in his dreams, he relived his parricide" (III, 8), the reader is invited to apply this knowledge to the final scene, the leper's visit, which begins with the words: "One night as he slept" (III, 22). Again, Julian's inability to distinguish reflection from reality in the following key scene influences our interpretation of the final scene as well:

> And one day as he happened to be at the edge of a spring, while he was stooping over it to judge the water's depth, there appeared before him a very emaciated man, with a white beard and of such piteous aspect that he found it impossible to hold back his tears. The other also wept. Without recognizing his face, Julian had a blurred recollection of features resembling it. He cried out; it was his father; and he gave up all thought of killing himself.
> [III, 13]

Indeed, in the words *immediately* preceding the final scene, the narrator insists on the fact that "the ghastly visions continued" (III, 21), the continuation seemingly becoming the final scene itself, the "ghastly visions" appearing to describe the leper.

Julian and Christ

Each scene also contains some association between Julian and *Christ*, particularly through the use of the crucifixion image. In the first scene, Julian, in his anxiety to kill a pair of mountain goats, trips on the body of the first and falls into a position quite like that of a crucified figure: "face downward above the abyss and both arms spread out" (I, 53). In the second scene, after having killed his parents, "he lay flat on his belly, in the middle of the entranceway, his arms spread out, and his forehead in the dust" (II, 84), a crucifixion image reinforced by further references to the cross (II, 58) and to Christ (II, 79) within the same scene. The final association in this series occurs when Julian, embracing the leper, "ascended toward the blue expanses, face to face with Our Lord Jesus, who was carrying him into the heavens" (III, 57). This important conclusion to the story had been prefigured early in the first section, when the narrator had noted that Julian "looked like a little Jesus" (I, 21).

The Stag, the Leper, and the Father

However, the most surprising, consistent, and significant of the linkings among the three scenes, never before pointed out, to my knowledge, involves a series of associations that link the physical appearance of the *stag* which Julian kills in the first scene and the *leper* of the third scene with that of Julian's *father*, particularly at the moment of his death in the second scene.

In the first of these scenes, when Flaubert describes Julian's killing of the deer, one notices that its family constellation—"a stag, a doe, and her fawn" (I, 63)[9]—is identical to Julian's. This association is reinforced by the appearance of the stag, who recalls Julian's father in several ways, the most evident of which are its "white beard" (I, 64)—mentioned prominently in the description of Julian's father in III, 13—and the fact that it is "of monstrous size" (I, 64), as is Julian's father (see II, 50). Flaubert reinforces this association directly when he compares the stag to "a patriarch" (I, 67) and indirectly in comparing it to "a justicer" (I, 67), since this is one of the very first qualities he mentions concerning Julian's father: "Always wrapped in a foxskin cape, he strolled about his estate, rendered justice among his vassals" (I, 9). The stag's death, of course, is directly associated with that of Julian's father by the stag's own prediction ("—'Accursed! accursed! accursed! One day, ferocious heart, thou shalt murder thy father and thy mother!'" I, 68) and by the stag's voice, which Julian hears at the moment when he strikes down his parents in the second scene: "Faint at first, this long-drawn, plaintive voice, drew nearer, grew louder, turned cruel; and he recognized with terror the bellowing of the great black stag" (II, 75). In addition, the "beard" common to Julian's father and the stag is mentioned twice in the parricide scene (II, 73 and 74), and his father's eye—"a lifeless eye that scorched him like fire"

---

9. "This 'family group' does not appear in any previous version" (Duckworth, *Trois contes*, p. 201).

(II, 79)—recalls rather specifically the "eyes aflame" (I, 67) of the stag just before its death.[10]

The description of the leper/Christ figure in the final scene of the story picks up many of these same points of association. The leper's eyes, like those of the stag and of Julian's father, are described as "redder than coals" (III, 31). The leper is said to have "a king's majesty" (III, 31), while Julian's parents possessed a "majestic softness" (II, 79) at the moment of their death. Julian's parents were "dressed in coarse linen" (II, 33), and the leper was "wrapped in coarse linen rags" (III, 31). The leper is "motionless as a column" (III, 35), whereas Julian's father "looked like a statue in a church" (II, 50). Julian must use a "torch" (II, 79) to perceive the murdered corpses of his parents, and it is "when he brought the lantern closer" (III, 31) that he is able to see the leper. Furthermore, the leper's rotting flesh strongly suggests that of a cadaver, as does Julian's vision of his father as a "very emaciated man" (III, 13), and several other aspects of the leper mark a direct association with a dead person: he is clothed in a "shroudlike garment" (III, 37), his body is compared to a "skeleton" (III, 37), his face to a "plaster mask" (III, 31). Finally, the "quickening death rattle" (III, 47) issued by the agonizing leper directly recalls the "two almost equal death rattles" (II, 75) of Julian's dying parents.

What, in fact, is the significance, the reason, for this astonishing association of the stag, the leper, and Julian's parents, particularly his father? What is the role of his mother—her relationship to the father and to Julian? How is the stag able to make such a prediction, particularly if he is a creature of Julian's own imagination rather than a "real" exterior figure endowed by God with predictive power and speech? Why does Julian enjoy killing animals so much? What does this desire stem from and what does it mean to him? Why does he fail to kill the animals in the second scene, particularly if this is his own dream? Why does Julian kill his parents, either in reality or in a dream? What

---

10. Michael Issacharoff (" 'Trois contes' et le problème de la non-linéarité," *Littérature*, 15 [1974], pp. 27–40), Bart ("Psyche into Myth," p. 321) and Brombert (*The Novels of Flaubert*, p. 229) all discuss the importance of eyes in *Saint Julian*. Brombert's interpretation is quoted in note 35 of Chapter 1.

is the significance of the leper, particularly if he is a creature conjured up by Julian during an hallucination? Why does Flaubert choose not to have Julian's wife accompany him into exile as in all the other versions of the legend? Where, if at all, does the Christ imagery fit into this puzzle?

"... more than a single interpretation"

The complexity of these questions reaches beyond the scope of traditional literary approaches and quite apparently in the direction of psychoanalytical criticism. The references to dreams, the psychological dimension created by Flaubert's additions to the legend, the parricidal (Oedipal) subject matter, push even the most reluctant reader toward Freud and his followers, as is verified by Victor Brombert's remark that "Freudian exegetes and symbol hunters could hardly hope to find a more rewarding document."[11] But the use of psychoanalysis in literary criticism has several major pitfalls, two of which are hinted at in Brombert's comment: First, there is the danger of approaching a literary work with a preconceived system and merely "hunting out" symbols that will establish the validity of the system rather than determining how the symbols function within the framework of the story. Second is the danger of calling all psychological criticism "Freudian" and refusing to take account of the variety of approaches and directions within psychoanalysis. Even the "Oedipus complex," at the very core, to be sure, of Freudian psychology, has been interpreted differently (and sometimes radically so) by all the major psychoanalysts—Jung, Adler, Rank, Fromm, Lacan, and Kohut, among others.[12] A third problem is to determine who or what—author, character, reader, or work—is being psychoanalyzed.

I hope to have minimized the first of these dangers—the distortion of the literary text which often accompanies the imposition of a preconceived system of analysis—by setting up the

---

11. *The Novels of Flaubert,* p. 229.
12. A useful work that capsulizes the theories of several major psychoanalysts and gives the references to those of their works which treat the Oedipus complex is Patrick Mullahy's *Oedipus/Myth and Complex* (New York, 1948).

problem initially, independently from any psychoanalytical "so-lution," and fairly objectively, insisting only on the structural patterns and associations which the text seems to yield without undue imposition and interpretation. The following chapters offer several solutions to the problem, by different critics repre-senting various psychological viewpoints—Freudian, Jungian, Kohutian, Sartrean, and others. There are also some dif-ferences of opinion concerning the delineation of the problem. Finally, each critic has had to define the subject of his inquiry and specify whose mind is being analyzed.

To those readers skeptical about the eclectic nature of such a format, we would address the following remark by Freud, which might also serve as a preamble for this book:

> But just as all neurotic symptoms, and, for that matter, dreams, are capable of being "over-interpreted" and indeed need to be, if they are to be fully understood, so all genuinely creative writings are the product of more than a single motive and more than a single impulse in the poet's mind, and are open to more than a single interpretation. [*Interpretation of Dreams*, IV, 266][13]

13. All references to Freud's works, in this and following chapters, are based on *The Standard Edition of the Complete Psychological Works of Sigmund Freud*, trans. James Strachey et al., ed. James Strachey, 24 vols. (London, 1953-74). Following the title of the individual work are a Roman numeral, indicating the *volume*, and an Arabic numeral, indicating the *page* in that volume where the quotation appears.

Essays

1

Displacement and Reversal in *Saint Julian*

William J. Berg

••

We must, at the outset, deal with two questions which have important methodological consequences for subsequent textual analysis: To what extent are the major scenes in *Saint Julian* analogous to dreams? And who or what is the subject of our analysis?

"Dream or Fact"?

As we saw in the Introduction, the narrator marks the major scenes in *Saint Julian*, those which terminate the three sections of the tale, as more akin to "dream" than to "reality." This strategy clearly influences the reader's approach to the text. We are encouraged to relax our defenses, to accept the rather unpalatable occurrences depicted in the scenes as figments of someone's imagination rather than as "real" events.[1] The narrator seems particularly bent on reorienting the reader of the 1870's, a period dominated by realism and naturalism, which posit the text as an imitation of external reality. Finally, in suggesting that these scenes are similar to dreams, the narrator signals them as mental projections with potential psychological value.

However, having accepted this orientation, the modern (post-Freudian) reader may still wonder whether the scenes can be analyzed or approached as dreams. Can the discoveries of dream theory and the techniques of dream analysis be applied to these passages? Certainly psychoanalysts as well as literary critics are fond of comparing the dream to literature, as evidenced by the quotation from Freud that ends our Introduction and by Norman Holland's statement that "the literary work dreams a dream for us."[2] Indeed, Freud's classic description of the dream as "a (disguised) fulfillment of a (suppressed or repressed) wish" (*Interpretation of Dreams*, IV, 160) can be profitably applied to literature and myth, where many of the early discoveries in psychoanalysis originated. Recent studies have also shown that an analogy can be drawn between the dream's mechanisms of disguise or transformation (the dream work) and literary processes such as metaphor and metonymy.[3] However, it is precisely in the *nature* and *extent* of the "disguise," in the *modes* of transformation, that the text emerges as a distinct object with its own pertinent properties. The first of these is suggested near the beginning of *Saint Julian*, in a remark attributed to Julian's mother. Since it corresponds with the first "hallucination" scene, it can be read as a metatextual comment,[4] one designed to

1. Norman Holland (following Coleridge) terms this type of reaction the "willing suspension of disbelief." See *The Dynamics of Literary Response* (New York, 1973), pp. 63–103.

2. *Ibid.*, p. 75.

3. The most influential, albeit controversial, of these has been Jacques Lacan's "L'Instance de la lettre dans l'inconscient," in his *Ecrits* (Paris, 1966). A translation of this essay appears in *Ecrits: A Selection*, trans. Alan Sheridan (New York, 1977).

4. The term "metatextual" stems from Roman Jacobson's description of the "metalingual" function of language, that is, where certain aspects of a given communication are designed to clarify the code being used (see his "Linguistics

orient the reader in all such subsequent scenes. Questioning the appearance of the old hermit who has predicted Julian's saint-hood, the mother concludes: "Whether dream or fact, this must be a message from heaven" (I, 15). Indeed the text itself is neither dream nor reality, it is a *message*, a coded communication transmitted from a sender (narrator) to a receiver (reader).[5] Un-like the dream, which is self-directed, the text involves a trans-mission which can be gratifying to both parties, independently from or at least in addition to the content (overt or covert) of the message. Furthermore, the medium of the message, the printed word, has its own properties—paragraphing, punctuation, con-nectors, typographical space, syntax, grammar, tropes—which cannot apply, except by analogy, to the dream, and these prop-erties entail their own means of encoding and decoding. Finally, the text has its particular type of organization or form,[6] some-times quite conventional and at any rate highly visible due to the fixed nature of the text, which contrasts with the fleeting quality of the dream.

In short, the text, like the dream, is a repository of elaborate and often disguised fantasies, a privileged realm which favors the dramatization of basic impulses and lays bare the fundamen-tal mechanisms and structures of the personality. As such, the

---

and Poetics," in *Style in Language*, ed. Thomas A. Sebeok [Cambridge, Mass., 1960], pp. 350–377). Several recent studies have extended this notion to self-commenting aspects of the literary text: see, for example, Jacques Dubois, "Code, texte, métatexte," *Littérature*, no. 12 (1973), pp. 3–11, and my "Crypto-graphie et communication dans *La Chartreuse de Parme*," *Stendhal Club*, 78 (1978), 170–182.

5. Although it might be interesting to approach the dream as a coded mes-sage transmitted from a sender (a source of desire) to a receiver (a conscious or preconscious system with a censoring agency), the visual and spatial nature of the dream, its immediacy, and the difficulty of identifying a sender (the dream seems to dream itself) render it substantially different from the text and gener-ally inaccessible by modes of textual analysis. However, when a dream is re-counted, whether orally or in writing, the very verbalization makes of it a text, requiring modes of analysis which are properly literary. This suggests the poten-tial value of studying literary processes for the psychoanalyst.

6. By "form" I mean those organizational principles which do not pertain to syntax (sentence structure) but to the overall composition of the text. These principles can range from the title of a work to its plot, from the rhyme scheme of a sonnet to the division of a play into acts or the use of letters in an epistolary novel.

text is a valuable psychological document, but it must be examined through its own modes—narration, linguistic detail and literary form; this is precisely what the psychocritical method proposes to do.

Having specified the *modes* of textual elaboration, we must now return to our second preliminary question and attempt to identify the *subject* of our analysis. In spite of my best efforts to remain neutral, I have frequently referred to "Julian" in terms similar to those one would use in speaking of a real person. It is imperative, therefore, that we begin our examination of this question by discussing the status of the literary character.

The Literary Character

The main character in a work of fiction marks the intersection of two lines of force. One is within the work and includes the narrator, other characters, relationships and situations; as Charles Mauron states, "the principal element of all drama is not the character, but the relationship set up between at least two figures—the dramatic situation."[7] A second line of force runs from the author[8] through the character to the reader (and back again), defining the process of reading, which, according to Holland, works in the following way: "The psychoanalytic theory of literature holds that the writer expresses and disguises childhood fantasies. The reader unconsciously elaborates the fantasy content of the literary work with his own versions of these fantasies. . . . And it is the management of these fantasies, both his own and the work's, that permits their partial gratification and gives literary pleasure."[9] In short, we are analyzing a series of relationships within the text and the process of reading

7. "Les Personnages de Victor Hugo: Etude psychocritique," in *Victor Hugo: Oeuvres complètes*, vol. II (Paris, 1967), p. ii.

8. By "author" I mean Gustave Flaubert (1821–1880). The "narrator" is the mode, voice, stance, or persona temporarily adopted by Flaubert for the sole purpose of telling a particular tale. The author cannot be directly present in the text any more than the narrator can exist outside of it. This chapter concentrates on the narrator (in addition to the character and the reader) and will not involve the author until the final pages.

9. *Dynamics*, p. 52.

"through" the text. When, then, I refer to "Julian," it is not as a real, autonomous person but as an economical reduction where the character stands for the entire fictional situation and the complex process of reading which encompass him. However, the convenience of this convention must not lead us to neglect the impact of the text on the *reader* nor the role of the *narrator*, whose psychological situation is, as we will see, sometimes more analogous to the author's and more fulfilling for the reader than the character's. Furthermore, we must remember that to bridge the gaps of time, space, and culture (not to mention personality) that separate author from reader, the relationships within the text must point to nearly universal psychological phenomena[10] and must be well marked. It is the task of the literary critic to uncover these markings, describe their mechanisms, and identify their psychological function, which is what we now propose to undertake for the first major scene, terminating Part I of *Saint Julian*, in which the stag predicts that Julian will kill his parents.

The Stag and the Father: Displacement

The numerous associations between the stag and Julian's father, detailed in the Introduction, would seem to indicate that the stag is indeed a "disguised" figure representing the father. But of interest here, as formerly stated, are the extent and modes of this disguise and its psychological functioning for Julian and/or the reader.

The disguise is effected by a process which, although involving large textual segments, is constructed precisely like a metaphor, that is, where two separate textual entities are compared through a series of common or overlapping features. It

10. It is for this reason that I have drawn much of my supporting material from Freud's theoretical and anthropological writings. I will also relate certain aspects of *Saint Julian* to Sartre's analysis of Flaubert in *L'Idiot de la famille*, 3 vols. (Paris, 1971–72). Most of Freud's and Sartre's remarks have been confined to footnotes, designed to demonstrate the "fit" of my analysis with their theories and to serve as an exposition of their basic tenets and terms. The reader who is already familiar with their thought may well want to skip many of these footnotes.

will prove helpful to our discussion to represent this process graphically, as in Figure 1:

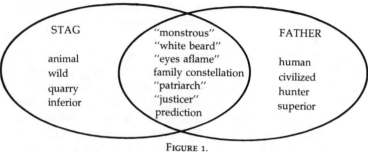

FIGURE 1.

The common features, which would be termed "grounds," "motivators," or "intermediaries" in rhetorical analysis,[11] are underscored by textual markings: In "The stag . . . bore sixteen points with a white beard" (I, 64) the "misplacement" of "beard" (which belongs with "stag," not "points") sets off this word, as does its position at the end of the sentence. The repetition of "like" in "solemn like a patriarch and like a justicer" (I, 67) serves to further reinforce these personifications. The expression "eyes aflame" (I, 67) is a metaphor, textual marker *par excellence*, since it introduces an alien context (flames) into this winter scene. It should also be noted that the reader is led to focus on the stag by the paragraphing, which makes "The stag" or "The great stag" the first and therefore foremost words in three of the four paragraphs directly preceding the "prediction."

However, though numerous, marked, and clustered, these features do not overwhelm the reader and can go unnoticed, as is indeed the case for most of the critics who have dealt with this text. In spite of the resemblance, the "disguise" remains effective. How and why does the narrator manage to keep these

11. The term "ground" comes from Ivor A. Richards (*The Philosophy of Rhetoric* [New York, 1965]), "motivator" from Gérard Genette (*Figures III* [Paris, 1972]), and "intermediary" from Jacques Dubois *et al.* (*Rhétorique générale* [Paris, 1970]). The graphic scheme of overlapping circles is borrowed from the latter work, whose authors are often referred to as the "Groupe MU" or "Groupe de Liège." These common features also correspond to Freud's notion of "fragments": "one form of the distortion which constitutes the dream-work is replacement by a fragment or an allusion" (*Introductory Lectures on Psycho-Analysis*, XV, 120).

associations unobtrusive? First of all, the remaining semantic features, those which do not overlap from stag to father, are highly differentiated and even opposite in terms of the thematic codes set up in the story (superior/inferior; hunter/quarry; civilized/ wild; human/animal). But of primary importance is the nature of the common features. Except for "patriarch," none is of a direct or conventional nature, which would allow the reader to make the association from outside the context of the story. And except for the "prediction," none of the remaining associations take place within this particular textual segment. Some depend upon the reader having gleaned details from earlier passages: the family configuration, the "justicer" (I, 9); while others will only be operative when reinforced in subsequent passages: "monstrous" (II, 50), "white beard" (II, 73–74), "eyes aflame" (II, 79).

Stretched out over the entire story, the common features are never obtrusive; the association is never explicit; the stag and the father are related but never equated. The features are sufficient to effect a shift or displacement from father to stag but sufficiently subtle to maintain the disguise. Of course, this is in keeping with the psychological content of the story. To kill the father, "the good lord," would be unthinkable for Julian, unpalatable for the reader, whose situation duplicates Julian's at this point in the story. The stag is a socially acceptable substitute upon whom Julian can unleash sanctioned violence. From the reader's standpoint as well as Julian's, the displacement allows for the pleasure of the hunt while avoiding the unconscionable realization of the motivation behind it. The stag, in announcing that Julian will kill his parents, is not only predicting a future event but is pointing out the actual state of events, what is really taking place on a covert level, behind the overt content of the massacre scene which we are witnessing.

In effect, the dream (for Julian) or the text (for the reader) is a meeting point of two opposed psychic systems—the unconscious, pushing basic desires toward realization, and a censoring mechanism that represses these desires, prohibits them even from reaching consciousness. It is precisely the distorting or disguising aspect of the text (or dream) which can resolve this conflict by creating figures and situations which are at once interesting to the unconscious desires and inoffensive to the censoring agency or "conscience."[12] In a sense, this "compromise" is effected by a sort of double delusion—the unconscious wish deluded by a substitute object (not the real object of its desires) and the censoring agency deluded because the real nature of the desire remains unstated.

The delusion is terminated, however, by the stag's prediction, which raises the desire to the consciousness of both Julian and the reader. And, in the following key passage, Julian is shown to be aware that his is indeed a *wish* ("supposing I wanted to") and not some arbitrary accident of fate:

> That night, he could not sleep. By the flicker of the hanging lamp, he pictured again and again the great black stag. Its prediction haunted him; he struggled against it. "No! no! no! I cannot murder them!" next, he would reflect: "Still, supposing I wanted to?..." and he feared that the Devil might instill the urge in him. [I, 72][13]

But if the nature of the wish is made explicit, the motives behind it remain unstated. Julian projects them onto the Devil, the foremost scapegoat in Christendom, and the "celebrated leeches" later attribute Julian's illness to an equally vague "baleful wind" or "desire for love" (I, 73). No clear statement of motive is made, and indeed this is hardly surprising due to the reprehensible nature of the desire. The task of unearthing this covert motivation falls to the critic and is among the most interesting, most pertinent,[14] and most intricate of all literary problems. How can it be approached?

12. This is not to say that all displacement takes the form of a disguise or defense against an illicit fantasy. Displacement may simply involve a shift from one element or level of the text to another without "hiding" the former. Note also that in order to fully understand the text the "initiated" reader must effect a displacement from stag to father, that is, in the opposite direction from Julian's. In effect, the reader duplicates but reverses Julian's situation, a process that will be examined throughout this study.

13. Colin Duckworth, ed., *Trois contes* (London, 1959), p. 202, suggests of this passage that "Julian is now obsessed by two fears: the fear common to all the Julians, that he might kill his parents accidentally, and a Freudian fear *avant la lettre* (analogous to the Oedipus Complex) that even though he finds the idea consciously horrifying, he might feel a desire to commit such an act."

14. "Pertinent" because, while most major psychoanalysts (Freud, Rank, Adler, Jung, Fromm, Lacan, *et al.*) acknowledge the notion of an Oedipus complex or rivalry between son and father, not all agree with Freud that motivation lies in the Incest-Motif or desire to possess the mother (see note 30).

Reading Strategies

In addressing the question of *why* Julian (the author? the reader?) might want to murder his parents, several psychological tactics seem possible. Five will be outlined here in order to set apart two which are, properly speaking, "psychocritical" strategies:

(1) One approach, which we might term "universalist" or "psychoanthropological," involves the application of general principles to the particular case. Julian desires as he does because all men do; he is simply acting out a universal fantasy, corresponding to the Oedipus complex, the motivational core of which is the Incest-Motif, an erotic attachment to and desire for the mother. An appropriate passage from Freud could be cited in evidence: "the boy's sexual wishes in regard to his mother become more intense and his father is perceived as an obstacle to them; from this the Oedipus complex originates. His identification with his father then takes on a hostile colouring and changes into a wish to get rid of his father in order to take his place with his mother" (*The Ego and the Id*, XIX, 32). Thus Julian wants to slay his father in order to possess his mother. Furthermore, such wishes are especially evident in dreams and, by extension, in texts purporting to be dreams:

> In the son's eyes his father embodies every unwillingly tolerated social restraint; his father prevents him from exercising his will, from early sexual pleasure and, where there is common property in the family, from enjoying it. . . .
> There is no need to feel surprised, therefore, if, in a large number of people, dreams disclose their wish to get rid of their parents and especially the parent of their own sex. We may assume that this wish is also present in waking life and is even conscious sometimes, if it can be masked by some other motive. [*Introductory Lectures*, XV, 206]

We could even account for the precise symbolism of Julian's disguised fantasy, the animal replacing the father, by citing from Freud's anthropological writings:

> Psycho-analysis has revealed that the totem animal is in reality a substitute for the father; and this tallies with the contradictory fact that, though the killing of the animal is as a rule forbidden, yet its killing becomes a festive occasion—with the fact that it is killed yet mourned. The ambivalent emotional attitude, which to

this day characterizes the father complex in our children and
which often persists into adult life, seems to extend to the totem
animal in its capacity as substitute for the father. [*Totem and
Taboo*, XIII, 141]

In fact, citing the above passage could have spared us the
painstaking task of tracing the associations between the stag and
Julian's father within the text. But this points precisely to the
danger of a "universalist" approach: reference to the general
text from Freud would have substituted for analysis of the particular text by Flaubert. We would not have uncovered the
modes of elaboration peculiar to Flaubert nor have examined
such questions as how the post-primitive reader, having lost
contact with the original symbol, could make the stag-father
connection in *Saint Julian*. Moreover, concerning Julian's
motivation, we would be assuming that Freud is correct about
the Incest-Motif, an assumption which by no means all psychoanalysts are willing to grant. We would have lost the opportunity
of discovering what this particular text might add to our understanding of literary and psychological mechanisms.

Certainly the use of general psychoanalytic theory has a valid
role in literary criticism. The citations illustrate and summarize
the system for the uninitiated reader, which is indeed the intent
of our footnotes. The aptness of the theoretical statement can
also assist in validating the system, though this hardly seems
necessary in Freud's case. Rather, the "fit" of theory to text can
serve to support our analysis. However, it must not substitute
for analysis, and we must look elsewhere for an approach to the
question of Julian's motivation and its particular modes of elaboration in Flaubert's text.

(2) A second approach, somewhat less general, might be
called the "psychobiographical"; here we would attempt to explain Julian's behavior in terms of Flaubert's. Julian is simply
acting out one of the author's favorite fantasies, which Sartre,
for example, does indeed find to revolve around the wish to do
away with the father. In *L'Idiot de la famille*, Sartre describes the
"semi-feudal practice" of Flaubert's father and Gustave's exclu-
sion from the family scheme, which make of him the "family
idiot." He concludes that "the essential aspect of living, for the
child, then for the young man, must be seen as a discourse

which is aimed at the father but cannot be spoken" (p. 1883). Sartre states that "the *death of the father* is among the fantasies which he caresses most willingly" (p. 464) and finds traces of the ritual murder of the father beginning with Flaubert's earliest literary efforts—*Passion et vertu, Quidquid Volueris, La Peste à Florence, Les Funérailles du Docteur Mathurin,* and others—and culminating with *Saint Julian,* which, although written in 1875, was conceived as early as 1845.[15] Sartre is particularly interested in the Oedipal aspects of Flaubert's famous but mysterious illness (often thought to be epilepsy) and entitles one section, a portion of which is included in Chapter 4 of this book, "Flaubert's Ailment as 'Murder of the Father'" (pp. 1883–1920). Thus Julian can be said to slay his father so that Flaubert can symbolically slay his own.

Using Sartre in this way would, as with Freud, summarize his thought and, by its "fit," validate our analysis of *Saint Julian.* But once again the text would be left behind, since the demonstration lies outside of it. We should stress, however, that we are speaking here about the temptation to use aspects of Flaubert's biography or a psychological study of Flaubert to explain Julian, not about Sartre's method itself. As the reader will observe in Chapter 4, Sartre's psychological conclusions are based on close textual analysis, and his approach is thus primarily "psychocritical."

(3) Another approach, which Norman Holland calls "psychoanalytic," will posit a hypothesis derived from psychoanalysis, then attempt to verify it through the details of the text.[16] One could assume, for example, that the notion of the Incest-Motif is correct, but here the assumption must be confirmed by textual evidence. Let us return to the text in question, the final scene in Part I of *Saint Julian,* where Julian slays the great stag, but we will focus this time on the doe. She is indeed

15. In fact, one study, unknown to Sartre—Alan W. Raitt, "The Composition of Flaubert's 'Saint Julien l'Hospitalier,'" *French Studies,* 19 (1965), 358–372—has shown convincingly that Flaubert may have conceived the idea for *Saint Julian* as early as 1835.

16. "Psychoanalysis seeks out those roots [of our pleasure in literature] by looking in literary works not so much for a central 'point,' as for a central fantasy or daydream, familiar from couch or clinic, particular manifestations of which occur all through the text" (*Dynamics,* p. 7).

referred to as a "mother" (I, 65), an association even more direct than that of the stag with a "patriarch." Her voice is described as "human" and "rending" (I, 65), whereas Julian's mother (human) utters a "rending scream" (I, 82) later in this very scene. While Julian's mother had been characterized as "very white" (I, 10), the doe is "blond like dead leaves" (I, 64). The comparison not only highlights the mother/doe association, but it introduces a detail which will reappear later as the material of Julian's bed (III, 19).[17] Furthermore, the family ties between the doe and the fawn are depicted as tighter than those with the stag, largely through the use of possessive adjectives. Julian first sees "a stag, a doe, and her fawn" (I, 63), and the doe is later referred to as "its mother" (I, 65). The fawn is also in the very intimate act of nursing from the doe: ". . . and the spotted fawn, without hindering her progress, sucked at her dug" (I, 64). This could be read as a projection of Julian's desire for his own mother's breast and attention, as could the fact that the mother's cry is caused by the death of the fawn. The killing of the doe could be seen as an act of possession with possible sexual overtones, as suggested by the narrator's word choice as Julian "laid her down on the ground" (I, 65).[18] After the killing, even because of it, Julian does manage, through his illness, to get his mother to his bed ("For three months, his mother in anguish prayed at his bedside," I, 73) while keeping his father at a distance ("and his father, moaning, continually paced the halls," I, 73). Finally, Julian's two "lapses" at the very end of Part I can be read from the perspective of rivalry and incest. Julian's father gives him "a large Saracen sword" (I, 76), which, when referred to as a "bare blade" (I, 78), doubles the opportunity for seeing it as a "phallic symbol," and with which Julian nearly kills his father by "accident." At that point Julian switches to a javelin, a weapon more in keeping with his boyish means: "He could send his [javelin]

17. All the occurrences of dead leaves in *Saint Julian* are traced and studied in Chapter 3, pp. 161–162.
18. This reading of a second sense into "laid," although highly suggestive, seems less solid than a "psychocritical" reading, which would link it to other crucial occurrences of the same word within the text; for example, "His father and his mother lay before him, on their backs, with a hole in their breasts" (II, 79).

into the neck of a bottle, break the teeth of a weather vane" (I, 80). Here "neck" and "teeth" seem to hint at an oral fantasy, perhaps related to the earlier nursing, while the penetration of the bottle might further suggest a desire for the mother. Finally (I, 83), Julian "nails" the mother's bonnet, which was "white" (like the mother) and which he took for a stork (where babies come from). In short, if we assume this particular type of reading stance, it is difficult not to read the final actions of Part I as sexual gestures revealing the motivation behind Julian's wish to do away with his father.

Such an approach does involve textual analysis, and, in the hands of a master like Holland,[19] it can be extremely revealing. However, the potential danger (as the reader will no doubt already have perceived by *my* attempt) lies in distorting the text to fit the initial hypothesis and in hunting out "symbols" which may establish the validity of the hypothesis, but at the expense of elucidating the text. In the above "analysis," for example, we avoided the fact that the doe is generally associated with the stag, as is Julian's mother with his father. The male/female roles appear to be similar, certainly not as different as the Oedipal configuration with the accompanying Incest-Motif would have it. Besides, a cigar, as Freud was fond of saying, is sometimes only a cigar, and the same could presumably hold true for Julian's javelin. We need an approach which not only returns to the text but makes it the *point of departure*, which not only tests hypotheses but *generates* them. The psychocritical is such an approach, and we will examine two forms of it here.

(4) The first type of psychocritical approach involves a purely internal reading of the text, concentrating on those modes which are properly literary—narration, linguistic detail, and form. No *prior* hypothesis is formulated;[20] rather, the text is

19. This is not to imply that Holland would stop here; he is primarily interested in the reader's re-enactment and management of those fantasies embodied in the literary text.
20. Of course, one cannot (and should not) approach a text without prior ideas and beliefs. Our discussion is naturally slanted by the fact that we are looking for *psychological motivation*. However, the critic can reduce bias by avoiding prior hypotheses, by continuously questioning those generated by the text, and by attempting to articulate the principles of his or her methodology as clearly as possible.

considered as a matrix of *possible* meanings which the critic must "process" or "work through" in order to uncover recurrent patterns and then assess their psychological significance.

In this final scene from Part I, however, the reader is immediately and quite thoroughly frustrated in attempting to determine Julian's motivation. But at least we can describe the narrator's means of withholding this information and generate several hypotheses concerning the psychological function of this very lack of explanation.

We note at once that the narrator portrays Julian as totally unaware of his own motives: he contemplates the massacred animals, "not understanding how he might have done it" (I, 62). The narrator further indicates that Julian "thought of nothing, remembered naught" (I, 56). When emotion is attributed to him—"The prospect of so great a carnage, for a few minutes, made him choke with pleasure" (I, 57)—it is the future hope, not the event itself, that affects him. Julian is depicted as completely remote from himself and his surroundings. He is the subject of perception verbs only five times—"he saw" (used three times), "wide-eyed, he gazed" (I, 62), "he pictured again" (I, 72)—all of them pertaining to vision, the least immediate of the senses. Some limited contact with a few small animals is suggested at the very beginning of the scene, and some key sounds appear at the end, where their rareness serves to highlight the importance of the stag's prediction, the accompanying bell, and the mother's "rending scream." But by and large the narrator insists on the *distance* between Julian and the other elements of the scene, which are "at the far end" (I, 53), "far away" (I, 55), "despite the distance" (I, 55), "on the opposite side" (I, 63) or "at a hundred paces" (I, 80). Furthermore, this distance grows progressively greater during the scene; Julian initially kills with sword, knife, or whip, later by arrow. And, if Julian is only semi-conscious throughout most of the scene, he is totally estranged during his three months of illness. Finally, the near killing of the father makes him lose consciousness altogether ("fainted," I, 77), while that of his mother causes him to disappear completely ("was seen no more," I, 84).

The narrative techniques deployed in the scene not only underscore Julian's distance from his surroundings but duplicate that same distance between the reader and Julian. The paucity of discourse—direct, indirect, or free indirect—deny us contact with Julian. The use of the past tense, particularly the past definite, also holds the reader at a great temporal distance. When we do shift to direct discourse and the present (or future) tense with the stag's prediction and Julian's self-query, these events acquire an enormous impact due to their very directness in an otherwise remote and distant scene. They emerge as forcefully for the reader as they are meant to for Julian.

Paragraphing, punctuation, sentence structure, and grammar are also mobilized to reinforce and recreate this predominant sense of distance for the reader. For example, Julian is the subject of the first sentence of the scene—"One winter morning, he set out" (I, 50)—and the reader expects to follow him on his adventures. By shifting immediately to a new paragraph and focusing on the dogs' actions—"His Danish jennet, with two basset hounds close behind, under its even tread made the ground ring" (I, 51)—the narrator thwarts the reader's expectations and moves us away from Julian, just as the character is removed from the center of the scene. The use of an impersonal pronoun and the plural indefinite article in I, 56 also add to the remoteness of the scene.[21] Making the weapon, rather than Julian, the subject of several sentences—"an arrow hit it" (I, 55), "The crossbow again twanged" (I, 65)—seems to distance the actions from Julian, remove them from his control. The impersonal reflexive construction ("Il se fit"), rendered in English by "Gaps appeared in their mass" (I, 58), makes the events self-accomplishing, diminishes Julian's role. However, the most consistent technique, adopted throughout the entire scene, involves the use of sentence structure and paragraphing to separate Julian, typographically, from his victims and to isolate cause from effect. For example: "Julian aimed, shot; and the arrows fell like shafts of rain in a storm. Maddened with terror the stags

---

21. It is often impossible or undesirable to translate a given part of speech by its counterpart in English. The passive construction "could be seen" is not an impersonal pronoun, although it does successfully capture the impersonal flavor of the French expression ("on voyait"). For a discussion of this type of translation problem and the various solutions adopted in this book, see "Poetics and Translation," pp. 256–267.

fought" (I, 59). Here the action ("Julian aimed, shot") is separated
from the agent ("arrows fell") by a semicolon and from the effect
("Maddened with terror the stags fought") by a period and a
new sentence. A more usual or "causal" structure might be
"Julian shot arrows which fell on the stags," and indeed we
encounter this type of sentence structure earlier in the scene,
when Julian's contact is more direct: "Julian, with a sweep of the
sword, cut off both its feet" (I, 52). In short, as Julian grows
progressively distant from objects and events, as he steadily
loses control, even consciousness, this separation is mirrored
grammatically, accomplishing the same effect in the reader. The
structure described above is prevalent from clause to clause,
from sentence to sentence, and especially from paragraph to
paragraph. Julian launches an arrow at the end of one paragraph
("he... began shooting," I, 57), but its effect is not felt until the
following paragraph ("With the whistling of the first arrow, all
the stags turned their heads simultaneously," I, 58), from which
Julian is totally absent. This same separation of cause from effect, of Julian from his milieu, of reader from Julian, is particularly evident in the final sentences (in separate paragraphs) of
Part I:

> He did not doubt but that it was a stork; and he threw his javelin.
> A rending scream rang out.
> It was his mother, whose cap and long streamers remained
> nailed to the wall.
> Julian fled from the castle, and was seen no more. [I, 81–84]

Again Julian's action ("he threw his javelin") is separated from
its effect ("A rending scream rang out"), itself isolated from its
source ("his mother") and in turn creating an effect ("Julian
fled"), which is removed to another paragraph.[22]

In short, throughout this scene Julian is depicted as distant
from his surroundings, even from himself, and this distance is
underscored by the sentence structure and paragraphing. Furthermore, the reader is held at a parallel distance from Julian by
the lack of information and customary means of obtaining it

---

22. Note also the use of commas to augment the feeling of distance from
clause to clause in the last two sentences.

(interior monologue, direct speech, and the like) as well as by the paragraphing, which at times shifts our focus away from Julian just when he begins to interest us. The entire scene is thus characterized by a separation of entities, a fragmenting of experience, a rupture of causal sequence.

What are the possible psychological meanings behind these techniques? What might they imply in terms of Julian's motivation or of the reader's reaction? The lack of information and accompanying distance suggest the extent of Julian's repression and thus the reprehensible nature of the motives and their power.[23] Further, the isolation, the alienation, the absence of direct contact might be read as the source of Julian's psychological problems. In this sense the nursing fawn could express a desire, its killing jealousy on Julian's part.[24] On the other hand, the fawn, Julian's avatar in this scene, is portrayed in a thoroughly *dependent* position, nursing from the mother and following in her steps, while the stag's "monstrous size" (I, 64) and repeated designation as "the great stag" (I, 66, 67, 72) seem to suggest Julian's own sense of *smallness*. Perhaps this state of dependence and weakness could be seen as the source of Julian's resentment and consequent need for vengeance.

But these hypotheses, generated from within the text, must also be tested from within the text, and the means of testing are removed by the very distance which we have just discussed. It is at this point that an overlapping but nonetheless distinct type of psychocritical strategy can be introduced.

(5) The second psychocritical approach involves the connection and comparison of the scene in question with other scenes where motivation may be more apparent and assumed to be operative, though obscured, in the initial scene. In the preceding discussion we remained *within* the final hunt scene from

---

23. Freud's analysis of distortion can also be applied to repression: "dream-distortion is proportionate to two factors. On the one hand it becomes greater the worse the wish that has to be censored; but on the other hand it also becomes greater the more severe the demands of the censorship at the moment" (*Introductory Lectures*, XV, 143). Thus it can be said that sometimes the *less* we see of something the *more* it may be assumed to be important.
24. See Chapter 3 for a discussion of the significance of nursing in *Saint Julian*.

Part I and concentrated on individual features (such as verb tenses and parts of speech) or their relationships with neighboring or contiguous features (as with sentence structure and paragraphing). Here textual elements are related to others *outside* the given scene, primarily on the basis of similarity. Interpretation is based on the juxtaposition and superimposition of separate textual segments. Mauron compares such a technique with "free association,"[25] but in Flaubert's case the reader's reactions seem rather well controlled by the narrator's suggestions. A clustering of similar, well-marked features leads us to associate two texts in much the same way that the overlapping of features led us to associate the stag with Julian's father. In the hunt scene, for example, a series of architectural comparisons are drawn directly from the description of Julian's castle at the very beginning of the tale: "a long, wall-like rock" (I, 53) recalls "the base of the walls rested upon the blocks of rock" (I, 2); "a frigid lake, which looked like lead" (I, 55) suggests the "lead scales" (I, 2) covering the castle's roofs; while the "enclosure" (I, 59) where the deer are trapped mirrors the "enclosure, made with stakes" (I, 4) of the castle. The sky "red like a sheet of blood" (I, 61) points the reader toward the chapel, for which the mother "embroidered altar cloths" (I, 10),[26] and this religious association is further reinforced by the tolling of the bell which accompanies the stag's prediction. Furthermore, the motif of killing animals harkens back to Julian's first killing, which indeed occurred in the chapel of the castle, and it is to this episode that the reader is led, by "controlled association,"[27] for possible information concerning the source of Julian's parricidal wish. It should be noted that it is not only in retrospect that this episode stands out; it strikes the reader the first time through the text, since it is the first specific event which is portrayed from Julian's life.

The reader will recall that Julian spies a mouse in church and

25. "Psychocriticism," trans. Barbara Blackbourn, *Sub-Stance*, no. 3 (1972), p. 54. For the full quotation see our Preface at note 1.

26. The French word "nappe" translates as both "sheet" and (altar) "cloth" and can also mean (deer's) "hide." On the difficulty of adequately translating this word, see "Poetics and Translation" in Part II of this book.

27. Indeed the extent of control is indicated by the fact that each of our four chapters deals with this scene, although from different perspectives.

registers more emotion over its presence than during the entire long hunt scene: "the idea of seeing the mouse again worried him" (I, 28); "he . . . was annoyed by it, felt hatred toward it, and resolved to do away with it" (I, 28). But what is the source of this irritation and of the immense pleasure obtained through killing the mouse?[28] Here we must look at the short paragraph immediately preceding the killing, remembering that in literature two *contiguous* clauses, sentences, or paragraphs will often be read as *causal* (witness the final four paragraphs of Part I).[29] In a single sentence the narrator gives us a complete picture of Julian's life and relationship to his parents: "His seat in the chapel was next to his parents; and, no matter how long the services lasted, he remained kneeling on his prayer stool, his cap on the floor and his hands folded" (I, 27). His world is ordered ("His seat"); his role is subordinate ("next to his parents"); his life boring ("no matter how long the services lasted"). He is submissive ("he remained kneeling"); he is dominated by taboo ("his cap on the floor") and restraint ("hands folded"), a detail which may also suggest a lack of power. He is motionless, speechless, and sightless (his head is lowered, as we learn when he raises it in the next paragraph). In short, this is a portrait of total dependence and inferiority. In this context, it is precisely the mobility of the mouse ("it trotted"), its freedom to go ("ran back") and come ("it returned"), its disregard for taboo ("on the first altar step," I, 28), which troubles Julian by making him conscious of his own weakness. His rage is at once an expression of self-hatred caused by his own sense of inferiority and a manifestation of revolt against the parental authority that binds him. Julian counters this situation by finding a victim smaller than himself—the word "little" is repeated twice: "a

28. The narrator illustrates this pleasure in the episodes immediately following this one, but it is interesting to note, from the perspective of withholding information, that the following direct comment, originally placed at the end of this episode, was later removed by Flaubert: "This act had given him immense pleasure. He wanted to begin it again" (given in *Flaubert, Oeuvres,* ed. Albert Thibaudet and René Dumesnil [Paris, 1952], II, 1049).

29. At this point we return to the first mode of psychocritical reading (internal analysis) before proceeding again to the comparison of separate textual segments. The two approaches, separated for the purposes of exposition and theoretical discussion, are inseparable in practice.

little... mouse" (I, 28) and "this little body" (I, 30)—and by duplicating the very configuration of submission and dependence in which he is enmeshed. He entraps the mouse ("having closed the door," I, 29), renders it dependent on him ("scattered some cake crumbs on the step," I, 29) and finally immobile ("no longer moved," I, 30). In so doing, Julian acquires a measure of masculine power through strategy ("he stationed himself in front of the hole," I, 29), bearing arms ("a stick in his hand," I, 29), and action ("he struck lightly," I, 30). In short, by *duplicating* then *reversing* the very scheme of superiority/inferiority that holds him, Julian is able to assert himself. The killing of animals is a way to achieve power with all the modes that infantile inferiority imposes: size, strength, freedom, mobility, and independence. Does this scheme and its attendant modes provide a clue to Julian's motivation in the larger hunt scene?

Certainly several comparisons in the later scene mark it as a proving ground of ritual combat. When Julian approached the forest, "he entered an avenue of tall trees, the tops of which seemed to form a triumphal arch" (I, 56), and later the stags occupy a valley "shaped like an arena" (I, 56). The animals are typically seen as weak ("They circled around him, trembling, with a meek and beseeching look in their eyes," I, 56), entrapped ("They leaped around the enclosure, trying to escape," I, 59), too small ("The rim of the valley was too high to climb," I, 59), and dependent, as we saw with the fawn. Julian kills the fawn, a reminder of his own weakness; he imposes silence on the doe, immobility on the herd ("Then all was still," I, 60), and submission on the stag ("He sank to his knees," I, 69). Weakness, silence, immobility, and submission were the very qualities used in the earlier chapel scene to suggest Julian's inferior situation.

May we not strengthen, if not yet confirm, our hypothesis that the motivation behind Julian's Oedipal desires are not all that "complex." His family situation is shown to be one of exaggerated dependence and weakness, imposed by rigid restraint. Killing animals appears as a means of duplicating this scheme yet reversing it so that Julian ends up on top. By perpetuating the pattern but exchanging the animals for himself, himself for his parents, Julian is able to achieve their power and superiority.[30] This reading would also account for the association of the two parents as co-holders of power and authority; the mother here seems less an object of sexual desire than a second authority figure toward whom Julian feels inferior and thus resentful.

Furthermore, as the animals grow progressively larger, within this scene and throughout the tale, they come also to represent the parents, the power figures themselves. That is, the parents, whom Julian has replaced in the power scheme, are now associated with the animals, who have replaced Julian on the bottom. The *displacements* from father to stag and mother to doe complete the *reversal* of Julian's situation, as in Figure 2.

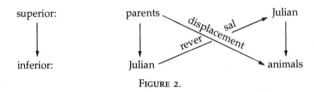

FIGURE 2.

However, it is this second symbolic dimension of the animals—who initially represented only Julian's own inferiority but who have come also to represent its cause, the parents—which ultimately leads to the failure of the hunt to procure psychic satisfaction, to lend Julian a sense of superiority. In fact, at the end of Part I, Julian is portrayed as weaker ("This weakness," I, 78), more immobile (three months in bed), more dependent ("he was taken on strolls in the courtyard, the old monk and the good lord each holding him up on one side," I,

---

30. This reading of the motivation behind Julian's Oedipal desires might be substantiated by psychologists such as Alfred Adler and Erich Fromm. "A proper insight for instance into the 'Oedipus complex' shows us that it is nothing more nor less than a figurative, sexually clothed conception of what constitutes masculine self-consciousness, superiority over women" (Adler, *The Neurotic Constitution*, trans. Barbara Glueck and John Lind [New York, 1926], p. 64). "The child's natural reaction to the pressure of parental authority is rebellion, which is the essence of Freud's 'Oedipus complex.' Freud thought that, say, the little boy, because of his sexual desire for his mother, becomes the rival of his father.... In my opinion, however, this conflict is not brought about primarily by the sexual rivalry but results from the child's reaction to the pressure of parental authority, which in itself is an intrinsic part of patriarchal society" (Fromm, *Man for Himself* [New York, 1947], p. 161).

74), more childlike ("he wept for a long time," I, 70), and more insecure ("forsaken," I, 71) than at any other point represented in the story. He seems to have regressed, to have failed in his psychic growth, and his failure is depicted in the very terms used to represent his initial problem. Why does this failure occur? Here, for once, the text leaves little doubt: it is directly related to the stag's prediction, which, as we saw earlier, simply raises to consciousness the motives lying behind the killing of the animals. The disguise is ended, the mask is down, and the displacement effected by the animals can no longer take place. And, as the displacement fails, so too does the reversal which it supports. Julian is abruptly returned to his initial subordinate position. But this hypothesis of a breakdown in the displacement mechanism, as well as that concerning Julian's motivation—the reversal of a superiority/inferiority scheme—remain to be further tested and clarified in Part II.

The Death of the Father: Replacement

When we again encounter Julian, in Part II, he seems fully recovered and pursuing the very pattern just described, that is, establishing his superiority through slaying. Having abandoned animals, he takes on monsters—the serpent of Milan and the dragon of Oberbirbach (II, 8)—along with a list of progressively more powerful figures, from fourteen horsemen (II, 3) to the Caliph of Cordova (II, 9). Their defeat also procures the dependence of a series of progressively more powerful personnages, beginning with "clergy, orphans, widows, and foremost the aged" (II, 4), and extending all the way up to the Emperor of Occitania (II, 9), who rewards him with his own daughter, whose silence and submissiveness would also seem to fulfill Julian's desire for adult superiority. She is depicted as "crouching in front of his feet... clasped hands" and addresses him as "dear lord" (II, 23), again duplicating and reversing Julian's earlier situation. In short, in terms of our hypothetical scheme, Julian seems to have reached the pinnacle of success and superiority, and yet he is not satisfied. An unfulfilled desire persists throughout the second section of the tale: "his other urge was growing unbearable" (II, 21); "Julian... could not bring himself to yield to this urge" (II, 26); and finally: "Temptation was too strong" (II, 27). Furthermore, this desire, indicated by the conditional past tense in the following passage, is clearly linked to hunting animals: "Dressed in crimson, he leaned on his elbows in the recess of a window, recalling his past hunts; and he longed to scour the desert after gazelles and ostriches, ... to reach the most inaccessible peaks" (II, 19). In spite of his regal situation ("Dressed in crimson"), Julian is again shown as immobile ("he leaned on his elbows") and closed in ("in the recess of a window"), while his desire takes the opposite form: mobility ("scour") and domination ("to reach the most inaccessible peaks") through hunting. In fact, killing animals constitutes Julian's supreme desire, as is revealed in the following key passage:

> Sometimes, in a dream, he fancied himself like our father Adam in the midst of Paradise, among all the beasts; by extending his arm, he made them die; or else, they filed past, by pairs, in order of size, from the elephants and the lions to the ermines and the ducks, as on the day they entered Noah's ark. From the darkness of a cave, he aimed unerring javelins at them; others would appear; there was no end to it; and he awakened, wild-eyed. [II, 20]

The passage illustrates several important points concerning Julian's motivation. First, it may appear surprising that Julian, having killed many human victims, who are more similar to the real target, the parents, than are animals, remains obsessed with killing the latter. It is as if his desire and its particular mode of displacement were "fixed" at the moment of the stag's prediction (perhaps because of it) and he can progress no further without resolving it. Indeed, another aspect that emerges from this passage, as well as from the previous one, is the desire to return to the past. Julian recalls "his past hunts," and Paradise itself may be read as the ultimate regression, a return to the lost innocence of civilization, the childhood of the human race. Finally, Julian's form of self-representation in the scene contains a clue which is important for confirming our hypothesis concerning his will for power and is also of potential significance in interpreting the final scene of the tale. Julian "fancied himself like our father Adam." Adam is at once the symbol of the exiled *son* (like Christ and Julian), revolting against God the Father by destroying His order, and, here, the *father* of mankind. That Julian sees himself in the role of the father enables us to substantiate the notion that the real goal in slaying the father is to assume his role. In this way, the killing of animals or parents, the obtaining of power and superiority, even possessing the mother, would all be subordinated to an ultimate drive: to become the father. At this point textual evidence is too slim to sustain such a theory, but we can well add it to those other hypotheses which we are testing as we weave our way through the text.

For the moment, we must return to the major "hunt" scene in Part II and review the questions of motivation and failure of displacement. We are struck immediately by the fact that, quite unlike the hunt scene in Part I, Julian is portrayed as very close to his surroundings, and the reader is placed at an accompanying short distance from Julian.

This closeness is stressed from the outset by the use of perception verbs; in the very first sentence Julian is the subject of "he heard" and "he caught a glimpse" (II, 27). In addition to ten vision verbs, there are two pertaining to sound ("he heard"; "He listened closely," II, 75) and two expressions involving smell ("enervating scents," II, 54; "foul beasts," II, 66). However, the sense that dominates the entire scene, and is completely absent from the earlier one, is touch, the most direct of all senses. From the moment Julian enters the woods, he is in "contact"[31] with his surroundings: "he was walking in the forest at a fast clip, enjoying the soft grass and the balmy air" (II, 52). Touch is the primary sense used to communicate his discovery of intruders in his wife's bed: "he felt" (II, 73); "his groping fingers" (II, 74); "again he passed his hand slowly" (II, 74); "Julian slipped his fingers" (II, 79).

Here contact with animals is as direct as it is repugnant: "The wild boar rubbed its tusks against his heels, the wolf the inside of his hands with the bristles of its muzzle. The monkeys pinched him and made faces, the weasel rolled over his feet" (II,

---

31. See Grimaud's discussion of the psychological significance of contact in Chapter 3.

66). Later he is bombarded directly and simultaneously through the senses of sound ("deafened"), touch ("bruised"), and smell ("choked"): "deafened by the buzzing of the insects, bruised by birds' tails, choked by their breaths, he walked with outstretched arms and closed eyes" (II, 67).

In both the above texts we also note that *contact* is reinforced by *causality*. In the first text, the transitive verbs serve to transmit the animals' actions directly to Julian; there is none of the separation so evident in the hunt scene from Part I. In the second passage, the repetition of the causal preposition "by," and the listing of the various agents ("buzzing," etc.) and causes ("insects," etc.), as well as the close proximity of their victim ("he") and their effects ("with outstretched arms and closed eyes"), again illustrate the directness of influence here. The same mechanism is operative when Julian strikes his parents: "Bursting into boundless rage, he sprang upon them thrusting his dagger" (II, 75). Again, cause ("boundless rage"), effect ("he sprang"), agent ("his dagger"), and target ("them") are clearly joined by the sentence structure.

If Julian is brought into close contact with his surroundings, the reader's distance is diminished in a parallel way by the narrative techniques. We draw closer to Julian through the increased use of direct speech ("'I am only obeying thee!'" II, 29) and indirect speech ("telling himself, trying to believe, that this was not possible, that he had made a mistake, that there are sometimes inexplicable likenesses," II, 79). And, of particular importance, from the moment that Julian returns to the castle and encounters someone in his wife's bed, is the high incidence of "free indirect discourse." Flaubert is particularly fond of this mode of discourse (also called *style indirect libre* or *erlebte Rede*), where the expressions are clearly those of the characters but are not designated as such by transitional words like "telling himself" or conventional typographic markings like dashes or quotation marks. Usually, conversational terms ("Doubtless, she was asleep," II, 71), italics and punctuation marks ("It *was* a beard, this time, and a man!" II, 74), or ellipsis (here of a verb: "a man lying with his wife!" II, 74) signal the presence of this mode of discourse for the reader. In addition to the above examples, free indirect discourse is used throughout the final paragraphs of Part II, where the obliqueness of the technique creates the effect of Julian speaking in "a voice different from his own" (II, 80).

Another technique that serves to lock the reader into Julian's perspective is the presentation of events in what might be called an "impressionist sequence"; that is, the events are given to the reader in the order in which they would occur for Julian, rather than in the more usual cause-effect sequence.[32] In the sentence "Suddenly, behind his back, sprang a darker mass, a wild boar" (II, 55), for example, the effects of time ("Suddenly"), position ("behind his back"), light ("darker"), and general impression ("mass") precede identification of the object itself ("a wild boar"), the cause of the previous impressions. Again with "shapes moved in the uncertain darkness... and out came hyenas, quite frightened, panting" (II, 58), the reader reconstructs the perceived objects along with Julian; we must share his perspective, identify with him. This procedure should not be confused with the breaking up of causal sequence so prevalent in the first hunt scene; here, to the contrary, the narrator follows and stresses the sequence of the *perceptual act* (often the reverse of causality in natural objects)[33] so that Julian is more closely engaged in the scene and we with him.

But what is the psychological significance of the closeness, the contact displayed throughout this scene? Once again, as with the distance described in the earlier hunt scene, the aim is double-targeted: the contact possibly suggests something about *Julian's* psychology and definitely has an effect on the *reader's* reaction to the scene. For Julian, we may hypothesize (and indeed we can do no better, since a character is a hypothetical entity) that the closeness suggests that he is approaching the real target of his murderous desires: the parents. Indeed, as the mediation of the animals fails, as the mask falls, Julian's contact with reality is depicted as more palpable, through the use of touch verbs; more immediate, through the extended impressionist sequence by which he progressively identifies who is in

32. Cause-effect sentence order is more usual in French than in English. See Jean-Paul Vinay and John Darbelnet, *Stylistique comparée du français et de l'anglais* (Paris, 1958), pp. 105, 221–222.
33. That is, we often perceive effects *before* identifying their causes.

his bed; and more heightened, through the amount of direct, indirect, and free indirect discourse, particularly after his return to the castle. The closeness seems especially designed to emphasize Julian's frustration; the facility of visual sensation in the earlier hunt scene is replaced by the encumbrance of the tactile in the final scene from Part II. Moreover, this frustration serves as a further indication of Julian's motivation (deep-seated inferiority) and takes the very form it had in his childhood. The claustrophobia ("the beasts . . . forming a narrow circle around him," II, 64), the immobility ("incapable of the slightest movement," II, 64), the sense of being powerless, sightless, and speechless ("with outstretched arms and closed eyes like a blind man, without even the strength to cry out 'mercy!' " II, 67)—all recall the infantile modes of inferiority discovered in the initial chapel scene and later duplicated with Julian's illness. This feeling of inferiority emerges rather forcefully and explicitly from the final scene of Part II; Julian notes that "Some higher power was destroying his strength" (II, 60). It would seem at first that this superior power belongs to the animals, who have become not only aggressive, but invulnerable. However, it is significant that Julian blames himself: "Then his soul collapsed with shame" (II, 60). This self-castigation is further stressed by the use of reflexive verbs (II, 55 and II, 63),[34] where the action turns back against the subject. Even the eyes of the animals—"to see him" (II, 57), "a monstrous jackdaw that watched Julian" (II, 62), "As they watched him out of the corners of their eyes" (II, 67), and "here and there, between the branches great numbers of large sparks appeared, as if the firmament had showered all its stars down into the forest. It was the eyes of animals, wildcats, squirrels, owls, parrots, monkeys" (II, 62)—seem to suggest here, as they do frequently,[35] the workings of the human conscience. Finally, the disdain of the animals (II, 66), their

34. Reflexive verbs are not always translated as such. See note 21.

35. Victor Brombert concludes, of this very passage, that "the peering eyes of the animals staring at him are like an exteriorization of his own ensnaring conscience. A chronic and inescapable sense of guilt is indeed one of the most fundamental traits of the Flaubertian psychology: not a Christian guilt, but a deep-rooted sense of the *péché d'exister*, almost Sartrean in nature, and which explains perhaps why Sartre has been for so long fascinated and at the same time repelled by Flaubert" (*The Novels of Flaubert* [Princeton, 1966], p. 229).

taunting ("irony was apparent in their devious manner," II, 67), and their hostility ("they seemed to ponder a plan for revenge," II, 67) appear to represent projections of Julian's psyche (note the use of "was apparent" and "seemed"), the terrible torture inflicted by the conscience in the violent repression of desire. In short, the barriers seem to be of Julian's creation not of the animals'.

It is at this point that we can return to our hypothesis concerning the failure of displacement. Indeed the animals' invulnerability seems to indicate, as did Julian's earlier illness, that his censoring agency, aware of and repulsed by the real motives behind the "hunt," will now prohibit Julian from killing animals. Indeed Julian is made to feel this link and articulate it: "he felt that murdering animals would determine the fate of his parents" (II, 21).

But this repression, this damming of desire, finally leads to an explosion, where a stream of psychic energy bursts past the barriers of censorship and rushes headlong and undisguised toward the real object of its desires, the parents. The highly revealing sentence directly following this night of frustration and failure—"His thirst for carnage was taking over again; animals lacking, he longed to massacre men" (II, 70)—points up the interchangeability of the objects and describes a curious process where, displacement having failed, desire returns toward the original object. One could well speak of a "replacement" of objects or a "regression" toward the infantile fantasy lying behind the substitute objects.[36]

---

36. For Freud, "regression" involves "a return of the libido to earlier stopping-places in its development" (*Introductory Lectures*, XVI, 342). In fact, he goes so far as to state that every dream is itself "*a substitute for an infantile scene modified by being transferred on to a recent experience*" (*Interpretation of Dreams*, V, 546). In Julian's case, we might say that when the sophisticated mechanisms of substitution and modification break down, when the real intent behind the recent experience (the hunt) becomes evident, Julian's psyche regresses to the infantile fantasy lying behind it, marking a return to "a direct, undisguised fulfilment of that wish" (*Introductory Lectures*, XV, 128). Thus, while the killing of the parents in Part II appears to represent a subsequent stage in Julian's life, a later event than the massacre of the animals in Part I, in another sense we might also read the later scene as a regression to an earlier stage of psychic development, which lays bare the basic desires disguised in the prior scene.

When Julian does kill the parents (whether "dream or fact"), the scene is again marked as a duplication and reversal of his initial situation. The decor of the death room is like that of a chapel, with its "lead-lined panes" (II, 73) and "an ivory Christ that hung in the alcove" (II, 79). The father himself had been compared, earlier in this scene, to a "a statue in a church" (II, 50). It is, in fact, in this room that Julian customarily kneels to pray, as we learn in the very first sentence of the scene ("while in their bedroom, she had just gone to bed and he was about to kneel in prayer," II, 27), and the narrator reinforces this detail near the end of the scene by noting that Julian's "abdication" instructions were left "on a prayer stool, in the death chamber" (II, 81). Again Julian appears to reverse his former situation by imposing immobility ("The dead . . . had not even budged," II, 75) and weakness ("they grew weaker," II, 75) on his victims, while he himself assumes a position suggesting physical superiority ("he bent over," II, 79). Finally, although the discussions of Moskos (Chapter 2) and Sartre (Chapter 4) concerning the motives of adultery/incest are very convincing, the killing may be read more simply as due, once again, to Julian's jealousy or sense of inferiority: "a man lying with his wife!" (II, 74); someone else has taken his place, his possession, and is thus better than he. Julian's vengeance is intended to restore his lost power.

Yet it is precisely as a result of the killing that Julian falls into a position of even greater inferiority, the nature of the negative effect serving to further justify our previous reading of his motivation as a superiority drive. Julian gives up all his possessions, his very identity—"henceforth he had ceased to exist" (II, 82)—and even his wife. The last detail is particularly interesting since, as we mentioned in the Introduction, it is entirely of Flaubert's invention. In the original legend, Julian's wife follows him into exile and shares his penitence. Sartre clearly shows the importance of Flaubert's eliminating the wife in order to em-

---

Furthermore, whereas Part I marked the triumph of the "censor," first in distorting, then in repressing, these desires, Part II bears witness to the dethroning of the censor, a psychic event which will result in the overwhelming sense of guilt which pervades Part III.

phasize Julian's solitude,[37] but could we not also read her absence as further confirmation of Julian's inability to assume the role of father. Julian remains so thoroughly entrapped in his former family situation that he is unable to establish a new configuration with himself on top.[38] Indeed, at the end of Part II, Julian is at the lowest ("flat on his belly," II, 84), most submissive ("his forehead in the dust," II, 84), solitary ("no one daring to address him," II, 83), and distant point in the story ("He . . . finally passed out of sight," II, 85).

The Leper and the Father: Reconciliation?

Whereas Part II of *The Legend* began with Julian in a position of seeming superiority and ended with its reversal in the final major scene, Part III has the opposite movement. That Julian begins the final section of the story in a position of submissiveness is obvious, but less so, perhaps, is the narrator's continued use of the same codes as in the initial chapel scene to signal this inferiority: "He held out his hand to horsemen on the roads, would bend his knee as he approached harvesters, or remained motionless in front of courtyard fences" (II, 2). Once more the hands are used to indicate a lack of power (see I, 27 and II, 23, 67) and, here, to further denote dependence, while genuflexion (see I, 27, 70; II, 23, 81) again suggests submission. As often before, Julian is depicted as immobile ("motionless") and alienated (fenced out). The major difference here, of course, is that Julian imposes this submission upon himself. He has internalized the voice of authority, and his "conscience" or "superego"[39] inflicts punishment on him for his crime, or rather the

37. See Chapter 4.
38. In fact, Julian's wife seems more like a mother than a wife, and he more like a child than a husband: "He did not reply, or burst into tears" (II, 24). On the absence of sexuality in Julian's marriage, see also Chapter 3.
39. Julian's guilt and self-punishment following his parents' death correspond rather directly to Freud's "anthropological" description of a universal human condition: "We cannot get away from the assumption that man's sense of guilt springs from the Oedipus complex and was acquired at the killing of the father by the brothers banded together. On that occasion an act of aggression was not suppressed but carried out; but it was the same act of aggression whose suppression in the child is supposed to be the source of his sense of guilt. . . . After their hatred had been satisfied by their act of aggression, their love came to

desire behind it ("despaired that he should have committed it," III, 10). This split in Julian's personality is indicated by the reflexive verb ("se désespérait") in the above passage, and the narrator identifies it rather explicitly in phrases like "His own person was so repugnant to him" (III, 11). This inner rift is particularly evident when Julian fails to recognize his own image in the fountain (III, 13), a scene which we will examine more fully later. Julian is again bent on regression to his childhood ("He often closed his eyes, yearning, through memory, to come back to his youth," III, 20), but he is blocked by the sudden surge of his parents' bodies ("suddenly, the two corpses were there," III, 20) and is continuously haunted by images of them ("the ghastly visions continued," III, 21). It is at this point that the leper (himself a "ghastly vision") makes his appearance and effects a resolution or at least a reversal of Julian's situation. In order to assess the psychological significance of this reversal, let us take a broad look at several recurrent features—characters, themes, situations, techniques—through which the final scene in Part III can be compared with those of Parts I and II.

The theme of death is again dominant, but here Julian himself dies and does not cause the death of those around him. A bed is also present, but whereas at the end of Part I Julian was in bed and his parents out, in Part II his parents in and Julian out, here Julian is in bed *with* the leper. There is also a progressive reduction in the number of characters involved with Julian: from the multitude of animals, finally reduced to three (the deer family) in I, to the two parents in II, Julian is here confronted by the leper alone. Furthermore, the leper incorporates or embodies traits from nearly all the previous characters. Of course the leper is primarily associated with Julian's father, by the series of common features detailed in the Introduction—"eyes redder than coals" (III, 31), "a king's majesty" (III, 31), "motionless as a column" (III, 35), the "coarse linen" (III, 31), and the various cadaverlike features: "death rattle" (III, 47), "shroudlike gar-

---

the fore in their remorse for the deed. It set up the super-ego by identification with the father; it gave that agency the father's power, as though as a punishment for the deed of aggression they had carried out against him, and it created the restrictions which were intended to prevent a repetition of the deed" (*Civilization and Its Discontents*, XXI, 131–132).

ment" (III, 37), "plaster mask" (III, 31), and so on. However, many of the latter features are equally applicable to Julian's mother, and the fiery eyes also relate to the stag, as is further suggested when the leper "closed his eyes" (III, 48), recalling the stag who "gently closed his eyelids, and died" (I, 69). Moreover, other features in this scene directly recall the doe: the leper, like Julian, lies down on "dead leaves" (III, 50), while the doe was "blond like dead leaves" (I, 64); Julian "laid ... down" (I, 65) the doe and "laid" (III, 46) a cover on the leper; the doe dies from "a shot right in the breast" (I, 65), and Julian is "chest upon chest" (III, 56) with the leper. And the last two features further evoke the dead parents, who "lay before him, on their backs, with a hole in their breasts" (II, 79). Of course the doe and the stag, through their many points of association with the mother and the father, would also be secondarily associated with the leper (*A* is like *B*; *B* is like *C*; therefore, *A* is like *C*). We can attempt to schematize this complex set of relationships as in Figure 3.

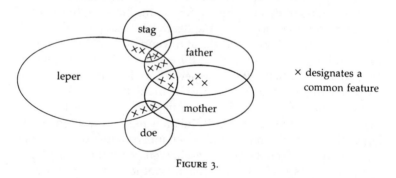

FIGURE 3.

The leper thus represents a "condensation"[40] for Julian and a crystallization of the main currents of the story for the reader. The narrator further underscores the monumental importance of the leper figure by the techniques deployed throughout this final scene.

40. According to Freud: "The laws that govern the passage of events in the unconscious, which come to light in this manner, are remarkable enough and suffice to explain most of what seems strange to us about dreams. Above all there is a striking tendency to *condensation*, an inclination to form fresh unities

Verbs of sense perception are used to stress Julian's contact with the leper. Three hearing verbs in the first short paragraph—"he imagined hearing," "He listened intently," "could make out nothing save" (III, 22)—rivet Julian into the scene. Here, as in the final scene from Part II, powerful transitive verbs suggest the direct effect of outside forces, particularly through the sense of touch: "Hail lashed at his hands, rain streamed down his back, the violent air made him choke, he stopped" (III, 34). Contact is rendered all the more vivid and direct here by the use of comparisons to evoke parallel sensations of great force. The leper's mouth emits "breath thick like a fog, and foul" (III, 37). Julian "could feel against his thigh the Leper's skin, colder than a snake and rough as a file" (III, 53). In this final scene, sense experience is shown to go beyond the physical, to penetrate beneath the surface to the very depths of Julian's being: "an aroma . . . gladdened his heart and his nostrils" (III, 42); "a superhuman joy flooded down into the soul of the swooning Julian" (III, 57).

The reader is also brought into close contact with Julian through the use of techniques similar to those identified earlier but whose incidence and impact are even stronger here. Julian's thoughts are depicted through the medium of free indirect discourse: "And this lasted a long, long time!" (III, 36); "It was wine; what a boon!" (III, 42). But the feeling of directness is especially accomplished by the increased amount of direct discourse: the leper speaks nine times;[41] not only does each occurrence do away with the mediating effect of the narrator, and thus draw us closer to the scene, but the accompanying use of the present tense diminishes the reader's temporal distance from the events as well.

Of special importance is the sustained "impressionist" sequence marking the leper's arrival. The reader, like Julian, must

---

out of elements which in our waking thought we should certainly have kept separate. As a consequence of this, a single element of the manifest dream often stands for a whole number of latent dream-thoughts as though it were a combined allusion to all of them; and in general the compass of the manifest dream is extraordinarily small in comparison with the wealth of material from which it has sprung" (*An Outline of Psycho-Analysis*, XXIII, 168–169).

41. For a list and lengthy discussion of the occurrences of direct discourse in this final scene, see Chapter 3, pp. 169–172.

progress through a long series of effects before coming to identify their source. The leper's presentation, extended over the
first ten paragraphs of this scene, can be schematized as follows:
"someone" → "the same voice" → "it" → "there was" → "the
loud voice" → "a church bell" → "a man" → "he" → "coarse
linen rags, his face . . . a plaster mask . . . both eyes" → "him" →
"leper's sores" → "there was" → "his demeanor" → "a king's
majesty" → "he" → "his weight" → "the eyes of the Leper."

This progressively constructed portrait, where the narrator
uses several "stalling" tactics—metonymy ("the voice," "his
weight"), synecdoche ("linen," "eyes," "sores"), simile
("church bell," "king"), impersonal nouns ("someone," "a
man"), pronouns ("it," "there," "he," "him," "his")—before
finally identifying the subject ("the Leper"), roots the reader into
Julian's perspective and signals the monumental importance of
the leper figure. This eerie apparition emerges from night and
fog, perhaps even from one of Julian's "visions," progressively
accumulating traits that suggest the stag (the church bell, the
eyes) and especially Julian's father (the eyes, the king's majesty,
coarse linen, a mask, *une lèpre*,[42] and so on). In this sense, the
leper is no less than the *ghost* of Julian's father.[43] But it remains
to determine the psychological significance of his appearance
here. There are several possible interpretations, varying in the
degree to which they appear to resolve the problems delineated
during the course of this study.

First, if the leper is seen as a disguised figure representing
Julian's father through a displacement operative for both Julian
and the reader, this scene or fantasy would appear to absolve
Julian of his father's death, since Julian does not cause it and
even attempts to save the leper/father.[44] This interpretation is

42. On a purely phonetic level, it would also be possible to see a link between
"le père" (l[ə] pɛr) and "lèpre" (lɛpr[ə]), perhaps reinforced by the typographical
anagram connecting Julian's present dwelling ("la cahute") with his former one
("le château").

43. And ghosts are frequently father figures. See Otto Rank's discussion of
Shakespeare's ghosts in *Das Inzest-Motiv in Dichtung und Sage* (Leipzig, 1912),
chapter VI, pp. 204–233 (cited by Norman Holland, "Shakespearean Tragedy
and the Three Ways of Psychoanalytic Criticism," in *Psychoanalysis and Literature*, ed. Hendrik Ruitenbeek [New York, 1964], p. 211).

44. In fact, the final scene can be read as a "rescue phantasy," which, according to Freud, nearly always involves the *father*: "he then forms the phantasy of

also consonant with the generally accepted religious significance of the legend: through penitence and acceptance of his guilt, Julian is pardoned by God and "reborn" in Heaven. Furthermore, returning to a more psychological level, Julian affords the leper the care, nourishment, and shelter generally provided to the child by the parents and can thus be said to repay a childhood debt. In short, by saving, succoring, and embracing the leper, who has the form of his father's cadaver, Julian appears to assuage his guilt and effect a reconciliation with the father.[45]

Even more, as Julian embraces the leper, abandons his body and identity to the leper, the reader detects a deeper desire—to identify with the leper, to become the leper and, by extension, the father. Indeed the leper and Julian exchange family roles: Julian is obedient like a son, provident like a father; the leper is authoritative like a father, weak like a son. This identification is further effected by extensive use within this scene of a grammatical construction where the same body part is repeated twice in close succession, the first applying to the leper, the second to Julian (or conversely), and thus equating them through the presence of common (in fact identical) features.

---

rescuing his father from danger and saving his life; in this way he puts his account square with him" ("A Special Type of Choice of Object Made by Men," XI, 172).

45. In L'Idiot de la famille Sartre finds just such a reconciliation with the father in Flaubert's personal life at the moment he was writing Saint Julian: "In this sense, if the dive in January, 1844 [i.e., Flaubert's breakdown], was—among so many other things—a parricide, the financial ruin, by bringing his entire pipe-dreamer's existence under scrutiny, achieves what analysts call a 'reconciliation with the father'" (p. 2131). Sartre sees the reconciliation reflected in the tale: "in 1875 a reconciliation with the father is achieved. The late Achille-Cléophas not only figures in the Legend, in the form of a gentle country squire who adores his only son; he is also God the Father: a God who is hidden but good" (see Chapter 4, pp. 200-201). Sartre's analysis of the suicide of a character representing both Gustave and his father in Les Funérailles du Docteur Mathurin—"Let us note that this ritual murder is also, in one sense, an attempt at identification: father and son, sewn in the same skin, die together" (p. 464)—seems like a direct preview of the final scene in Saint Julian, as does his description of the ramifications of Flaubert's ailment: "Thus, the late Gustave junior and his father, victims of a double murder (the father has killed the son whose death kills the father), achieve together, inseparably, the supreme dignity of Being-In-Itself. The father will always be the 'other' in this once-young heart, but an other who is power-less" (p. 1909). However, in neither case does Sartre relate these episodes to the final scene of Saint Julian, owing most likely to his not having established the link between the leper and Julian's father.

They are "side by side" (III, 50), "mouth against mouth" (III, 56), "chest upon chest" (III, 56), and "face to face" (III, 57). This grammatical "mirroring" parallels the earlier mirror scene, where Julian examined himself in the fountain:

> And one day as he happened to be at the edge of a spring, while he was stooping over it to judge the water's depth, there appeared before him a very emaciated man, with a white beard and of such piteous aspect that he found it impossible to hold back his tears. The other also wept. Without recognizing his face, Julian had a blurred recollection of features resembling it. He cried out; it was his father; and he gave up all thought of killing himself. [III, 13]

In short, Julian now resembles the father, is confused (identified) with the father, has become the father.[46] The associations between Julian and Christ, in this scene and elsewhere (see the Introduction), might also be explained from this perspective, since Christ, the very archetype of the exiled son, ascends to sit with the Father, indeed to become the Father in the mystery of the Trinity.[47]

Furthermore, Julian's change in status is accompanied by an increasing sense of power and superiority, whose modes of rep-

---

46. Indeed, Freud finds this desire to identify with the father to be at the root of the rescue phantasy (see note 44): "in the rescue phantasy he is completely identifying himself with the father. All his instincts, those of tenderness, gratitude, lustfullness, defiance and independence, find satisfaction in the single wish *to be his own father*" ("A Special Type of Choice," XI, 173). Indeed he sees it as a necessary step in normal psychic growth: "Along with the demolition of the Oedipus complex, the boy's object-cathexis of his mother must be given up. Its place may be filled by one of two things: either an identification with his mother or an intensification of his identification with his father. We are accustomed to regard the latter outcome as the more normal; it permits the affectionate relation to the mother to be in a measure retained. In this way the dissolution of the Oedipus complex would consolidate the masculinity in a boy's character" (*The Ego and the Id*, XIX, 32).

47. Per Nykrog, "Les 'Trois contes' dans l'évolution de la structure thématique chez Flaubert," *Romantisme*, no. 6 (1973), notes the link between Julian and Christ and interprets it in a religious framework: "Saint Julian, who chooses lucidly, voluntarily, the sacrifice of his terrestrial being, is a Christian Saint: the form of his saintliness, the consciousness he has of a sin which he inescapably inherited, and the salvation which he finds beyond bodily sacrifice, everything with him is modeled on Christ, and it is God the Son who leads him to Heaven" (p. 60). In *L'Idiot* Sartre reads Christ's sacrifice psychoanalytically, but primarily from the father's point of view: "The Passion represents the

resentation again conform to those described earlier. He displays great physical force: "Julian leaned his body forward, extended his arms, and, bracing his feet, arched himself back, twisting at the waist to apply greater power" (III, 34). And, as the leper acquires traits previously associated with weakness and inferiority—"motionless" (III, 35), "squatting" (III, 45), "trembled" (III, 45), "failing" (III, 45), "lifeless" (III, 45)—Julian embodies those affiliated with superiority: he is higher ("Julian ascended," III, 57) and freer ("The roof flew off, the firmament unfolded, " III, 57), finally ending up "on top" in the heavens.

However, we must remember that Julian is depicted as essentially *passive* and *dependent* throughout this scene. If he manages to muster physical force, it is because of "a command not to be disobeyed" (III, 34); if he rises to the heavens, it is through the intervention of the leper (father), not through his own doing; if the event causes joy, that emotion is experienced passively: "a superhuman joy flooded down into the soul of the swooning Julian" (III, 57). In the penultimate paragraph, describing his "ascension," Julian is the subject of only one of twelve clauses, he is the object in several involving the leper: "the Leper clutched him" (III, 57); "arms embraced him" (III, 57); "who was carrying him" (III, 57). The verbs themselves suggest the very passivity, enclosure, and restraint which Julian has been struggling since childhood to overcome: "Whenever his mother held him against her, he accepted her embrace coldly" (I, 48). Thus, in terms of the codes set up in the story, the ascension scene is depicted *negatively*.

The key phrase "naked as on the day he was born" (III, 53), which in some ways seems to suggest "rebirth," might simply be read here as a further regression, an ultimate return to an even more distant and primitive state where the child is totally dependent on the parents. Such an interpretation might also be borne out by the flooding, the passivity, and the detail "mouth against mouth" (III, 56), which suggests a fantasy of oral

---

generosity of the Lord, who becomes a man in order to save his vassal" (p. 608). It seems to me, however, that, from the son's point of view, Christ represents the exiled Son, whose suffering derives from a separation from the Father and whose salvation depends on rejoining the Father, becoming the Father in the melding of the triangle of the Trinity.

merger,[48] corresponding to the most basic stage of human development.

The consequences of such a hypothesis are somewhat disturbing, because they seem to contradict to a certain degree the commonly accepted religious interpretation of the story as a positive salvation and ascension. Rather, Julian would appear to be yielding to the ultimate temptation, that of Saint Anthony as well as so many of Flaubert's characters, self-annihilation, in short, suicide. Even more disturbing (at least in the framework of this study) is that such an interpretation contradicts our earlier description of identification as manifesting the desire to become the father and leaves unresolved the drive toward superiority, independence, and power which we have seen to characterize the main lines of the story. It would appear that Julian, confronted by his father's ghost (the leper), is driven to a state of greater submission and even regression to the most basic stage of his development.

Perhaps it is this interpretation which accounts for the narrator's unexpected intervention in the final words of the story,[49] where he cuts off Julian's ascension in midflight and brings him soundly back to earth: "So there is the story of saint Julian the Hospitaler, about as it is found on the stained-glass window of a church, in my birthplace" (III, 58).

However, this return to the narrator's perspective may well suggest the only context where reconciliation with the father can occur, where the will to power can be exercised, where the Oedipus "complex" can be transcended.

The Narrator's Space

In the last paragraph of *Saint Julian* the narrator marks the tale as belonging to his space ("my birthplace") and his time ("there

48. Holland notes, for example, that "In literature, this earliest phase appears as fantasies of losing the boundaries of self, of being engulfed, overwhelmed, drowned, ... But these fantasies can also be of a benevolent merger or fusion, ... the 'oceanic feeling' of the mystic. We would expect, then, to find poems and stories about love or about religious mysticism based on fantasies of oral merger" (*Dynamics*, pp. 35–36).

49. In quoting the ascension scene Sartre says: "Such are the final words of the *Legend*" (*L'Idiot*, p. 2106; see Chapter 4, p. 189). He is certainly not alone in

is"). He identifies it as an artifact ("stained-glass window"), a work of fiction ("the story") in which he is free to exercise his own license ("about"). The interruption of the third-person narration by a first-person singular pronoun ("my"), one of the rare occurrences in all of Flaubert's later works and in direct contravention of his narrative principles,[50] obliges us to take a very close look at this sentence. Indeed, this final cluster of details compels the reader to take another, closer look at the entire story, this time from the narrator's perspective. When the narrator declares himself a persona, he too, like the main character, becomes a possible repository of the author's fantasies, an eligible candidate for a psychocritical reading. What happens if the same problems raised in conjunction with Julian—the inferiority/superiority scheme, revolt of the son, identification with the father, failure of displacement, regression, reconciliation, reversal, and so on—are explored from the narrator's point of view?

Although Flaubert's narration is highly objective—one of the author's trademarks—the narrator's position remains clearly superior to that of the characters. In fact, this superiority is guaranteed from the outset by the form of narration: third person and past tense. Except for those infrequent (and thus highly noticeable) moments when we share Julian's point of view, the tale is dominated by the narrator's transcendent perspective. From the opening description of the castle, details are filtered through the narrator's vision and voice, and it is not before the twelfth paragraph that we share a character's perspective ("and she noticed," I, 12) or speech (" 'Rejoice, O mother! thy son shall be a saint!' " I, 13). While this proportion diminishes progressively, as we have seen, it is still the narrator's presence that dominates the story. Moreover, the use of the past tense implies that Julian's actions are already completed, his fate sealed, and that the narrator already knows the outcome. The character is, in effect, frozen, fixed in the past, deprived of his freedom to encounter a still-open world, and these are precisely

---

failing to mention, discuss, and integrate into his analysis what are really the final words of the story, where the narrator speaks of himself.

50. See, for example, the quotation from Flaubert's *Correspondance* on p. 67 of this chapter.

the grounds for Sartre's general objection to the use of third-person, past-tense narration.[51]

However, it is through these very conventions and their manipulation that the narrator is able to assert his own freedom and superiority. He can compress time ("For three months," I, 73), space ("He traveled through regions so torrid... and through others so icy," II, 7), objects ("There were fountains in the halls," II, 17), and people ("He gave assistance in turn to the Dauphin of France and the king of England, the templars of Jerusalem," II, 7). The narrator can shift focus away from the characters, as we saw in the first two sentences of the hunt scene from Part I or as in the following passage:

> Thus, the emperor's daughter was bestowed upon him, along with a castle she had inherited from her mother; and, when the wedding was over, leave was taken, after endless courtesies were exchanged.
>
> It was a white marble palace, built in the Moorish style, on a promontory, in an orange grove. [II, 14–15]

Here the narrator removes us from the characters by the use of an impersonal pronoun[52] and verbs in the passive voice, as well as by the paragraphing, which turns attention toward the palace, away from the young wife and Julian, whose wedding night would presumably be of greater interest to them and to the reader than their dwelling. The narrator's tendency to avoid proper nouns (Julian is the only major character who is named) and the overwhelming use of pronouns—"It grew. He became

---

51. Sartre finds this narrative form characteristic of late-nineteenth-century prose, where "the anecdote is recounted from an absolute—that is, ordered—point of view; it amounts to a local change in a system at rest; neither the author nor the reader run any risks, fear any surprises: the event is past, catalogued, understood" (*Qu'est-ce que la littérature?* [1948; rpt. Paris, 1970], p. 178), and links its prevalence to bourgeois society: "19th-century novelistic technique offers the French public a reassuring image of the bourgeoisie" (*ibid.*, p. 169). Roland Barthes develops a parallel argument, from a literary point of view; he finds these techniques too "conventional," too limiting of the freedom of the modern writer: "The past definite and the third person in the Novel are no more than the fatal gesture by which the writer points his finger at the mask he is wearing" (*Le Degré zéro de l'écriture* [Utrecht, Holland, 1968], p. 37); he links them to literary history: "The narrative past thus belongs to a security system for *belles-lettres*" (*ibid.*, p. 31).

52. The impersonal pronoun ("on") is translated by a passive. See note 21.

famous. He was in demand" (II, 6)—could also be read as a form
of mastery.[53]

Another, more overt means by which the narrator asserts his
superiority over the characters is by withholding information
from them and delivering it unto the reader. He names objects
unknown to Julian ("an animal that Julian did not know, a
black-nosed beaver," I,55) and speaks when the character cannot ("without even the strength to cry out 'mercy!' " II, 67). The
narrator and reader know before Julian what is lying in his bed
("he leaned over the pillow where the two heads were resting
close together," II, 73), and we are told that they are dead—
"The dead, pierced through their hearts, had not even budged"
II, 75)—a full six sentences before Julian is able to see this for
himself (II, 79). Indeed, the entire killing scene is constructed
ironically, since everyone but Julian knows of the parents' arrival. Finally, in the key fountain scene—"without recognizing his
face, Julian had a blurred recollection of features resembling it.
He cried out; it was his father; and he gave up all thought of
killing himself" (III, 13)—Julian never does realize that the face is
his own, that it is he himself who now resembles the father, has
become the father. Only the narrator is permitted to understand
and report the full significance of this event.

However, the primary means by which the narrator shifts
focus away from the characters and toward himself, by which he
transcends their world and creates his own, is through style.
The structure of a sentence can reorder the random occurrences
of reality into organized lists, where animals are associated by
species and size ("blackbirds, jays, polecats, foxes, porcupines,
lynxes, a host of beasts" I, 56) much as they appear in Julian's
dream of Paradise. In the first four paragraphs of the story, the
progressive reduction of "real" space (the characters' world), as
we move from outside the castle to inside its courtyard, is reversed by a progressive increase in textual space or paragraph
size (the narrator's world). Through *comparisons*, such as "The
stones of the courtyard were as smooth as the paving ["dal-

---

53. See, for example, Holland's analysis of Matthew Arnold's prose: "He
tends to turn actions or conditions into nouns or pronouns which he then ma-
nipulates as fixed entities" (*Dynamics*, p. 155).

lage"] in a church" (I, 3), the narrator foreshadows the description of the chapel several pages later, where the *detail* "A drop of blood stained the flagstone ["dalle"]" (I, 30) recalls the earlier comparison and adds an ironic dimension to it, since the church paving has now been "stained" by Julian's murder of the mouse. Separate *entities*, such as stag and father, as well as *scenes*, like the hunt and the chapel, are also associated, through the strategic use of clustered common features. In effecting these associations, the narrator and attentive reader transcend the chronological line of the story and impose a higher order upon it. Through a network of intersecting connections, running back and forth across the entire text, the narrator creates his own space, superimposed on the characters' world, which in turn becomes as static and immobile as the stained-glass window to which the narrator compares it in the final words of the tale.

In fact, the narrator's situation constitutes a *duplication* yet *reversal* of the characters', according to the very terms which emerged from our analysis of the story line. The narrator is higher, stronger, more mobile, more authoritative than the character, who is seen as silent, submissive, dependent on the narrator.

In this sense, and given the narrator's position as creator and purveyor of order, his role is more analogous to the father's than to that of Julian, the would-be destroyer of order. In sharing the narrator's point of view, we approach the Oedipal configuration from a different angle, that of the father, who seems to delight in the demise of the upstart son.[54] From this perspective, we can read the narration not only as a defense against a fantasy represented by the character,[55] but as a separate, even opposite fantasy, one perhaps more in tune with Flaubert's age and status as he wrote *Saint Julian*.

---

54. Note that here, as elsewhere, I am not alluding to the "masculinity" of the roles of father and son but to their differing degrees of power. Accordingly, the struggle depicted in *Saint Julian* is potentially as relevant to the female reader as to the male.

55. Holland, for example, views literary form (including narration) essentially as a defense mechanism: "The literary work, through what we have loosely termed 'form,' acts out defensive maneuvers for us: splitting, isolating, undoing, displacing from, omitting (repressing or denying) elements of the fantasy" (*Dynamics*, p. 189).

Indeed, there is ample extratextual evidence to show that this is precisely how Flaubert saw the literary work, not from the character's limited standpoint, but from that of the narrator, transcendent and omnipotent: "The artist must be in his work like God in Creation, invisible and all-powerful."[56]

If Julian is carried off by Christ, the son, the narrator can be said to hold the position of God, the father.[57] The reader who effects the *displacement* from character to narrator can join the author in accomplishing the ultimate *reversal*, from son to father, from creature to creator.

56. From a letter of March 18, 1857, to Louise Colet, in *Correspondance*, vol. IV (Paris, 1927), p. 164.

57. This hypothesis concerning Flaubert's attitude toward the literary text is also substantiated by two general psychological statements, which seem particularly pertinent to our previous analysis of the final scene in *Saint Julian*. Otto Rank notes: "I compared to the creative drive of the individual as treated in 'Der Kunstler' the creation of the individual himself, not merely physically, but also psychically in the sense of the 'rebirth experience,' which I understood psychologically as the actual creative act of the human being. For in this act the psychic ego is born out of the biological corporeal ego and the human being becomes at once creator and creature or actually moves from creature to creator, in the ideal case, creator of himself, his own Personality" (*Truth and Reality*, trans. Jessie Taft [New York, 1968], p. 210). Rank's mention of rebirth recalls Julian "naked as on the day he was born" (III, 53) and suggests a link between this final scene and the drive for artistic creativity. This link would be further reinforced by Freud's discussion of another dimension that emerged from the final part of the tale—the desire to become the father: "there is no doubt that the creative artist feels towards his work like a father" ("Leonardo da Vinci," XI, 121).

2

The Individuation Process in *Saint Julian*

George Moskos

Flaubert creates the life of Saint Julian from birth to apotheosis in three chronological frames: childhood (with the parents), the conquests of the hero (separation from the parents which ends in their murder), and the "dark night of the soul" (which culminates in reunification with the parents and spiritual transformation). This progression leaves the reader with the impression of an inexorable movement, seemingly controlled only by visionary indices: the predictions of his destiny made to Julian's parents at his birth, the stag's prediction to Julian that he will murder his parents, and the leper's call near the end of the story. If we look to the extended scenes to understand Julian's "psychology" (his personal feelings and obsessions), we will find only the most superficial of clues. He is indeed obsessed with the slaughter of the animals and, after the stag's prediction, with the murder of his parents. Beyond his painfully repressed desire to murder his parents, what do we in fact know, or what can we even infer, about his relationship with them? As though to block our way even more efficaciously, the narrator insists on Julian's almost total ignorance of both his actions and their motivations: he is stupefied when he realizes that he has killed the mouse in the chapel; the long chase scene is like a dream; after the slaughter of the herd of deer, Julian does not understand how he could have done it; even the murder of his parents takes place in the dark.

I am not suggesting that conscious awareness of action and motivation is equivalent to the existence of a personal psychology, simply that this combination of elements renders a "personal" reading of the text much more problematical. From the very beginning, Julian is presented as "extraordinary," a miracle child (like Jesus) whose birth is accompanied by visions. He even cuts all his teeth without crying once. Even as he attains mythical proportions, Julian is curiously "absent" from the story. The tremendous psychological upheavals which we sense in the three major scenes seem unattached to a personal history. The drama moves on step by step, as though ignorant of its own toll of sorrow and pain. Julian, simultaneously present and absent, suffers.

Each hallucinatory scene effects a decisive change in Julian's life, and serves as a bridge from one part of the story to the next. Most important, the last scene (with the leper) differs markedly from the others in that it is illuminated for the first time. Figuratively and literally, Julian is no longer "in the dark," and he *understands* what he must do. There is not only a movement from one section to the next, or a simple correspondance of motifs, but also a clear progression from incomprehension to understanding, from darkness to light. If Julian is absent from a great part of his own story, it is because he is *not born as an individual* until the last page. The only possible object of our analysis is the progression itself, and the only sign of this progression, the text.

How then can we decipher this textual progression? If Julian is both present and absent, who "experiences" this progression? C. G. Jung's theories of the collective unconscious and the individuation process can help us to answer both these questions. Put quite simply, individuation is the process by which the integration of the personality is realized. The catalyst of this process is the collective unconscious, not to be confused with the *personal* unconscious. The contents of this collective unconscious do not originate in personal experience, but rather "in the inherited possibility of psychic functioning in general."[1] The collective unconscious reveals itself to the conscious mind "in images which, as in dreams and fantasies, initiate the process of conscious reaction and assimilation."[2] The activation of any of these "archetypes" that demands its assimilation by the conscious mind is ultimately a manifestation of the drive toward psychic wholeness, the integration of the psychic systems (consciousness and the unconscious) in the process of individuation. I will show that the textual progression in *The Legend* can be understood in relation to the stages of individuation outlined by Jung.

Julian's fantastic birth marks him as the mythological hero through whom the phases of a "regular, instinctive psychic occurrence"[3] are realized, carrying him to his birth as an individual. The atmosphere of dream or hallucination, combined with the seemingly unmotivated yet unfailing mechanism of progression and transcendence which leads from one section to the next, suggests a description of the story as the psychic projection of a collective process which works itself out in the life of an individual. In his evolutionary study of the development of human consciousness, *The Origins and History of Consciousness,* Erich Neumann maintains that such an exemplary individual permits us to become aware of what we ourselves have *already* experienced:

> In the course of its ontogenetic development, the individual ego consciousness has to pass through the same archetypal stages which determined the evolution of consciousness in the life of humanity. The individual has in his own life to follow the road that humanity has trod before him, leaving traces of its journey in the archetypal sequence of mythological images.[4]

1. From *The Collected Works of C. G. Jung* (hereafter *C. W.*), ed. Sir Herbert Read, Michael Fordham, and Gerhard Adler, Bollingen Series 20 (New York and Princeton, 1953–79), VI (*Psychological Types*), 485.
2. Erich Neumann, *The Origins and History of Consciousness,* Bollingen Series, 42 (Princeton, 1970), p. xv.
3. C. G. Jung, "A Psychological Approach to the Dogma of the Trinity," in *Psychology and Religion: West and East* (*C.W.*, vol. 11), p. 193.
4. Neumann, *Origins,* p. xvi.

In realizing his own wholeness, Julian must recapitulate the psychic experiences of the collectivity. Julian carries the burden, and the promise, of our history.

The World of the Parents

Saint Julian opens with a description of the castle of Julian's parents before his birth. Each part of the castle is neatly laid out in a geometric, stable order: "The four towers at the corners" (I, 2), "A second enclosure" (I, 4), "A pasture of green grass, . . . itself enclosed by a thick thorn hedge" (I, 4). The running of the household is as ordered as its construction: "Her household was ruled like the inside of a monastery" (I, 10). The imposing figure who controls and maintains this order is the father. In his role as "justicer," the father is supported by a long and seemingly universal ancestral legacy. In his armory there are "weapons of all nations and of all ages" (I, 7). An eternal and fixed order reigns over the world: "Life had been peaceful for so long that the portcullis could not be lowered anymore" (I, 5).

Although an event of miraculous portent, Julian's birth does not effect any change in this stable parental order. To the contrary, he is completely assimilated by it. Until the murder of the mouse in the chapel, Julian *always* appears surrounded by his father and mother. Through an analysis of the repeated use of the imperfect tense, Benjamin and Heidi Bart arrive at a similar description of the story's opening pages. They conclude that in Julian's childhood world there "is neither Beginning nor end: everything has always been thus 'depuis si longtemps,' and the imperfect tense mirrors it."[5]

5. Heidi Culbertson Bart and Benjamin F. Bart, "Space, Time, and Reality in Flaubert's *Saint Julien*," *Romanic Review*, 59 (1968), 32. See also Jean-Paul Sartre, *L'Idiot de la famille: Gustave Flaubert de 1821 à 1857* (Paris, 1971–72), I, 13–648. In his "reconstruction" of Flaubert's childhood, Sartre presents many details that parallel my analysis of Julian's experience. He discerns a basic dichotomy between "Faith" and "Reason" which haunts Flaubert throughout his life. This division is accompanied by the dream of a state of unity: "Nonetheless he retains the nostalgia for unity, all the more strongly since this nostalgia is nourished by an obscure reminiscence comparable to the memory of another life. . . . a state of innocence" (p. 332). Sartre associates this state of innocence with the adoration of the Father, perceived as a medieval "Lord": "And this state is *always* characterized by adoration. When the subject considers himself as inessential and holds as essential his Lord, then he becomes 'infinite' and 'profound.' This . . . is

Erich Neumann describes the "symbolic self-representation of the dawn state, showing the infancy both of mankind and of the child"[6] in terms which parallel my analysis of Julian's early childhood: "Enfolded and upborne.... Nothing is himself; everything is world. The world shelters and nourishes him, while he scarcely wills and acts at all.... Everything is still in the 'now and for ever' of eternal being... yesterday and tomorrow, genesis and decay, the flux of life and birth and death, have not yet entered the world."[7] The infant lives in a state of unconscious bliss. Analytical psychologists use the term *Self* to describe this totality which envelops the child (the nascent ego). The starting point for all psychic development is the Self, "the archetype of wholeness" and "the ordering and unifying center of the total psyche (conscious and unconscious)."[8] The ego grows out of the Self, and it is the relationship of these two centers of the psyche (ego and Self, consciousness and the unconscious) which determines psychological development. In the pre-ego and earliest stages of ego development, the child lives in a state of participation mystique with the Self, a state in which no opposites have been constellated. The primal relationship is one of complete ego-Self identification, in which the Self is "experienced" in projection onto the parents. In *The Child*,

---

an indistinction of the heart and the mind united in an act of total love" (pp. 332–333). Thus the Father is all, and controls the Son, who need only passively submit to his control.

6. Neumann, *Origins*, p. 11.

7. *Ibid.*, pp. 12–15.

8. Edward F. Edinger, *Ego and Archetype: Individuation and the Religious Function of the Psyche* (reprint; Baltimore, 1973), p. 3. As the ego is the center to which all the contents of consciousness are related, the Self is the center of the unconscious. The activation of this archetype of the Self begins the process of individuation, which culminates in the reunification of the psychic systems, with the Self as the center of the integrated personality. This new totality, a synthesis of the conscious and unconscious systems, is the Self. Jung writes that the object of the individuation process "is the *self* in contradistinction to the *ego*, which is only the point of reference for consciousness, whereas the self comprises the totality of the psyche altogether, i.e., conscious *and* unconscious" (C. G. Jung, *Mandala Symbolism* [from *C.W.*, vol. 9, pt. II], Princeton/Bollingen Paperback Edition [Princeton, 1973], p. 5). The conception of the Self, as Edinger points out, "is a paradox. It is simultaneously the center and the circumference of the circle of totality" (Edinger, p. 6).

Neumann states that "symbolically, the relationship of the ego to the totality-center is that of a son. In its relation to the development of the ego, the totality-center, or Self, is closely bound up with the parent archetype."[9]

The scene of the murder of the mouse in the chapel (beginning with "One day, during mass," I, 28) marks the beginning of a decisive rupture of this state of participation/unity which characterizes the opening pages of *The Legend*. Although in the preceding paragraph Julian's place is next to his parents, just as it has been from the beginning ("His seat in the chapel was next to his parents," I, 27), they disappear as soon as the mouse is spotted for the first time. Julian observes it over an indeterminate period of time ("and every Sunday, he would watch for it," I, 28), with no hint of his parents' presence. The preparation of the murder takes us one step farther, in that Julian actively seeks this isolation: he closes the door ("So, having closed the door," I, 29). In this scene, and the two that follow, Julian is alone for the first time in the story. In all three cases, his solitary state is accompanied by murderous violence. Although this distancing from his parents, and their subsequent murder, may tempt us to infer that this aggression is directed against them, a close analysis of the text reveals a more ambiguous situation.

In the first scene, the physical description of the mouse—"a little white mouse" (I, 28), "this little body" (I, 30), "a pink snout" (I, 30)—corresponds quite closely to two traits of the infant Julian: "his pink cheeks" (I, 21), "a little Jesus" (I, 21). After killing the mouse, Julian throws it outside, directly mirroring his own state of separation. The scene contains the same dream or hallucinatory clues as the long chase scene: an indeterminate span of time translated by the use of the imperfect tense and the notation "After a very long while" (I, 30), and Julian's disbelief when confronted with the body of the mouse ("stunned before this little body which no longer moved," I, 30). Through an unconscious displacement mechanism, Julian seems to eliminate himself from what was a charmed existence. The contiguity of the scene with his parents, and the fact that

9. Erich Neumann, *The Child: Structure and Dynamics of the Nascent Personality* (New York, 1973), p. 9.

the murder takes place in the same spot, clearly indicate that the state of unity with the parents has been shattered. At this point it is not at all clear *who* has ended it: the parents have been "absent" since the beginning of the scene, but it is Julian who has literally shut them out.

This short scene ends on a highly ambiguous note which surreptitiously reintroduces the parents: Julian will not speak of his violence ("said not a word about it to anyone," I, 30). The only other secrets in the text thus far are the predictions of Julian's destiny made to his parents, and hidden by them: "The couple kept their secret from each other" (I, 21). Their visionary "secret" leads both parents to respect Julian as marked by God. The fact that the murder takes place in the chapel suggests a sort of sacrilege of this now empty sanctuary of parental protection. It is by their very absence—verbal (their secret) and physical (the empty chapel)—that the parents are implicated in Julian's violence.

The following episode, in which Julian kills the small birds in the garden, is constructed as a violent reply to the earlier description of the first lessons given to Julian by his parents. In the passage beginning "When he turned seven" (I, 22), Julian's mother teaches him to sing. In the garden, Julian uses a hollow reed, not to devise a flute to accompany the warbling of the birds, but rather as a weapon to kill them. Again in the earlier passage, Julian's father lifts him up onto a horse, "to make him brave" (I, 22). Now Julian himself raises up his weapon ("then lift the tube," I, 31), assuming what was the prerogative of the father. In both this scene and the one in the chapel, Julian's use of phallic objects (the reed, the stick) serves to reinforce this assumption of paternal force. (We should not forget that the mother's lesson is likewise violently deformed by Julian.) Again, this violence appears to be directed against the infant Julian: his prey is small (not "oiseaux," birds, but "oisillons," *small* birds) and in French the "chirping" of birds ("gazouiller") has come to be used to describe the prattling of small children.

Julian raises the tube to his mouth, blows up his cheeks, and—glaring textual lapsus—without his blowing out the peas, as if by magic, the birds fall from the sky: "then lift the tube, swell his cheeks; and the little creatures rained down on his shoulders" (I, 31). This lapsus, coupled with the abundance of animals killed (characteristic of the major chase scene that follows), once again places us in a hallucinatory dream world. More importantly, the missing breath marks the absence of the parents. References to expiration and death are present in all the major scenes and are constellated about the parental figures: the doe who bellows when her fawn is slaughtered (she is killed immediately thereafter), "the two almost equal death rattles" (II, 75) of the parents in the murder scene itself (note the presence of "small birds" in II, 51), and the "quickening death rattle" (III, 47) of the leper in the final scene. This lapsus situates Julian in a world *already* abandoned by the parents, one in which the "life breath" is missing. Only death, his parents' and his own, is a certainty. Inversely, since this breath comes from the parents, the lapsus reinforces the notion of Julian's assumption of parental force: he quite simply *assumes* that their power is at his service. The associations with the death of the parents, and Julian's symbolic suicide, betray a fundamental *impotence* just below the surface of this *power*. Life and strength will return only in the last scene, when the leper repeats the father's gest of raising Julian up, while at the same time transmitting the heretofore absent "breath of life" to him. The leper's transformation begins when Julian lies on top of him ("mouth against mouth," III, 56), close enough to feel the breath from his nose ("the breath of his nostrils had the sweetness of roses," III, 57).

The killing of the small birds, like the preceding scene in the chapel, is structured around five principal elements:

1. The atmosphere of dream or hallucination.
2. The absence of the parents. They are "a priori" not present, having disappeared when Julian spots the mouse.
3. The reintroduction of the parents by way of their absence (lapsus, secret). The transposition of the education scene in the imaginary structure of the bird massacre reinforces this hypothesis. The close association of these elements with Julian's violence suggests an implicit involvement of the parents.

4. Julian's assumption of magical powers (properly those of the parents), masking a fundamental impotence.
5. Julian's self-directed violence (against the infant that he was): a suicide.

The last of these three short scenes shares a similar five-part structure. When Julian spots a pigeon on the ramparts of the castle, he happens to be standing at a spot on the wall where there is a break. A small piece of stone, the murder weapon, appears under his hand: "where he stood, his fingers happened upon a loose stone" (I, 32). This series of events, coincidental at first glance, seems less so when we remember that the mouse appeared out of a hole in the wall of the chapel, corresponding to the crack in the wall. The solidity and stability of the parental world, so carefully delineated *architecturally* in the opening passage, is cracked and split, paving the way for Julian's violence. (The image of the "hole" ["trou"] will reappear in the scene of the parents' murder: "His father and mother lay before him, on their backs, with a hole in their breasts," II, 79.) The use of a reflexive verb to describe Julian's "finding" of the rock ("se rencontra") underscores the dreamlike, magical nature of the sequence. Effortlessly, Julian wounds the pigeon: "He swung his arm, and the stone squarely hit the bird which fell straight into the ditch" (I, 32). Julian simply swings his arm, and as if by magic, the stone reaches its target. As in the slaughter of the birds, there is an empty space which "assumes" the force of the parents (it was his *father's* arm which lifted Julian up), and at the same time marks their absence. A symbolic challenge to, and removal of, the father? Certainly. More clearly, however, there is the unspoken, and *passive*, assumption that this power is at the disposition of the son. The passive nature of this "challenge" is evident in the preceding scenes: the mouse is killed with only a light blow, leaving Julian stupefied; the birds fall in great abundance with little effort on Julian's part. This time the charm is broken. The pigeon is only wounded, and clings to life. For the first time, Julian is obliged to engage his *own* energy in order to finish it off, giving us a foretaste of the ferocity which will characterize the long chase scene.

He scurries into the ditch, "ferreting on all sides, nimbler than a young dog" (I, 33). Pushed into a world of death, Julian cannot tolerate the existence of an impulse to life. Finding the pigeon in the bushes gasping for breath, Julian's reaction is one of extreme irritation: "Its protracted life irritated the child. He began to strangle it" (I, 35). What follows is a double dance of death and suicide. The convulsions of the pigeon are mirrored in Julian's quickened heartbeat, and his death is accompanied by Julian's loss of consciousness: "With the final stiffening, he felt faint" (I, 35).

For the first time the parents also seem to be *directly* touched by Julian's violence. In the preceding scene, the missing breath, although linked *prospectively* with the murder of the parents, functioned as a sign of their *absence*. Julian now actively seeks to cut off this life breath as he strangles the pigeon. The description of the pigeon, its wings broken, "throbbing, hung in the branches of a privet" (I, 34), anticipates the final scene of Part I (I, 81–83), in which Julian mistakes his mother's bonnet for the wings of a stork and nearly kills her. His javelin pierces the bonnet and its long streamers, nailing them to the wall, a position analogous to that of the pigeon suspended in the hedge.

The erotic tone of the passage is unmistakable: Julian's quickened heartbeat, the "wild and tumultuous delight" (I, 35) that grips him, the final stiffening accompanied by his lapse into a faint which resembles orgasm. Given the textual correspondences between the wounded pigeon and Julian's mother, can we view this scene as an incest fantasy?

Such an interpretation confronts us with a complex web of textual correspondences that paradoxically seem to indicate not only incest but also matricide *and* patricide, and suicide. The description of Julian's mother which resembles in some details that of the wounded pigeon is taken from a passage in which Julian nearly kills her. (Julian is in fact *also murdering* the pigeon.) At the same time, the descriptions directly preceding this later scene are replete with blatant phallic imagery: the heavy sword with which he nearly kills his father, the bare blade which makes Julian go pale, the javelin which he throws through the necks of bottles. It is in fact with a javelin that Julian pierces his mother's cap.[10] Unlike a previous "accident" involving his father ("Julian imagined he had killed his father," I, 77), it is not explicitly stated that Julian thinks he has *killed* his mother ("Julian fled from the castle, and was seen no more," I, 84). This narrative silence only serves to heighten the ambiguity of Julian's action. Nonetheless, even *if* we read this second scene as an incest fantasy, we must conclude that this incestuous desire is inextricably linked, as in the pigeon scene, with a mortal threat to the mother.

The reference to the *strangulation* of the pigeon obliges us to take into account the "contamination of identity" which has characterized the symbolic absence/presence of the parents in all of these short scenes: the secret known to each parent, the deformation of the education scene involving both parents, the holes, the missing life breath. In their presence, absence, and death, the parents are systematically presented *together* (except in the intersection between this sequence of short scenes and the first long massacre scene). This "contamination of identity" is evident even in the later "accident" scene with the mother. Flaubert refers to the "barbes" (streamers) of her bonnet, linking her by semantic similarity to both the father and the stag. This bonnet appears in the first description of the mother which includes a reference to its "cornes" (horns) reminding us of the stag's "andouillers" (antlers). This systematic "contamination of identity" strongly suggests the possibility of an incestuous desire which involves both Julian's mother *and* father. In any case, it is clear that the murder of *both* parents is projected in this scene.

Neumann's mythological analysis of the child's (nascent ego's) "experience" of the world can help us to understand this "contamination of identity" and inseparability of the parents in the first part of *The Legend:*

> The question . . . about the origin has but one answer, and of this there are two interpretations: the womb and the parents. . . . The uroboros appears as the round "container," i.e., the maternal womb, but also as the union of masculine and feminine opposites, the World Parents joined in perpetual cohabitation. . . . The

10. See Chapter 1, pp. 36–37.

World Father is joined to the World Mother in uroboric union, and they are not to be divided. They are still under the rule of the primordial law: . . . father and mother, heaven and earth . . . reflect one another, and cannot be put apart. . . . Their unity is a state . . . independent of the opposites.[11]

This union is undissolved as long as the child exists in a state of complete ego-Self identification. The breakdown of this Paradise state and the dissolution of parental unity are always more or less simultaneous. This sequence of three short scenes is a first step, although halting and incomplete, in that direction.

This movement is interrupted by the appearance of the father, temporally linked by the notation "That evening" (I, 36) to the preceding scene, which took place "One day" (I, 28). The contiguity and continuity of these two scenes create an atmosphere in which dream and reality are complementary. Julian "wakes" from his faint only to hear his father's admonition that he learn to hunt: "his father announced that at his age one must learn venery" (I, 36). The slaughter of the animals is an order, or at least an obligation, imposed by the father!

In this section, which I will call the intersection, extending from his father's admonition to the beginning of the long chase scene, Julian is almost always alone. His father appears only twice: to make up a pack of dogs for Julian, and indirectly when it is mentioned that his money permitted him to buy the most exotic birds of prey. Both references not only reinforce his father's encouragement of the hunt but also detail the extent to which Julian's apprenticeship is in fact *dependent* on his father. His mother appears only once. Returning from the hunt, reeking of the odor of ferocious beasts, Julian unwillingly accepts her embrace: "Whenever his mother held him against her, he accepted her embrace coldly" (I, 48). It is also important to note the particularization and textual separation of the parents in this section. Julian's father assumes the *educative* function which heretofore was exercised by both parents. On the other hand, the mother assumes the *affective* function which had also been shared in the opening passages ("both cherished the child with

11. Neumann, *Origins*, pp. 12–18.

equal love," I, 21). It is evident that another step in the break-down of the primordial unity has taken place. No longer does he hunt with the others from the castle: "he preferred hunting far from the crowd" (I, 44). The increasing amount of time Julian spends outside the walls of the castle and his growing perfection in the art of the hunt are accompanied by an accentuated ferocity. As Julian's prey become larger and more vicious—bears, wild boar, wolves—he begins to resemble them.

The massacre scene, beginning with "One winter morning" (I, 50), is centered about the five elements of the preceding shorter scenes, with the essential difference that this structure crystallizes around the murder of the parents, and breaks to the surface. The entire scene takes place in a timeless dream world: "He was hunting in some indeterminate land, for an indefinite time, solely because of his very existence, everything fulfilling itself with the ease which one experiences in dreams" (I, 56). All geographical specificity has been lost: the castle, the chapel, the garden, the ramparts have all been left far behind. The very facility of the slaughter translates Julian's assumption of almost Godlike powers, which are the domain of the parents. He is confronted with "a host of beasts, with every step more numer-ous" (I, 56), yet he never tires of killing them. Even the decor reflects his fantasy of power: "Next he entered an avenue of tall trees, the tops of which seemed to form a triumphal arch" (I, 56).

Up to this point, the unfolding of this fantasy strictly follows the pattern of the others. The sighting of the family of deer rapidly changes what is a very delicate balance. For the first time, the three "victims" of Julian's aggression appear as *individ-ual* figures and as members of the *family* group. The configura-tion of the stag's family is exactly that of Julian's: "A stag, a doe, and her fawn" (I, 63). The dependence of the fawn still sucking on the mother's tit, the father as authority figure standing above the group, and the simplicity and unity of the group recall the harmony of the first days of *The Legend*. The fawn is Julian's first victim: "The fawn, immediately, was killed" (I, 65). The cry of the doe, "deep, rending, human" (I, 65), undermines (even for Ju-lian?) the illusion of animal slaughter which is the principal sup-port of the fantasy. The doe/mother is killed. Julian uses his *last* arrow against the stag, who seems not even to feel it. He advances toward Julian, who, now stripped of his power, "recoiled with unspeakable terror" (I, 67). The identification of the stag and the father breaks to the surface: "solemn like a patriarch and like a justicer" (I, 67). His prediction of the parents' murder completely drains Julian of the ferocious energy which has propelled him throughout the massacre scene: "Julian was stunned, then overcome with a sudden weariness" (I, 70). Like a child, Julian breaks down in tears, and he is suddenly afraid to be in the forest alone: "The solitude all about him seemed fraught with ill-defined perils" (I, 71). The ferociously independent Julian is reduced to a crying child lost in the woods. What has happened? What path has brought him to the horrible realization that he will murder his parents?

To answer these questions, we must go full circle back to the Julian of the origins (so close in fact to the helpless child after the stag's prediction), and to the idea of ego-Self identification. Since the latent ego (the child) is completely identified with the parents who are the center and the totality of being (the Self), it "experiences itself as a deity. . . . His total being and experience are ordered around the *a priori* assumption of deity."[12] Edinger uses the term "ego-inflation" to describe the passive assumption of omnipotent parental power which characterizes the magical and effortless slaying of the animals in the sequence of three short scenes and at the beginning of the long massacre scene.[13] This state of Paradisical containment cannot last forever. The child must grow up, and the "criterion for being 'grown up' is that the individual is led out of the family circle and initiated into the world."[14] In psychological terms, the coalescing and separation of the ego complex from the Self (ego-Self differentiation) is the next natural step in the development of the psyche. The movement in *The Legend* from the envelopment of the first part to the disappearance of the parents and Julian's solitude beginning with the episode of the mouse in the chapel can be understood as the first push toward this differentiation. The geo-

12. Edinger, p. 7.
13. See Chapter 3, p. 141.
14. Neumann, *Origins*, p. 408.

graphical configuration of the three short massacre scenes traces a line which runs from the center to the periphery of the castle—from the chapel to the garden, and then to the moat (although barely so, Julian is outside of the confines of the castle for the first time in the story). During his apprenticeship of the hunt, Julian is more and more often outside of the castle. Finally, in the long chase scene, all reference to the castle is completely absent.

The line I traced in the text was not a straight one. This "push" loses momentum at two points: Julian faints after strangling the pigeon, and he is immensely tired after the stag's prediction. In both instances this loss of strength is followed by the reappearance of the parents: the father's admonition at the dinner table and the return to the castle. Even the linear distancing from the parental center is not a clean break. In the first group of short scenes, Julian stays within the walls of the castle (and when he does overstep the boundary, there is dissolution back to the father). The equipment and training for his hunts come from his father; Julian carries his parents with him even in his fleeting moments of solitude. The disidentification of the ego and the Self is by no means an easy task. At the beginning of this process there is no real continuity of consciousness. The nascent ego can be compared to an "island" which "rises up with whatever contents it then has, but soon sinks back again into the unconscious."[15] The schematic diagram in Figure 1 will help us to visualize this movement.[16] It is the first two frames which interest us for the moment: the ego contained in the Self, and the ego moving out of the Self. (The first frame, for the sake of clarity of presentation, is a bit misleading in its portrayal of the ego as an already organized system. More exactly, it should be presented as a diffuse constellation of small points within the Self.) As the ego coalesces and moves out of the Self, we notice the large area still "under the control" of the unconscious. If we imagine the first two frames repeated interchangeably several times *before* the introduction of the third frame, we have a close approximation of the "rising and sinking" of

15. *Ibid.*, p. 15.
16. From Edinger, p. 5.

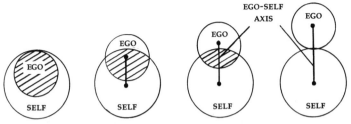

FIGURE 1. The disidentification of the ego and the Self. From *Ego and Archetype* by Edward F. Edinger, copyright 1972 by the C. G. Jung Foundation for Analytical Psychology, Inc.

the nascent ego, and a rather precise structural diagram of *The Legend* up to this point. After each section in which Julian has distanced himself from the parents, there comes a point of weakness which ends in a return to the previous state of containment. Any movement by the ego requires an extraordinary effort to break away from the "psychic gravitation" of the unconscious. The ego, easily tired, has a tendency to fall back into his Paradise world where no effort is required.

It should not surprise us that the three short scenes are ended when the magically thrown stone fails to kill the pigeon and Julian is forced to use his own hands to strangle it. The effort is too demanding—blackout, and back into the world of the parents. This notion of falling back into the world of the parents will also help us to begin to untangle the complex web of elements associated with the incest fantasy of this third scene. Neumann shows that in mythology this return of the weak ego to the previous state of containment and unity (in the uroboros) is represented as a form of incest:

> Being oneself is still a wearisome and painful experience, still the exception that has to be overcome. It is in this sense that we speak of "uroboric incest."... The term "incest" is to be understood symbolically.... Uroboric incest is a form of entry into the mother, of union with her.... it is more a desire to be dissolved and absorbed; passively one lets oneself be taken.[17]

17. Neumann, *Origins*, pp. 16–17.

Here we must be very careful not to forget that the uroboros (the mythological representation of the state of primordial unity, and of the Self) is *both* masculine and feminine, "and they are not to be divided."[18] This inseparability of the mother and the father of the primal union was Julian's particular experience in the opening passages. Neumann's exclusive reference to the mother in his description of uroboric incest is a function of the predominance of the maternal side (containment, protection, shelter) for the weak ego seeking reabsorption. However, as Neumann himself emphasizes, entry into the mother is also *reunion with the father* (who appears *first* in the intersection). Finally, this "uroboric incest" is presented as the dissolution or "dying" of the child in the pleroma, a passive suicide of the ego.

As a general schema, this explanation by uroboric incest does significantly associate certain elements of the scene: the "incest" with both parents culminating in Julian's faint (death, suicide) back into the parental world. By its emphasis on the *passivity* of this return, however, it runs counter to the evidence of Julian's *active* participation in the scene. The positive suppression of the parents (matricide/patricide) indicates, to the contrary, a resistance to this dissolution. In my discussion of the *movement* of these passages I have emphasized the dynamic of the birth of the ego. Their *content* (violent murder/suicide, images of death) differs markedly from what we might then expect. The network of images of rupture, the massacre of the animals, the deformation of the parental lessons, the absence/murder of the parents, and the stag's prediction all point to the destructive nature of this movement toward consciousness. It is in the third scene that this violence is not only directed against the parents but also linked to the motif of incest. The decisive element in this drama is that the distancing from the parental world is "experienced" by the nascent ego as a traumatic loss, as the expulsion from the garden of Paradise. What is more, "this separation is not experienced only as passive suffering and loss, but also as an actively destructive deed. It is symbolically identical with killing [and] sacrifice."[19] The birth of ego-consciousness *demands* the slaying

18. *Ibid.*, p. 18.
19. *Ibid.*, p. 121.

of the parents. Consciousness must be freed from the hold of the unconscious.

This parent murder is inextricably linked to the notion of *active incest* as opposed to the *passivity* of *uroboric incest:* "the hero's 'incest' is a regenerative incest. Victory over the mother, . . . taking the form of actual entry into her, . . . brings about a rebirth."[20] To slay the mother is to penetrate her (as in the myth of the dragon fight).[21] This "incest," and victory over the mother, is a profoundly symbolic act which liberates the ego from the hold of the unconscious. However, since the world of the unconscious is both masculine and feminine, paternal and maternal, this struggle involves *both* the First Parents. In mythology, it is presented as "a fight in which the murders of both father and mother, but not of one alone, have their ritually prescribed place."[22] (The victory over the father is often presented separately as a dismemberment or castration). "Incest" with the mother symbolizes her death, and that of the father.

The borderline state of Julian's consciousness in the three short scenes accounts for the coexistence of indications of uroboric and active incest. In the last short scene Julian is at the greatest distance yet from the parental center, but still far from an independent position. At the first real hint of what this independence means in relation to his parents (*strangulation* of the pigeon/*active incest/murder*), Julian is still able to slip back into the security of the parental world (uroboric incest). Activity and passivity, independence and dependence confront one another in a still largely unequal battle. The primal unity of the parents, although showing some signs of disintegration, is still stronger than the ego's movement toward differentiation. The "contamination of identity" determines the double-targeted desire (and possibility) for incest with both parents—that is to say, reunion with the parents in the Paradise state.

In the intersection, as the ego complex gains in strength, the specific maternal and paternal "characteristics" (affective and educative) are precipitated out of this perfect union. After the

20. *Ibid.*, p. 154.
21. See discussion of the dragon fight in *ibid.*, pp. 152–191.
22. *Ibid.*, p. 153.

stag's prediction (which is the result of this affirmation of the ego and its distancing from the parental center), Julian can no longer simply slip back into Paradise. He is obliged to "recreate" it through his illness—to seek *actively* a primordial *passivity* that has been lost forever. He forces the parents to be rejoined in their common concern and care for him.

As his strength returns, the illusion of unity becomes more difficult to maintain. The two accidents at the end of Part I are vivid evidence of the breakdown of the primordial unity of the parents. The "accident" involving Julian's mother can be read as an incest fantasy (and a deadly one for her). In the preceding "accident" involving his father, Julian drops a sword which narrowly misses him, tearing his cloak. Here it is the authority function of the father that is attacked in a symbolic castration-murder fantasy. Dissolution in unity (uroboric incest) is no longer possible, for the primordial parents are separated. Now *both* parents are viewed as a threat to the continued development of the ego. Its double fixation by paternal authority and maternal affection must be overcome: both parents must be killed. Standing behind this differentiation of function, the essential unity of the parents as representatives of the unconscious is intact. When Julian stumbles into his bedroom, he will find both his mother and his father lying together, and he will kill them both.

An intriguing aspect of this first sequence of three short scenes is the fact that the images of suicide are more clearly discernible, and earlier, than those of parricide. Why does Julian turn his destructive energy on himself first? The structural correspondance between the second short massacre scene and the earlier education scene from Julian's childhood is crucial to our understanding of this suicidal tendency. My analysis showed that the "tools" (music, the elevation to courage) furnished by Julian's parents are deformed to become the imaginary structure of the scene, and the instruments of his self-destruction. In the education scene, our attention is drawn to the repeated use of the preterit tense ("eut," "apprit," "hissa") and to the notation of age ("When he turned seven," I, 22). These details single out the passage against the backdrop of the other scenes of Julian's childhood, almost all of which are recounted in the imperfect tense. The educational function of the scene (preparing Julian for the moment he will stand on his own as an individual) is marked out as an *event* which interrupts the continuity, the *timelessness* of his childhood. We can measure the gravity of this interruption by comparing Julian's smile at the end of this scene to his malicious laugh as he watches the dead birds fall all about him in the later one.

Within the context of the images of rupture and destruction linked to the absence of the parents and Julian's suicide, the fantasy replay of the education scene strongly suggests an unconscious cause-effect relationship which we might "formulate" as follows: "My parents prepared me to be an individual, to leave them. But why? I was perfectly happy with things as they were. They must want everything to change, to be rid of me. They must not love me anymore. I must have done something wrong. All this is my fault. I am guilty." Suicide. The suicide fantasies of these three short scenes reveal a guilt which *precedes* the guilt for the murder of the parents. It stems from what Julian "experiences" as a rejection by his parents, a denial of their love. Erich Neumann calls this the primary guilt feeling:

> Surprising as it may seem, the need to counteract [what the child perceives as] the lack of love . . . causes the child not to blame the world . . . but to feel guilty. . . . The primary guilt feeling . . . is not a matter of conscious reflection in the child, but it leads to the conviction, which will play a determining role in the child's existence, that not-to-be-loved is identical with being abnormal, sick, "leprous," and . . . "condemned."[23]

Although this primary guilt feeling cannot be derived from the guilt connected with the murder of the parents, its primordial role in Julian's development is a determining factor in his reaction to the stag's prediction. (Even in this scene, Julian kills the fawn first.) The doctors who care for Julian after his return to the castle declare that "Julian's illness . . . was due to some baleful wind, or to a desire for love" (I, 73). The significance of this diagnosis can only be understood within the context of Julian's regressive behavior after the stag's prediction. Horrified by the necessity of his own *birth* as an independent being, which de-

23. Neumann, *The Child*, p. 86.

mands the *death* of the parental world, Julian flees on the very
path which will take him back to the castle, to the sheltered
world of childhood: "Then, impelled by terror, he started running across the countryside, chose a path at random, and found
himself almost immediately at the gates of the castle" (I, 71).
Julian lapses into a condition analogous to the existence of an
infant in the cradle, surrounded and protected by the parents:
"For three months, his mother in anguish prayed at his bedside,
and his father, moaning, continually paced the halls" (I, 73). He
need not even *walk* on his own: "and he was taken on strolls
in the courtyard, the old monk and the good lord each holding
him up on one side" (I, 74). Julian's sickness *forces* his parents
to give him back what he feels they have denied him: their love.[24]

However, the intervening prediction of the stag has introduced two new elements, the murder of the parents and *conscious volition*, which shift the responsibility for the rupture
squarely onto Julian's shoulders. Obsessed by this prediction,
"That night, he could not sleep" (I, 72). What follows is *not* a
dream: " 'No! no! no! I cannot murder them!' next, he would
reflect: 'Still, supposing I wanted to?...'" (I, 72). Is it not he
who wishes their death, who therefore does not *merit* their love?
Julian's refusal to hunt when his strength returns functions as
both a repression of his now conscious murder desire and a
positive strategy conceived in function of his other desire, to win
back the love of his parents.

Dreaming

In Part I Julian exists in a kind of twilight or borderline state,
vacillating between ego-formation (consciousness) and the un-

24. See Jean-Paul Sartre, *L'Idiot de la famille*, II, 1862–1882. Julian's regression
to the state of the infantile ego is strikingly parallel to Sartre's analysis of
Flaubert's passivity as manifested in the accident ("chute") near Pont-l'Évêque
in January, 1844: "naked, fragile, without defenses, his powerlessness is meant
to render him as helpless as a nursing infant. Through death and madness, he
aims to *regress* to his protohistory. He prepared himself to receive the medical
treatments *as though they were the first maternal caresses.* ... he aspires to pure
passivity. It is no accident if the crisis took the form of a fall followed by
paralysis: he lost the use of learned gestures, he can no longer speak, or walk or
even hold himself up; it is a newborn infant that Achille brings back to the
Hôtel-Dieu" (p. 1865).

conscious state of unity. The atmosphere of dream or hallucination in these scenes is characteristic of the dawn state of consciousness of both the child and humankind in general: "The ability of all contents to change shape and place, in accordance with the laws of similarity and symbolic affinity, the symbolic character of the world . . . all this the world of dreams shares with the dawn period of mankind."[25] It is in dreams that we most readily return to the "infantile" state of the psyche and confront the contents of the collective unconscious.

If this primordial state of containment is comparable to a dream state, why are the dream clues (magical gests, lapsus, vagueness of time and place) clustered in the two massacre scenes? If the first section of the story is also interpreted as a manifestation of this unconscious state of containment, why does it become so clear to us that these specific sections are the result of dream or fantasy? In fact, the use of the imperfect tense and the notation "so long," which are indicative of the uroboric nature of the opening passages, are also found in the dream sequences. The use of the chapel as the transition to the first dream sequence and the fade-out at the end suggest a certain continuity of the sections. The essential difference is Julian's solitude, the distancing from the parental center signaled by their absence and his movement from chapel to moat. This *distance* is the determining factor that permits the precipitation of dream (archetypal) images. Julian, completely enveloped by the parents in the opening pages, lives in a state of continuity with them. While he inhabits this world, it cannot be the *object* of anything, it simply *is everything*. The contents of this world can become images (archetypes) only where consciousness is present. It is the first feeble apparition of *consciousness* which is marked by the activation of *dream* contents. In the first two scenes of the first sequence the primary dream contents are: the absence of the parents, Julian's passive assumption of their power, and Julian's symbolic suicide. Each content functions in terms of a "hidden" correlative: the absence of the parents/ lapsus, secret, breath, all linked prospectively to their murder; Julian's passive assumption of parental power/Julian's impo-

25. Neumann, *Origins*, p. 76.

tence without them; Julian's symbolic suicide/the primary guilt feeling. The third short scene functions as an active reversal of content and correlative while tracing out in embryonic form the dramatic structure of the end of the long chase scene. The absence of the parents, a negative component in the first two scenes, is a result of a positive suppression in the third one (strangulation, discernible physical resemblance to the mother).

Jung maintains that the dream is a *"spontaneous self-portrayal, in symbolic form, of the actual situation in the unconscious."*[26] It is an "expression of an involuntary, unconscious psychic process... [which] shows... inner truth and reality... as it really is."[27] As these formulas would indicate, Jung expressly rejected Freud's theories of the censor and of the dream as disguised wish fulfillment. How then can we understand the "hidden" correlatives of the first two scenes? Although distanced from his parents, Julian remains within the castle, still heavily dependent on their world. The result of this continued immersion coupled with the minimally increased energy of the ego is evident in the second scene. The transposition of the education scene into the structure of this "massacre" introduces the notion of rupture with the parents, although it is Julian who assumes *total responsibility* for it. This "confusion" corresponds to Neumann's analysis of the perception of archetypal images by the historically emerging ego: "Originally it was impossible for the ego to distinguish the source of these images, for at the stage of *participation mystique* an outside could not be perceived distinct from an inside; the two sets of images overlapped."[28] When we return to the infantile state in dreams, we are in a position analogous to that of the emerging ego. This historical perspective coincides with Jung's explanation of the obscurity of dream content as due to the general contamination of unconscious contents and the opaque background of the psyche.[29] At this stage in Julian's

26. C. G. Jung, "General Aspects of Dream Psychology," in *The Structure and Dynamics of the Psyche* (C.W., vol. 8), p. 263.

27. C. G. Jung, "The Practical Use of Dream-Analysis," in *The Practice of Psychotherapy* (C.W., vol. 16), p. 142.

28. Neumann, *Origins*, pp. 295–296.

29. See Jung, "General Aspects."

development, this "opaque background" still occupies the "foreground" of the dream.

Jung also observes that certain dreams exhibit a much clearer organization of both structure and meaning, and leave a correspondingly stronger and more lasting conscious impression on the dreamer. He attributes these particularities to an increase in psychic energy tension: "With an increase of energy-tension, the dreams acquire a more ordered character; they become dramatically composed and reveal clear sense-connections, and the valency of the associations increases."[30] He compares this "big dream" to "an illuminating idea that irrupts." Again, "the underlying factor here is a considerable tension of psychic energy."[31] The metaphor of "irruption" makes it clear that "this considerable tension of psychic energy" can only be created *between* two poles: ego-consciousness and the unconscious. In the first two scenes (within the walls of the castle), sufficient coalescing of the ego has not taken place to create the "tension" necessary for the precipitation of a "big dream." Only in the third scene, when Julian goes beyond the castle's boundaries, does the *distance*[32] between the systems become minimally sufficient to generate this psychic tension. This "irruption" takes place in a frenzy of murder and suicide. Nonetheless, the entire scene takes place within the shadow of the castle, and the energy charge is extremely weak. Although the essential elements and structures of the drama to follow begin to become distinguishable, they do not yet form a coherent, significant whole. An exhausted Julian falls back into the world of the parents in an attempt to short-circuit *all* psychic tension. The "big dream" must wait.

End of a Dream: The Intersection

Dreaming brings pain. Julian seeks solace in the "real" world of his parents, their castle, his childhood. However, everything

---

30. C. G. Jung, "The Transcendent Function," in *Structure and Dynamics*, p. 77.

31. C. G. Jung, "Brother Klaus," in *Psychology and Religion*, p. 320.

32. Berg approaches this notion of distance from another perspective in Chapter 1.

now seems to be turned around. His dreaming *is* the reality of his life, and the "real" world of his childhood has faded—like a dream. The functional and textual separation of the parents and Julian's increasingly frequent solitude are two indications of the radical upheaval of this world. Julian has "returned," but he does not find the perfect unity which he left (how long ago?) in the chapel: the child, in his place, next to his parents. He has literally already *gone too far*.

This separation/differentiation is accompanied by a marked shift in Julian's attitude toward his parents. (The first hint of this change came in the deformation of the education scene in the slaughter of the small birds.) In fact, it is evident that Julian's parents *have not changed* in any way. Julian's *perception* of them, however, is radically altered. If his father's two appearances underline Julian's dependence on him for his apprenticeship of the hunt, it is also clear that he rejects the accepted forms to which this instruction is meant to lead: "But Julian scorned such convenient contrivances; he preferred hunting far from the crowd, with his horse and his falcon" (I, 44). In the same way, he rejects the affection offered by his mother: "Whenever his mother held him against her, he accepted her embrace coldly, as if dreaming of profound things" (I, 48). This reference to Julian's dreaming sends us back to the preceding short sequence, and suggests that the rejection of the mother's embrace and the father's instruction are related both to one another and to the destruction necessary for Julian to be "born" as an individual.

"To become conscious of oneself," Neumann writes, "begins with saying 'no' to the uroboros, to the Great Mother, to the unconscious."[33] The parental embrace which characterized the security of childhood has become a *threat* to the continued development of the ego. Furthermore, after the separation of the parents, this tendency of the uroboros to fix the nascent ego in its embrace is specifically perceived as a negative maternal function: "the clutching Earth Mother . . . twines herself about the son and seeks to hold him fast as an embryo . . . by making him the eternal babe in arms. . . . She is the deadly uroboric mother."[34] Julian's reluctance to accept his mother's embrace

33. Neumann, *Origins*, p. 121.
34. *Ibid.*, p. 164.

and his desire to be far away from the castle are the first signals of this reversal of perception (which will reappear even more explicitly in the abortive massacre scene in Part II).

A closer analysis of the father's encouragement of the hunt will show that it functions in a fashion analogous and complementary to the mother's embrace. Beginning in the opening passage, Julian's father is identified with the use of arms, whether in conquest or the hunt: "In the armory could be seen, between banners and heads of wild beasts, weapons of all ages and of all nations" (I, 7). There is a rather evident confusion of the hunt and the father's military feats: banners and animal muzzles are found side by side, and the profusion of arms could have been used for either the one or the other. It is clear that violence, and perhaps even ferocity, are not entirely new and unknown elements in the father's world. Paternal violence, however, survives only in what we might call an "institutionalized" form. The description of the armory could well be that of a museum, the repository of a cultural heritage "of all ages and of all nations." The image of the father dispensing justice and settling the quarrels of his neighbors while wrapped in a cape of fox skins is a striking example of this "domestication" of violence. The active phase of past violence laid the foundations for the present peaceful state. Violence is now fixed in the form of *authority* which guards the stability of this now unchanging and eternal order, and gives it the force of law.[35]

Julian is expected to abide by this law, to shape his life by it. His father's exhortation to him concerning the hunt is expressed in terms of a duty which Julian must fulfill. This duty is connected to ancient traditions and rules which are the property of his father, who presents Julian with "an old writing-book which contained, in question and answer form, the whole pastime of hunting" (I, 36). What a person of Julian's age must know is fixed into written rules which he must recite from memory before his father recognizes him as worthy of the hunt: "When Julian was able to recite all this by heart, his father put together a pack of hounds for him" (I, 37). Julian must assume the subordinate position of a pupil who accepts a complete body of knowledge given by his master.

35. See Grimaud's discussion of societal violence in Chapter 3.

Neumann's discussion of the role of the father archetype in the development of consciousness closely parallels my analysis of the significance of the functions exercised by Julian's father: "'The fathers' are the representatives of law and order.... The world of the fathers is thus the world of collective values.... These fathers are the... supervisors of all education... as pillars of the institutions that embody the cultural canon, they preside over the upbringing of each individual and certify his coming of age.... The monotonous sameness of fathers and sons is the rule."[36] This conservative function assures cultural continuity until the advent of the hero signals the necessity of change. At this juncture, the father's role becomes a negative one, and can be seen as complementary to the fixative power of the Terrible Mother: "The Terrible Male... functions... as a principle that... fixes it [ego-consciousness] in a wrong direction. It is he who prevents the continued development of the ego and upholds the old system of consciousness. He is the destructive instrument of the matriarchate."[37] When the developing ego has achieved a certain degree of stability, it is the negative aspects of the parents that come to the fore. In order to continue his development, the hero must slay them both.

Weak and frightened after the first "revelations" of the three short scenes, Julian falls back into a world which, during his "absence," had ceased to exist. Rather than effecting the expected "short-circuiting" of psychic tension, the intersection serves as its radical confirmation. The "big dream" is inevitable.

The Big Dream

Up to a certain point, the long massacre scene follows the same pattern as the earlier ones. Even within the hallucinatory atmosphere of this scene, there are repeated precise indications of time and place which serve to guard the point of departure (the castle) as a reference. Soon the distance traveled becomes so great that this point of reference becomes meaningless, and is forgotten. All that counts is Julian, the *independent* individual

36. Neumann, *Origins*, pp. 172–174.
37. *Ibid.*, p. 186.

("solely because of his very existence," [I, 56]). Julian has arrived at a critical point of tension far more advanced than in the third short scene. However, all that precedes still takes place "with the ease which one experiences in dreams" (I, 56). This precision, simultaneous with the assertions of independence, defines the other, the unconscious pole. The facility of dreams betrays a continuing dependence on the power of the Self (ego-Self identification, and the resulting ego-inflation). The tension created between these poles is now extreme.

The massacre of the herd of deer which follows is the last step toward the final rupture. The references to the "breaths" (I, 56) of the deer, and to Julian's suffocating from the pleasure afforded by such an enormous slaughter ("The prospect of so great a carnage... made him choke with pleasure," I, 57), remind us of his *strangulation* of the pigeon (murder, suicide). The conclusion of the scene, however, sends us back to Julian's stupefaction when he murders the mouse in the chapel: "Wide-eyed, he gazed at the magnitude of the slaughter, not understanding how he might have done it" (I, 62). This correspondance makes it clear that the energy expended in the scene still has its origin in the *passive* assumption of power, ego-inflation. Due to the critical point of rupture which has been reached, this omnipotent power can no longer be "assumed" (ego-inflation, see p. 81) by Julian. His need to lean against a tree for support is the first indication of this "deflation." As we discover in the scene that follows, Julian has now used all but three of his arrows (after killing the fawn and the doe, Julian will have only one arrow left).

In my earlier analysis of the configuration of the family of deer I noted its *evident* correspondance with Julian's own family. As in a high-energy "big dream," the associations which the dream content establishes become clearer. If we compare the killing of the family of deer with the third episode of the short sequence, we find that the players are the same: Julian, his mother, and his father. This time, however, each one is represented by an *individual* within a *family group*. The condensation of the figures is replaced by an ordered presentation which, in conjunction with the clarity of association with his own family, begins to reveal clear sense connections within the dream. The action itself is ordered, "uncondensed." First, the fawn is killed (the dependent child who *should* no longer exist). If Julian is to stand independently, then the parents too must die. The mother is killed next. Julian then uses his last arrow on the stag. However, "magic" arrows are no longer sufficient: "The great stag did not appear to feel it" (I, 67). It is the stag's resistance, and his prediction, which crystallize (and *express quite clearly*) the significance and the orientation of both dream sequences. At this transitional point in the development of consciousness, the magic world of childhood *must* end, the parents *will* be slain.

The clarity and precision of the dream has the effect of "waking" Julian: "That night, he could not sleep" (I, 72). Julian is now consciously obsessed by the stag's prediction ("he pictured again and again the great black stag. Its prediction haunted him," I, 72), which he begins to recognize as perhaps his own volition. The irruption of the "big dream" at the point of transition between two psychic attitudes functions as the *revelation* and the *orientation* of this change. It indicates the path which should be followed: "the very dreams which disturb sleep most... have a dramatic structure which aims... at creating a highly affective situation, and builds it up so efficiently that the affect unquestionably wakes the dreamer.... They break through when their function demands it... when... [there is] a vital significance for conscious orientation."[38]

Julian refuses this conscious orientation because of his still unrecognized primary guilt feeling which engenders an excessive dependence on the valorization of the parents. Already "condemned" through some fault of his own to a denial of parental love, Julian must at any cost guard or *recreate* the primordial state of unity, without which he would be obliged to recognize his own "unworthiness." This "desire for love" cannot be reconciled with the stag's prediction. Julian cannot allow himself to accept as his own this "other desire." Therefore, he rejects it onto the already condemned "other" within him: "he feared that the Devil might instill the urge in him" (I, 72). Julian's sickness and his refusal to hunt allow him (the "real" Julian, the obedient child) to remain as one with his parents. The aggressiveness of the stag serves, at least in part, as an oneiric com-

38. Jung, "General Aspects," p. 252.

pensation for this excessive dependence on the parents. Jung writes, "It frequently happens that if the attitude towards the parents is too affectionate and too dependent, it is compensated in dreams by frightening animals, who represent the parents."[39] The stag's striking attitude change at the end of the scene makes it clear that his ferocity and his malediction have their source in Julian's own prior judgment of himself as guilty and condemned: "He sank to his knees, gently closed his eyelids, and died" (I, 69). This same gentleness will characterize the faces of Julian's dead parents: "and the majestic softness of their faces seemed to cherish some eternal secret" (II, 79). The similarity in the descriptions of the *eyes* of the stag and the father also underlines the internal origin of this ferocity. In the murder scene, when Julian leans over to verify that the corpse is indeed his father, "he saw, between his half-closed lids, a lifeless eye that scorched him like fire" (II, 79). It is strange that what is *extinguished* should *burn*. It is less so if we return to the eyes of the stag, which are "aflame" (I, 67) at the moment of his malediction/ prediction. In both cases, the condemnation (ferocity) is not pronounced by the stag/parents, but rather by Julian himself. The stag/parents do not condemn, they simply *reveal*, and *gently* die. The dream tells Julian that *he* is the "other" whose existence he refuses to recognize. This "ferocious heart" (I, 68) beats in his own chest.[40]

   Part I ends with Julian's self-exile after the second accident. The murder of the parents, necessary for Julian's birth as an independent individual, does not take place. The murder guilt is a *prospective* one, not yet in fact experienced as such. Julian rejects even the *desire* to kill his parents onto the "other," his shadow personality.

The Son and the Murder of the Parents

Immediately after Julian's exit from the castle, "He joined a troop of adventurers who were passing by" (II, 1). He is constantly surrounded by, and defending or fighting, a group. Ju-

39. C. G. Jung, *Symbols of Transformation* (C.W., vol. 5), p. 181.
40. See my discussion of the eyes of the animals in the second massacre scene and of the leper in the final scene. See also Chapter 1, note 35.

lian is never alone, and he even forms his own army, a grab-bag collection of every type. Jung views this plunge into the collectivity as a compensation mechanism of the weak ego, still seeking the participation mystique of the primal relationship: "The parental archetype is... driven into the background; it is no longer 'constellated.' But now a certain *participation mystique* begins with the tribe, society, the church, or the nation."[41] Even in the midst of his conquests, Julian remains obsessed with his parents and lives in fear that he may inadvertently kill them one day: "he protected the clergy, orphans, widows, and foremost the aged. Whenever he saw an aged person walking ahead of him, he would call out to know his face, as if he had feared to kill him by mistake" (II, 4). Those who enjoy Julian's protection are mirror images of his own psychic state of abandonment (orphans, widows), and his dependence on an authority figure (the clergy, the aged).[42]

Now the time of conquest has passed. Julian marries the daughter of the emperor of Occitania. The description of the castle he inhabits with his wife, as well as his daily activities, is entirely narrated in the imperfect tense (an abrupt change from the almost exclusive use of the preterit tense to recount his conquests). This use of the imperfect, coupled with the harmony of the description (for example, "The sky unceasingly was blue, and the trees were swayed in turn by the ocean breeze and the wind from the distant mountains that closed the horizon." II, 15), remind us of the opening passages of the story, the perfect world of childhood. A curious detail in the description of Julian's marriage also contributes to this reconstitution of his childhood world: "Thus the emperor's daughter was bestowed upon him, along with a castle she had inherited from her mother" (II, 14). As much emphasis is placed on the maternal origin of the castle as on his young wife. This castle will serve the same protective, enveloping function as did that of his parents.

Julian, to all outward appearance, fulfills a role remarkably similar to that of his father in Part I: "Julian no longer made

41. C. G. Jung, *Contributions to Analytical Psychology* (New York, 1928), p. 124.
42. See Chapter 3, p. 150; Chapter 4, p. 182.

war. He rested . . . ; and every day, throngs came before him, kneeling and kissing his hand in Oriental fashion" (II, 18). Peace and stability characterize Julian's kingdom just as they did his father's. The world of the mother meets that of the father in a harmonious and peaceful totality—too harmonious, and too peaceful. The entire description of the castle and Julian's life is suffused with an almost stage-set "prettiness" and emptiness. Everywhere there is "such silence that one could hear the rustle of a scarf or the echo of a sigh" (II, 17). Julian is "playing a role," that of the placid monarch, happily married, benignly ruling over a tranquil people. Here there is no assumption of paternal prerogative or power. As a consequence, it would be a mistake to consider his wife as a mother-substitute who enables him to satisfy an incestuous desire "on the sly." Julian has "imitated" the world of his parents (and his childhood) to prove to himself that he does not wish to murder them.[43] After all, how could a son whose life is so closely patterned after that of his parents possibly have any reason or desire to kill them? Moreover, the unity of this "fantasy" world (father and mother/Julian and his wife), unlike that of his childhood world, is intact. It is Julian's best defense against the "echo of a sigh"—the terrible knowledge that will not go away, and threatens to destroy the silence and the perfection of this life he has constructed.

The sigh comes from Julian as he sits at the window, dressed in all the trappings of his authority, and recalls the hunts of his youth: "he leaned on his elbows in the recess of a window, recalling his past hunts" (II, 19). The Paradise dream is recounted in the next paragraph. The contiguity and content of these descriptions betray an unresolved obsession with the parents.

The Paradise dream reveals the orientation of Julian's daydreams. The killing of the animals in Paradise, exactly parallel to the slaughter of the animals in Part I, is a means of rivaling with God the Father, and of assuming his power through ego-inflation: "he fancied himself like our father Adam" (II, 20). However, the dream also betrays Julian's assumption that he

---

43. Berg also notes the regressive nature of Julian's marriage (Chapter 1), while Grimaud analyzes the absence of sexuality (Chapter 3).

has *not* been created in God's image, and reveals the continuing presence of the primary guilt feeling. In *The Child*, Neumann analyzes the "normal" significance of the Paradise image: "the fact that man . . . created in God's image . . . names the animals and knows order, and forms the world centered around himself, is the basis of the development of man, who believes himself destined to dominate the world of nature and the psyche. Man's feeling that he was created in the image of the creative God is the leading symbol of this central position of man."[44] Julian's dream is an indication of a severe psychic crisis which reverses the terms of Neumann's description. Rejected by the parents, Julian is tossed into a world that has no intrinsic order. His presence in the garden is a disruptive, foreign element. Julian is *not* made in the image of God; unable to name the animals, he kills them.[45] The primary guilt feeling has in fact been evident since the beginning of Part II. Julian, exiled from the primary relationship with his parents, performs his penance by aiding orphans, those who, like him, have lost their parents. He wakes from his dream "wild-eyed" (II, 20), a far cry from the persona of the sage, tranquil ruler which he has assumed. His eyes remind us of those of the father and the stag, reinforcing my analysis of their ferocity as Julian's projection of his own shadow.

Julian's high level of psychic tension, and his method of dealing with it, have not changed since his return to his parents' castle after the stag's prediction: "Princes, friends of his, invited him to hunt. He always demurred, believing that, by this sort of penance, he might ward off his misfortune; for he felt that murdering animals would determine the fate of his parents" (II, 21). What sin does this penance expiate? The dual propositions of the sentence which immediately follows clearly delineate the source of this tension: "But he suffered from not seeing them, and his other urge was growing unbearable" (II, 21). Julian's still immature and dependent ego continues to yearn for the state of

44. Neumann, *The Child*, p. 155.
45. Sartre finds that the underlying "moral" assumption of *The Legend* is that God did *not* create humans in His image, and even taunts them with His absence (Chapter 4). See also Chapter 1, note 35. Might we read this *péché d'exister* as analogous to the primary guilt feeling?

unity with the parents—the perfection of the completely protected and dependent infant. It is Julian who is *guilty* of having
destroyed this perfection (primary guilt feeling). At the same
time, the instinctual drive toward ego-differentiation (sym-
bolized by the massacre of the animals/murder of the parents) is
becoming even more powerful. Again, as at the end of Part I,
Julian's refusal to hunt serves as a *repression* of his conscious
murder desire, and as a *positive strategy* which allows him to
punish the undesirable shadow, thus meriting his parents' love.
The designation of Julian's need to hunt as "his other urge"
functions to distance this desire from the infant/model son of the
first proposition, and to attribute it to the ferocious shadow.

In confessing his "dreadful thought" (II, 24) to his wife, Julian takes what appears to be the first step toward a recognition
and eventual assimilation of the shadow. However, his wife's
arguments, which conclude with a negation of the possibility
that Julian could commit such an "abomination," present Julian
with a reasoned denial of the "other's" existence. Julian's reaction to his wife's reasoning betrays the unconscious "logic"
catalyzed by this coming together of emotional and reasoned
denial: "Julian smiled as he listened to her, but could not bring
himself to yield to this urge" (II, 26). This smile recalls the only
other one in the story, the smile of the seven-year-old child still
secure in the love of his parents. This is the way everything
should be, just as it was before the existence of the "other"
child, the one who laughs maliciously as the dead birds drop all
about him. Although Julian is still undecided, the dynamic of
this logic "discharges" the tension in the preceding paragraph:
now there is only *one* desire, which no longer seems either to
contradict or to endanger Julian's wish to be reunited with his
parents (which disappears as a counterbalancing proposition of
this phrase). The total denial of the shadow, and its replacement
by the smiling child, means that a decision to hunt would be
made with the illusion that it would in fact restore this unity.
Specifically, it would do so through renewed ego-Self identification and ego-inflation, which confer omnipotent power on Julian. Such a "solution" would permit Julian to channel the continuing surge of energy which demands differentiation into the
killing of the animals while maintaining (or, more precisely,

reestablishing) the state of undifferentiated unity with the parents.

One night, as Julian is kneeling for his evening prayer, "he heard the yelping of a fox, then light footsteps under the window; and he caught a glimpse in the dark of some animallike shadows. Temptation was too strong. He took down his quiver" (II, 27). From the very beginning, this second long chase scene presents the same atmosphere of dream as the first ("distance," "dark," "shadows"). The descent into the forest is couched in the terms of darkness and depth associated with symbolic representations of the unconscious: "The woods grew thicker, darkness deep" (II, 54). However, all the animals who had surrounded the castle only minutes before have disappeared. What follows is an inversely parallel massacre scene. Rather than allowing the illusion of ego-Self identification (through their death), the animals confirm the power of the unconscious and the weakness of the still dependent ego: Julian cannot kill them. To the contrary, they turn on him: the victim becomes the aggressor.

After their first aggression in the cemetery and Julian's inability to kill a bull, his strength is gone, crushed and destroyed by "some higher power" (II, 60). This condition exactly parallels Julian's exhausted state after the stag's prediction ("overcome with a sudden weariness," I, 70). His power, which flowed freely from its unconscious source in the earlier scenes, is now cut off ("deflation," see p. 95). His first thought, as in the earlier scene, is to return home. This time, however, there are no magic roads that lead back.

The path is in fact a tortuous one, covered with plants that impede Julian's progress: "It was a tangle of vines; and he was cutting them with his sword" (II, 61). This motif of entwining and impediment is continued in the image of the animals forming a circle around Julian, who is unable to move. He breaks away through "a supreme effort of his will" (II, 64), but the animals track his every step. Although Julian is able to make some painful headway, near the end of the scene he is again reduced to a blind and helpless state: "and deafened by the buzzing of the insects, bruised by birds' tails, choked by their breaths, he walked with outstretched arms and closed eyes like a blind man, without even the strength to cry out 'mercy'" (II, 67). For the second time in the scene, Julian's impotence is described in terms of suffocation, a lack of breath ("choked," "choked by their breaths"). I have delineated the associations which link the life breath (and its absence) to the parents (and their death) and also to Julian's passive assumption of parental power. In this scene, the aggression of the animals functions to cut off Julian's access to this life-giving breath; he can no longer passively assume its presence. The tables are now turned; it is Julian who is being strangled.

The ferocity of the animals and their superiority over Julian are reflected in their gaze (as opposed to his own blindness): "Among its leaves was a monstrous jackdaw that watched Julian; and, here and there, between the branches great numbers of large sparks appeared, as if the firmament had showered all its stars into the forest. It was the eyes of animals" (II, 62). What a difference from the infinite number of animals who surround Julian in the first massacre scenes, "with a meek and beseeching look in their eyes" (I, 56). Likewise, the image of the rain of stars which renders the multiplicity of animals' eyes is the inverse of the description of the small birds who are killed in such great numbers that they literally fall like rain out of the sky in the second short scene. Earlier, I analyzed the gaze of the stag and of the father as revelatory of Julian's own denied ferocity. If Julian finally yielded to the temptation of animal slaughter again, it was because he imagined that he could recover the omnipotent power which would reconfirm his unity with the parents (thus permitting him to discharge the ego energy which pushes to differentiation without harming his parents). It is the innocent and gentle Julian-child who descends into the forest, only to discover that everything has been turned around. Julian's refusal of his own ferocity makes him the prey. The animals take a perverse pleasure in reminding him of his impotence and their superiority: "The monkeys pinched him and made faces, the weasel rolled over his feet. A bear, with its paw, knocked off his cap; and the panther, disdainfully, dropped an arrow it was carrying in its mouth" (II, 66).

This attempt to return to his childhood, to find everything just as it was before, is doomed to failure. Julian is not a child anymore. Paradise has become hell, and threatens his very life. Neumann considers that this transformation originates in the developing ego's changing perception of the unconscious, necessitated by its establishment as an independent complex:

> With the emancipation of consciousness and the increasing tension between it and the unconscious, ego development leads to a stage in which... the devouring side of the uroboros is experienced as the tendency of the unconscious to destroy consciousness. This is identical with the basic fact that ego consciousness has to wrest libido from the unconscious for its own existence, for, unless it does so, its specific achievement falls back into the unconscious, in other words is "devoured."[46]

It is this wresting of power from the unconscious (the murder of the parents) which Julian has systematically refused since the stag's prediction. The effect of this denial has been a continued dependence on the unconscious, evident in the large amount of time Julian spends daydreaming and fantasizing about the hunts of his youth, and his frequent depression, in the first section of Part II. Repression leads to a draining of energy from the conscious mind into the repressed contents of the unconscious. This loss of energy also leads to ego regression: "The regression caused by repressing the instincts always leads back to the psychic past, and consequently to... childhood..."[47] After prolonged repression, the unconscious contents have become so highly charged that they present a threat to the ego's very survival: "Repression... creates an underworld with a dangerous emotional charge which tends to erupt, to overwhelm and destroy...; repression does not transform the powers; it merely chains them temporarily."[48] It is this highly charged instinctual world that Julian confronts as he descends into the forest. The psychic tension which Julian has deliberately left unresolved now threatens to destroy him. This draining of energy into the unconscious has left him with greatly diminished ego strength (he goes into the forest as a child), and has exposed the devouring aspect of the unconscious. The motifs of twining, impedi-

---

46. Neumann, *Origins*, p. 299.
47. Jung, *Symbols*, p. 180.
48. Erich Neumann, "Creative Man and Transformation," in *Art and the Creative Unconscious*, Bollingen Series 61 (Princeton, 1971), p. 161.

ment, and aggression all dramatize the struggling ego's perception of the threatening attempt of the unconscious to keep him fixed in a primitive stage of development. Julian's rejection of his mother's embrace and his father's instruction was the first manifestation of this changed perception.

With the coming of the day, the nightmare dissipates: the animals disappear, and Julian spots his castle in the distance. Everything seems to be returning to normal. "Next, at the edge of a field, he saw, three paces away, some red partridges fluttering around in the stubble" (II, 69). One last temptation, one last chance. Julian throws his cloak over them, to no avail: "When they were uncovered, he found only one, and long since dead, rotten" (II, 69). His reaction is immediate and vicious: "This disappointment exasperated him more than all the others. His thirst for carnage was taking over again; animals lacking, he longed to massacre men" (II, 70). Julian's failure to capture such simple prey is the ultimate ironic provocation, one last proof of his impotence. Is the resulting "exasperation" sufficient to explain the curious process of replacement described by Berg in Chapter I?

The significance and impact of this passage become clearer when we consider the correspondences that link it to the end of the first long massacre scene. Indeed, it is the placement of the passage which first draws our attention: day is breaking when Julian spots the partridges midway between the forest which he has just left and his castle. Julian is "waking" from the dream. There is no explicit description of his "state of mind" at this point, simply the notation "he recognized, beyond the orange trees, the top of his palace" (II, 68). However, we will remember that he redescended into the forest *in order to return home* when his strength failed him. This reaction of *flight* at a moment of *weakness* is precisely what motivated Julian's return to his parents' castle in the earlier massacre scene. The essential remaining motive in the first scene, *fear*, is certainly Julian's primary emotion as the animals encircle him in the passage directly preceding the sudden appearance of daylight.

What surprises us in this second massacre scene is that up to the point when Julian spots his castle, an "irruption" similar to the stag's prediction has yet to take place, despite the evident high affectivity of the sequence. Julian's total subjection to the animals in the preceding encirclement scene is "suddenly" interrupted by the cock's crow. More precisely, the scene simply *dissolves* at that moment. How did Julian escape from his dangerous position? What happened to the animals? The dream shifts without transition. The continuity of dramatic structure of the "big dream," with its increased valency of associations and clear sense connections, is broken. The dissolution of the danger, the primacy given to the sighting of the castle, and Julian's lack of affectivity suggest a return to the *status quo ante* in which the mortal threat posed by the aggression of the animals will be forgotten, just as it blanks out of the dream and the text.

Julian's failure to trap the partridges radically changes this evolution of the scene: his *ferocity*, curiously absent during his encounter with the animals, repressed since his flight from his parents' castle, irrupts again. The day is breaking on the ferocious shadow, and he, not the child who left the night before, returns to the castle: "He climbed the three terraces, burst open the door with his fist" (II, 71). This reversal of attitude, in the context of the associations that link it with the first massacre scene, suggests that the partridge scene functions in a fashion analogous to the stag's prediction, as a *crystallization of meaning*.

Approached from this perspective, the various elements of the scene become more easily comprehensible. Julian's failure to snare such simple prey continues the provocation of the animals which revealed Julian's impotence. What of the one dead partridge which he finds under his cloak, "long since dead, rotten"? The specification of his prey as small animals links them to the first sequence of short scenes in which the mouse, the small birds, and the pigeon (two of the three are also birds) all stood as symbolic representations of the infant Julian. In the abortive massacre, Julian's impotence when faced with the attack of the animals revealed the inability of the young child (the weak ego) to break free from the embrace of the "devouring" unconscious. The long-dead and decayed partridge is the symbolic representation of Julian's self-deception: this infant, symbol of the state of unity and dependence which Julian has attempted to maintain, in reality died long ago.[49] The death of the innocent

49. See Chapter 3, p. 154.

infant and the revelation of his replacement by the "ferocious heart" were the principal elements of the stag's prediction. Julian refused to recognize any change. He transferred this ferocity onto the condemned shadow of the primary guilt feeling, and attempted to "recreate" the state of unity with the parents. The revelation of this infant's death in the long-dead partridge triggers the irruption of the repressed, ferocious shadow. Not only, then, does the replacement process involve humans for animals, but also the "ferocious heart" for the innocent child (this replacement being the reverse of the replacement of the "ferocious heart" by the dependent child after the stag's prediction).

The level of affect falls again as Julian prepares to climb the steps to his bedroom: "but, at the foot of the stairs, the memory of his beloved wife soothed his heart" (II, 71). The "ferocious heart" which irrupted in the previous scene is again repressed ("soothed"). This repression and lowering of tension are comprehensible when we remember that Julian's married life represents yet another defense against the knowledge of the fragmentation of his childhood world and the existence of his shadow. In this sense, it is a recreation of that state of unity, inviolable and intact. After the "revelation" of the dead partridge, it stands as the last bulwark in a crumbling system of defenses.

Julian enters the bedroom, which is *still* plunged in darkness. Unable to see, he trips over clothes on the floor and bumps into furniture. The bed, where the murder will take place, is completely "lost in the darkness at the back of the room" (II, 73). This entire description evokes the darkness of the primeval forest and Julian's blindness when surrounded by the animals. His stumbling over objects reminds us of the earlier images of entwining and impediment. The massacre scene has shifted its geographical location but not its psychic one. Julian once again faces the devouring power of the unconscious.

When Julian leans over to kiss his wife, he feels "the touch of a beard" (II, 73). Unwilling to believe that his wife would be unfaithful to him, he verifies twice more. Julian's final thought before losing all control is "a man! a man lying with his wife!" (II, 74). The shattering of the recreated unity of his marriage is a replay of the revelation of the dead partridge—only this time there are no other defenses, this last one having fallen like all the others. Julian yields finally and completely to the "ferocious heart" within him, which quite literally explodes out of his unconscious after prolonged repression: "Bursting into boundless rage, he sprang upon them thrusting his dagger; and he stamped, foamed, with howls like a wild beast" (II, 75). Julian *becomes* an animal, finally accomplishing the long dreaded act. It is only *after* the murder that he is able to see what he has done. Julian picks up the torch which his wife has dropped. Aided by the "scarlet reflection of the window, just then hit by the sun" (II, 79), he inspects the bodies and the scene of the massacre. Julian does not know what he has done until the light of the torch and the rising sun reveal it to him.

The murder of the parents corresponds to the mythological motif of the night sea journey analyzed by Neumann in *The Origins and History of Consciousness*. The journey is another mythological variation of the dragon-fight motif which also involves the slaying of the parents.[50] The hero of consciousness must descend into the darkness of the unconscious in order to slay it (active incest), and to liberate the ego from its embrace. He faces and conquers the devouring forces of the unconscious—both the mother and the father united against him—and ensures the progress of conscious development. Accordingly, the movement of the journey is always from west to east, from the darkness toward the light of the rising sun. In many of the related myths, the hero is portrayed as lighting a fire in the dark belly of the monster, an "act [which] 'kills' the . . . state of union."[51] The ritual act of dissociation is always performed in the darkness, and is instinctually controlled; it is "archetypal, i.e., collectively conditioned."[52] Julian's journey, like the hero's night sea journey, has carried him from the darkness to the light.

Religion

The Christ motif reappears at the moment of the murder of the parents: "Splashes and blotches of blood spread over their white skin, on the bedclothes, on the floor, down an ivory Christ that hung in the alcove" (II, 79). The association between Julian and

50. See the discussion of the dragon fight and active incest above.
51. Jung, *Symbols*, p. 211.
52. Neumann, *Origins*, pp. 415–416.

Christ is most often made through the use of the crucifixion image. What is of special interest at this point is the coincidence of the murder of the parents and the imagery of the crucified Christ, and Julian's voluntary assumption of this pose during his parents' funeral (as opposed to tripping and falling into it as in the scene with the wild goats in the first massacre, I, 53): "During the mass, he lay flat on his belly, in the middle of the entranceway, his arms spread out, and his forehead in the dust" (II, 84). The story begins to take on the appearance of a religious drama: Julian tells his wife that she obeyed the will of God by causing his crime, he appears dressed as a monk at the funeral, then he leaves to become a hermit and finally a saint. This religious turn of events should serve to remind us that both his parents considered Julian to be "marked by God." Even as an infant he is described as a "little Jesus."

What, then, does religion have to do with the murder of Julian's parents, and how is it related to the individuation process? The answers to both questions are found in the number *three*, everywhere present in the text up to this point: the three members of the family, the three days of celebration at Julian's birth, the three nurses who care for him, the three squires who wait to hunt with him, the three months of anguish for his parents during Julian's illness, the thrice-repeated prediction of the stag, and so on. The events preceding and following the parents' murder, and the murder itself, generate the most dense accumulation of references to the number three to be found in the story. The path which leads Julian back from the forest to his castle is measured out in threes: he spots the partridges three steps away from him, and later climbs the three terraces to his castle. The murder scene itself involves the three members of the family, reunited for the first time since Julian's flight from his parents' castle. (When his wife comes to the door, she is presented as extraneous to this reconstituted three-person unit; she appears as a phantom before fleeing in horror.) Before exploding in a murderous rage, Julian touches his parents three times. The two death rattles are continued and finally replaced by a third sound, the bellowing of the stag. The horrible event which he had predicted, and repeated three times, has come to pass. It takes three days to reach the monastery where his parents are buried. Finally, and perhaps most importantly, these events take place at the end of Part II, and effect a radical change in Julian's life which leads to his apotheosis at the end of Part III. The process of Julian's psychological development (his individuation) is also controlled by a three-part movement.

Given the religious orientation of *The Legend,* and the primordial role which the number three plays in the story, it is natural that our thoughts should turn to the Christian doctrine of the Trinity. In "A Psychological Approach to the Dogma of the Trinity," Jung establishes correspondences between the individuation process and a psychological reading of the Trinity which will help us to understand the role of religion in *The Legend:* "As a psychological symbol the Trinity denotes... the ... essential unity of a three-part process, to be thought of as a process of unconscious maturation taking place within the individual. . . . The three Persons are personifications of the three phases of a regular, instinctive psychic occurrence [individuation]."[53] The symbol of the Trinity, as an archetype of wholeness, is "a collective phenomenon [whose development] is a collective process, representing a differentiation of consciousness that has been going on for several thousand years."[54] The persons of the Trinity are projections of critical stages in the development of human consciousness. In the process of realizing psychic wholeness, Julian must pass through those critical stages experienced by humankind before him. In doing so, he relives the drama of the Trinity. In *Ego and Archetype: Individuation and the Religious Function of the Psyche,* Edward Edinger relates the stages of the Trinity even more specifically to those of the individuation process (see page 83 for a diagram of Edinger's scheme):

> Development of consciousness occurs via a threefold cycle ... : (1) ego identified with Self, (2) ego alienated from Self and (3) ego reunited with Self through the ego-Self axis. In briefer terms these stages could be called: (1) the stage of the Self, (2) the stage of the ego and (3) the stage of the ego-Self axis. These three stages correspond precisely with the three terms of the Christian trinity: the age of the father (Self), the age of the son (ego) and the stage of the holy ghost (ego-Self axis).[55]

---

53. Jung, "A Psychological Approach," p. 193.
54. *Ibid.,* p. 180.
55. Edinger, p. 186.

Part I of *The Legend* corresponds quite closely to Jung's description of the first stage in the drama of the Trinity, the stage
of the father: "the father denotes the earlier state of consciousness when one was still a child, still dependent on a definite,
ready-made pattern of existence which is habitual and has the
character of law."[56] Thus far I have for the most part analyzed
the relationship of Julian and his parents as the symbolic expression of the ego-Self dialectic. However, in patriarchal western
culture, the archetype of the Self has also often found its projection in the image of God the Father. The notion of man's filiation
to God, which will assume a pivotal role in *The Legend*, corresponds to the relationship of the ego to the Self: "The ego's
relationship to the Self is a highly problematic one and corresponds very closely to man's relation to his Creator as depicted
in religious myth. Indeed the myth can be seen as a symbolic
expression of the ego-Self relationship."[57] Both his parents consider Julian to be "marked by God" at his birth. The visionary
predictions made to them, the complementary determinants of
Julian's destiny, can themselves be traced back to a "supernatural" source. The Paradise dream is yet another example of
this projection of the Self in both God the Father and the parents. The double functioning of the symbolism of the Self—
parental and sacred—will be most explicitly clear in Part III.

The murder of the parents in Part II is the radical destruction
of ego-Self identification. This differentiation of Self and ego is
precisely the task Jung assigns to the Son of the Trinity.[58] In a
chapter entitled "Christ as Paradigm of the Individuating Ego,"
Edinger writes that Christ "recognized the danger of psychic
identification with parents and family.... A man's foes are
those of his own household because it is those to whom he is
closest with whom he is most apt to be identified unconsciously.
Such identification must be dissolved because an awareness of
radical separateness is a prerequisite for individuation."[59] The
conflict situation represented by the Son stage results in the
disidentification of ego and Self necessary for further development. Edinger points out that "Jesus singles out the father for

56. Jung, "A Psychological Approach," p. 181.
57. Edinger, p. 4.
58. Jung, "A Psychological Approach," p. 182.
59. Edinger, pp. 133–134.

special mention: 'And call no man your father on earth, for you have one Father who is in Heaven.' "[60] Christ's admonition exactly parallels Neuman's description of the "exemplary, archetypal way of the hero . . . [who] must slay the father . . . and seek an unknown directing authority, namely the Self that is so hard to experience, the unknown Heavenly Father."[61]

The appearance of the crucified Christ at the moment of the murder of the parents and the pervasiveness of the number three evoke the ongoing developmental drama—both individual and collective—that Julian is experiencing. Julian's first night sea journey has taken him from the darkness to the light. He now consciously chooses the mode of life he will lead, and voluntarily assumes the position of the crucified Christ. Having lived with the Father, Julian must be crucified as the Son before his "resurrection" into eternal life. This one remaining step corresponds to the conscious reunification of the ego and the Self by means of the ego-Self axis, and is likened by analytical psychologists to the third term of the Trinity, the Holy Ghost.

The Holy Ghost: From Solitary to Saint

Julian kills his parents and begins the third stage of his development, "the dark night of the soul," which culminates in a resolution of the tension. This resolution, however, does not come quickly. Julian's life in Part III is essentially that of a hermit in the wilderness. The entire world becomes a projection of his all-pervasive sense of guilt and unworthiness:

> He sought out lonely places. But the wind brought to his ears sounds resembling death rattles; the tears of the dew falling on the ground reminded him of other, weightier drops. The sun, every evening, spread blood over the clouds; and each night, in his dreams, he relived his parricide. [III, 8]

Parricide is the most radical form of ego-Self disidentification, and leads to a deep state of alienation which closely resembles the mystical experience: "We find again and again in the documentation of religious experiences a profound sense of de-

---

60. Matthew 23:9, quoted by Edinger, p. 134.
61. Neumann, "Creative Man," p. 165.

pression, guilt, sin, unworthiness. . . . The classic symbol for alienation is the image of the *wilderness.*"[62]

The ego that necessitated his action is now the primary object of Julian's disgust and horror: "His own person was so repugnant to him that in the hope of freeing himself he risked it in perilous tasks" (III, 11). The use of the direct object ("risked it") indicates that the psychic tension present in Part II is even stronger after the murder. Julian still considers his ego as "other," as an object that is not, or at least should not be, an integral part of his personality. The guilt for the murder of the parents only serves to intensify his feeling of unworthiness stemming from the primary guilt feeling. Although Julian is consciously doing penance for both these "sins," he refuses complete responsibility for either one. Both are rejected onto the "other," whether it be ego or shadow. There seems to be a clear indication that the ego has been assimilated by the shadow, or at least closely identified with it.

Julian's positing of his ego as unworthy, indeed as a "stranger," makes it evident that even the murder of the parents has not liberated him from their hold. Julian is still obsessed by the pristine unity of his childhood: "He often closed his eyes, yearning, through memory, to come back to his youth;—and a castle courtyard would appear, with greyhounds on the steps, servants in the armory, and, under a vine-covered arbor, a blond youth between an old man wrapped in furs and a lady with a high cap" (III, 20). However, standing between Julian and this perfect state of envelopment by the parents is the development of ego-consciousness which discriminates and divides. The murder shatters this idyllic dream of unity: "suddenly, the two corpses were there. Sprawled on the bed, flat on his belly, he would sob, repeating:—Ah! poor father! poor mother! poor mother!" (III, 20–21).[63]

The goal of the individuation process is to recreate consciously the state of uroboric plentitude, to eliminate the opposition introduced by consciousness. Out of the psychic tension between ego and unconscious "a third term [must] be born,

62. Edinger, p. 50.
63. Sartre provides a biographical link for this scene (Chapter 4, p. 183).

which 'transcends,' or surpasses, the opposites and so combines parts of both positions into ... [a] new creation."[64] To recreate this unity does not mean to repeat it. Such a repetition would only lead to ego-Self identity (and not union) and would signify a reduction of consciousness. In this sense, Jung maintains that the stage of the Son "is in itself a 'transitus' and amounts therefore to a bridge ... to the third stage."[65] In the meantime, Julian must suffer the psychic tension that divides his world, ravaging both body and soul. The new third term can be created only if this suffering is endured.

After Julian's "vision" at the fountain, Flaubert reinvokes the Christ image as a symbol of his suffering: "Thus, burdened with the weight of his memories, he traveled through many countries" (III, 14). An analysis of the scene at the fountain will enable us to understand this indirect reference to the "cross" that Julian must bear. Immediately prior to this scene, Julian's suffering "was becoming intolerable. He resolved to die" (III, 12). It is at this lowest point of his despair and alienation that Julian mistakes his own reflection for that of his father. It seems indeed strange that, at the very moment Julian is besieged by feelings of guilt and is on the brink of suicide, the appearance of what he assumes to be his father's image should *prevent* him from killing himself, rather than driving him to do so immediately.[66]

This sudden reversal of his decision is comprehensible if we realize that this episode marks the transition from the second to the last stage of psychic development. Edinger writes that, in the experience of the "dark night of the soul," "when the wanderer lost in the desert is about to perish, a source of divine nourishment appears.... Psychologically this means that the experience of the supporting aspect of the archetypal psyche is most likely to occur when the ego has exhausted its own resources and is aware of its essential impotence by itself."[67] Julian has reached an extreme low of self-regard and of the strength necessary to endure the tension. The mistaken image of

---

64. Neumann, "Creative Man," p. 192.
65. Jung, "A Psychological Approach," p. 182.
66. See Chapter 4, pp. 182–183 for Sartre's "biographical" reading of this scene.
67. Edinger, p. 50.

the father gives him the support and the strength he needs to go on. The old man who appears in the fountain is not the father of Julian's childhood, the strong authority figure. His apparition cannot be construed as an effort by Julian to *repeat* his childhood, to dissolve his consciousness by plunging headlong into the primordial state, unchanged by the intervention of consciousness. This "vision" is not an attempt at ego-Self identification, for in his subsequent behavior Julian displays no trace of ego-inflation. To the contrary, he pursues a course of ego-diminution by dedicating his life to the service of others. The discord brought by the Son stage effectively ends the psychic projection of the son's identity onto the parents. The goal of disidentification, especially in the case of the father, is "to withdraw all projections of the father archetype and discover it within."[68] The discovery of the "father archetype within," or the "other being, the other person in ourselves," is the signal for a major psychic advance. The son is now called on to give birth to the Father within him: "Just as the 'Son' proceeds from the 'Father,' so the 'Father' proceeds from the stage of the 'Son,' yet this Father is not a mere repetition of the original Father or an identification with him, but one in whom the vitality of the 'Father' continues its procreative work."[69] The appearance of the Father is an experience of the supporting aspect of the Self which serves to counterbalance Julian's interior alienation stemming from the quasi-identification he has established between ego and shadow. Glimpsing the "other being" within himself, Julian cannot commit suicide.

Jung writes that "since man knows himself only as an ego, and the self, as a totality, is . . . a God-image, self-realization [individuation] . . . amounts to God's incarnation."[70] Julian must give birth to this "image of God," this "other being" within himself: the son must recreate the Father. The task is not an easy one: "Because individuation is an heroic and often tragic task . . . it involves suffering, a passion of the ego. . . . The analogous passion of Christ signifies God's suffering on account of

68. *Ibid.*, p. 134.
69. Jung, "A Psychological Approach," pp. 184–185.
70. *Ibid.*, p. 157.

the injustice of the world. . . . The cause of the suffering is in both cases the same, namely 'incarnation,' which on the human level appears as 'individuation.' "[71] The "passion of the ego" is the cross which Julian has to bear: "The whole world is God's suffering, and every individual . . . who [gets] anywhere near his own wholeness knows that this is the way of the cross."[72] The cross that Julian carries is the "weight" of the memory of the murder of his parents, but also of his father's face in the fountain. He carries these memories as a burden, but also as a woman carries an unborn child within her.

Julian is now prepared for the final stage of his drama. Again the action is played out as if in a dream: "One night as he slept, he imagined hearing someone call him" (III, 22). Listening intently, he can make out only "the roar of the waters" (III, 22). The voice repeats his name. It comes from the other side of the river, "which amazed him, considering the breadth of the river" (III, 25). The "breadth of the river," with Julian on one side and the leper on the other, is the symbolic geographical configuration of the separation of the conscious and unconscious systems in Julian's psyche. However, Flaubert's description of the return trip with the leper emphasizes the notion of depth rather than width, suggesting more an ascent than a crossing: "The water, blacker than ink, rushed furiously along both sides. Abysses formed, mountains rose, and the boat bobbed on top, then went pitching down and whirled around, buffeted by the wind" (III, 33). The solution to the radical differentiation of ego and Self is another *descent* into the depths of the unconscious to confront its repressed contents, and *to raise* them to consciousness.

In this first movement of the last section, there are numerous details that reveal the leper to be a symbol of the transpersonal psyche, the Self (the dynamic of the crossing is an important clue in itself). The voice of the leper has "the tone of a church bell" (III, 28), linking it immediately with the God image, one of the principal conceptions by which the ego can "know" the Self. The totalizing function of the Self already becomes evident in this allusion to the church bell, since it links the leper to the stag

71. *Ibid.*
72. *Ibid.*, p. 179.

who made his prediction as a bell tolled in the distance (I, 67). The stag, of course, sends us back to the parents, whose household was run like a monastery (I, 10), and who kept the stones of their courtyard so clean that they resembled the paving in a church (I, 3). When Julian gives in for a moment to the violence of the storm, his boat is carried off course. However, he does not give up, "realizing that this was a matter of import, a command not to be disobeyed" (III, 34). Writing of the manifestation of the Self as an "inner authority," Jung maintains that it is often conceived as the "will of God." A decision made in obedience to this inner authority "appears to be . . . the result [of] divine intention."[73]

We also discover that although the leper is hideous in appearance, "there was in his demeanor something of a king's majesty" (III, 31). In his analysis of the Gnostic symbols of the Self, Jung concludes that "every king carries the symbol of the self. . . . The Gnostics . . . constantly endeavoured to give visible form . . . to this being, suspecting that he was the matrix and organizing principle of consciousness."[74] Jung quotes the alchemical allegory of the King, which corresponds in all major points to the sequence of events in this section of *The Legend*:

> He lives and calls from the depths: Who shall deliver me from the waters and lead me to dry land? Even though this cry be heard of many, yet none takes it upon himself . . . to seek the king. For who, they say, will plunge into the waters? Who will imperil his life by taking away the peril of another? Only a few believe his lament, and think rather that they hear the crashing and roaring of Scylla and Charybdis. Therefore they remain sitting indolently at home, and give no thought to the kingly treasure, not to their own salvation.[75]

For the alchemists, the King was the hidden transformative substance which had to be distilled from matter in order to complete the Work. Interpreting this allegory psychologically (as a psychic projection of individuation), Jung writes:

73. C. G. Jung, *Aion: Researches into the Phenomenology of the Self (C.W.,* vol. 9, pt. II), p. 26.
74. *Ibid.*, p. 198.
75. Michael Maier, *Symbola aureae mensae,* p. 380, quoted by C. G. Jung in *Alchemical Studies (C.W.,* vol. 13), p. 145.

> The darkness and depths of the sea symbolize the unconscious state of an invisible content that is projected. Inasmuch as such a content belongs to the total personality . . . there is always an attraction between conscious mind and projected content. Generally it takes the form of a fascination. This, in the alchemical allegory, is expressed by the King's cry for help from the depths of his unconscious, dissociated state. The conscious mind should respond to this call: one should *operari regi,* render service to the King, for this would be not only wisdom but salvation as well. Yet this brings with it the necessity of a descent into the dark world of the unconscious, . . . the perilous adventure of the night sea journey.[76]

It is my contention that the crossing of the river with the leper represents Julian's second night sea journey, and signals the beginning of a profound psychic transformation. The murder of Julian's parents was an activation of the archetypal motif of the first night sea journey. However, the night sea journey, like the uroboric symbol, has both a beginning and an ending symbolism. The full development of the personality necessitates another descent into the unconscious. The crucial difference between these two journeys is the conscious nature of the second as opposed to the collective conditioning of the first. According to Neumann, "archetypal materials . . . are assimilated consciously and by an individual who attains self-experience through his . . . union with the transpersonal worlds."[77]

The crossing of the river, like the murder of the parents, takes place in the dark. This time, however, Julian lights a lantern *before* venturing out of his shack. The voice of the leper, like the stag's, comes from far away and is almost indistinguishable at first. As with the two sources of light, what differentiates the voices is their placement in these pivotal scenes. It is only *after* hearing the voice of the stag that Julian becomes conscious of his crime. The voice of the leper, however, calls him to *begin* the final movement of individuation. The storm abates long enough for Julian to reach the other bank. Repeating the action by which he perceived his dead parents, Julian holds the light close to the waiting figure: "When he brought the lantern closer to him,

---

76. C. G. Jung, *Psychology and Alchemy* (C.W., vol. 12), p. 329.
77. Neumann, *Origins,* pp. 415–416.

Julian found that he was covered with hideous leper's sores"
(III, 31). Once again, the fundamental difference between these
two scenes is that in the first one the light (and conscious recognition) comes only *after* the murder, while in the second scene,
Julian is conscious from the outset of what confronts him.

The process of lifting an unconscious content to consciousness is a difficult and perilous one, threatening the ego with
extinction by the "devouring" aspect of the unconscious. In the
abortive massacre scene, and the murder scene that follows,
Julian's weak and unstable ego cannot hold its own against the
highly charged unconscious. The effect of the storm is similar to
the effect of the animals: Julian seems to lose strength. The ego's
energy is being drained by the unconscious. Just as he was
"choked by their breaths" (II, 67) in the second massacre scene,
during the crossing "the violent air made him choke" (III, 34).
When the animals surround Julian in "a narrow circle," he is
incapable of any movement. Weakened by his constant struggle
against the storm, "he stopped" (III, 34). It is at this moment
that "the boat was sent drifting away" (III, 34). Finding himself
at the critical point of impotence and subjection in the massacre
scene, Julian can depend only on his own will to extricate himself; "a supreme effort of his will" (II, 64) permits him to take
only one step. When he cannot go on battling the storm, it is the
will of the "other" (God's will, the Self's will: "a command not
to be disobeyed") which gives him the strength to persevere and
to reach the other side. During the abortive massacre scene, a
supernatural power *weakens* rather than strengthens Julian
("Some higher power was destroying his strength," II, 60). Even
this "other will" is assimilated as a content of consciousness:
Julian understands ("comprendre") that he must obey. The crossing does not end in the extinction or the abdication of consciousness; even at the height of the storm, "The small lantern
burned before him" (III, 35). However, now another light also
guides him: when the lantern is occasionally hidden by the
birds, "he could see the eyes of the Leper" (III, 35). The light of
consciousness has its unconscious counterpart in the
"eyes redder than coals" (III, 31) of the leper. No longer is the
other's gaze threatening or ferocious. Both lights are present,
and the one *aids* the other in this final stage of psychic growth.

Julian and the leper return to his shack, where the final scenes of the drama will be played out. At this point, we should examine more closely the figure of the leper. I have suggested that he is the symbol of the Self. However, this characterization does not answer two questions which his description raises. First, how are we to understand the striking similarities in the descriptions of the father, the stag, and the leper? Second, why is he portrayed as a leper? And finally, how do the responses to these questions relate to the archetype of the Self?

It is the function of the Self to gather all the disparate elements of the psyche about itself, and for this reason the symbol of the Self is a polyvalent one. The similarities in the appearance of the leper, the stag, and the father are one manifestation of this polyvalency.[78] The psychic projection of the father in the stag has its origins in Julian's "infantile" consciousness, which, too dependent on the parents, experiences them as frightening animal figures. At the same time, the stag's prediction is a revelation of the instinctual drive toward ego-Self differentiation, which Julian perceives as parental rejection and which he will not accept as his own desire. At this point it is sufficient to observe that many of the same similarities that have been noted between the stag and the father also exist between the father and the leper. Both the stag and the leper are projections of the father image, and we should expect to find certain repeated resemblances between the stag and the leper (the eyes, for example). What is of fundamental importance is that Julian experiences the father projection in the stag as threatening and frightening, while his projection in the leper does not elicit these emotions. Julian, with no sign of undue coercion, accedes to the leper's demands. He does feel a compulsion ("a command not to be disobeyed") to accept his presence, but it seems to be as much internal as external. If anything, he experiences the leper's presence as supportive (it gives him the strength to finish the crossing in spite of the storm). This change in Julian's projection of the father image indicates a fundamental reversal in attitude which leaves the way open for psychic transformation. The im-

78. Berg explains the polyvalent symbolism of the leper in terms of condensation (Chapter 1 at note 40).

mature and too dependent ego experiences the father as a frightening authority figure. The stabilized ego, free from ego-Self identification, is now ready to accept the father (hence the Self) again. This change in perspective (evident already in the vision in the fountain) between the father's projection in the stag and in the leper is the significant conclusion to be drawn from the similarities in their descriptions in Part III.

The points of association between Julian's parents and the leper refer almost exclusively to his parents immediately prior to, or following, their murder This fact points to a projection and eventual assimilation of the secondary murder guilt. That the majority of these points of comparison touch both parents should serve to remind us that Julian's guilt is not exclusively in relation to his father. Nonetheless, it is evident that the emphasis is on the paternal image, the leper himself being male. The father is the symbol of authority who once overthrown must be recreated. Several details of the leper's description remind us only of Julian's father ("eyes redder than coals," "motionless as a column"). Although the rotting flesh of the leper can be associated with both parents, it is more directly reminiscent of Julian's vision of his father in the fountain ("a very emaciated man"). It is immediately following this vision that Julian is implicitly compared to Christ bearing his cross ("burdened with the weight of his memories"). As soon as the leper steps into the boat, "it sank wondrously, borne down by his weight" (III, 32).

I have described this cross borne by Julian as the "passion of the ego" necessary for the incarnation of the Self. The person undergoing this process of individuation "suffers, so to speak, from the violence done to him by the self,"[79] which in order to be born requires a diminution of ego-dominance. Perhaps the most salient characteristic of Julian's attitude toward his "person" (his ego) is one of rejection because of his inability to accept the "shadow" personality with which he identifies it. This rejection determines the conduct of his life and is fundamental to our understanding of the manifestation of the Self as a leper. The shadow was first constellated in the primary guilt feeling, catalyzed by Julian's experience of his own drive toward inde-

79. Jung, "A Psychological Approach," p. 157.

pendence as rejection by the parents. "Not to be loved," we will remember, "is identical with being abnormal, sick, 'leprous,' and . . . 'condemned.' "[80] The leper is a symbol of this dark, unacceptable part of Julian's personality. He is ugly and repulsive: "his shoulders, his chest, his thin arms were hidden under blotches of scaly pustules" (III, 37). Several details of the leper's description are related to images which have tended to cluster about the notion of primary guilt: "he had a hole in place of a nose; and out of his bluish lips came breath thick like a fog, and foul" (III, 37). Here the "hole" which first appeared in the short massacre scenes as the symbol of the breakdown of the primal unity reappears directly linked to the "missing life breath" (p. 75) which signaled the absence of the parents in these same scenes. (Both motifs are also present in the murder scene: Julian *makes* the hole which deprives his parents of their life breath.) The association of both images with the secondary murder guilt is the first indication of the eventual identification of ego and shadow. The leper's breath, "thick like a fog," reminds us of the breaths of the herd of stags, "which could be seen steaming in the fog" (I, 56), in the first massacre scene. This view, and the prospect "of so great a carnage," made Julian "choke with pleasure." However, to have accomplished the slaughter only confirms the existence of the "ferocious heart" which Julian rejects. He will choke again, but not with pleasure, as the animals surround him with their breaths in the abortive massacre scene of Part II. The ironic provocation of the animals and the reversal of roles (Julian is being strangled, not the animals) show that the child he wishes to be no longer exists. The life breath of the parents is denied him—or, more precisely, it aggressively seeks to destroy him. The description of the leper's breath as "foul" reminds us of the partridge, "long since dead, rotten," which "revealed" the destruction of the illusion of primal unity which Julian had so long tried to maintain. This revelation is immediately followed by the irruption of the shadow. The leper not only confronts Julian with this unwanted and denied part of himself, but also demands that he "rescue" and protect him.

Why is this guilt feeling raised to consciousness at this particular moment? Edinger writes that "the way of indi-

---

80. Neumann, *The Child*, p. 86.

viduation . . . requires the total efforts and resources of the personality. Nothing may be held back."[81] If the conscious and unconscious systems are to be reunited with the Self as the new center, then all the components of the psyche, including the shadow, must participate. For Jung, the acceptance of the shadow is the first step in the individuation process, which is "invariably started off by . . . becoming conscious of the shadow, a personality component usually with a negative sign."[82] Julian must accept the leper, the dark side of his own personality, if he is finally to give birth to the Self.

When we compare the demands the leper makes of Julian to the parable of the Last Judgment in Matthew, we find significant parallels:

—"I am hungry!" he said.
Julian gave him what he had. . . .
Next, he said:—"I am thirsty!"
Julian fetched his jug; . . . It was wine; what a boon! but the Leper stretched out his arm, and at one draught emptied the whole jug.
Then he said:—"I am cold!"
Julian, with his candle, ignited a bundle of ferns. . . .
The Leper came over to warm himself; . . . he whispered:—"Thy bed!"
Julian helped him gently to drag himself there. . . .
—"My bones feel like ice! Come near me!"
And Julian . . . lay down on the dead leaves, near him, side by side. . . .
—"Undress, I need the warmth of thy body!"
Julian took off his clothes. . . . [III, 38–53]

Then the King will say to those at his right hand, "Come, O blessed of my Father, inherit the kingdom prepared for you from the foundation of the world; for I was hungry and you gave me food, I was thirsty and you gave me drink, I was a stranger and you welcomed me, I was naked and you clothed me, I was sick and you visited me, I was in prison and you came to me." Then the righteous will answer him, "Lord, when did we see thee hungry and feed thee (etc.). . . ?" And the King will answer them, "Truly, I say to you, as you did it to one of the least of these my brethren, you did it to to me." [Matt. 25:34-40][83]

81. Edinger, p. 144.
82. Jung, "A Psychological Approach," pp. 197–198.
83. Quoted by Edinger, p. 144.

Edward Edinger considers the parable of the Last Judgment to be extremely important in understanding the dynamic of the individuation process. His psychological interpretation of the parable both reinforces my analysis of the leper as a symbol of the rejected shadow and sheds more light on the intimate relationship between shadow and Self in the final stage of individuation:

> The King is the central authority, a symbol of the Self. He identifies himself with "the least"—that aspect of the personality which is despised and is considered to have no value. "The least" is hungry and thirsty; that is, it is the needy, desirous side of ourselves. It is a stranger, referring to that aspect which is lonely and unaccepted. It is naked, that is, exposed, and unprotected. It is sick, the side of the psyche that is diseased, pathological. . . . And finally it is in prison—confined and punished for some transgression. . . . All these aspects of the rejected shadow are equated with the "King," which means psychologically that acceptance of the shadow and compassion for the inferior inner man are equivalent to acceptance of the Self.[84]

There are evident similarities in Edinger's analysis of "the least" and the leper as a symbol of the "primary guilt feeling." This guilt was imprisoned in Julian's psyche, a repression of the loneliness and lack of love which the child experiences as guilt. The leper is the shadow side of Julian's personality which he has not been able to confront. To Julian's conscious mind, he is ugly and intolerable. Like "the least," the leper is also a symbol of the Self. After prolonged neglect, he demands to be recognized and helped. He is a stranger who must be welcomed into the hut as if it were his home. Only when Julian has done all these things will he finally give birth to the Self. Julian's *salvation* is the true subject of the scene.

Julian's acceptance of the shadow is simultaneous with his progressive "denuding": all his food goes to the leper, then his wine and his clothes, and finally, naked, he must also give his body. This "denuding" is the final "passion of the ego" necessary for the incarnation of the Self. Edinger links this "passion of the ego" with the *Kenosis* doctrine of the incarnation based on a passage from Philippians: "Christ Jesus who, though he was in the form of God, did not count equality with God a thing to be

84. *Ibid.*

grasped, but emptied himself, taking the form of a servant, being born in the likeness of men."[85] Echoing Jung's characterization of individuation as "incarnation on the human level," Edinger concludes: "This image of 'incarnation by emptying' fits precisely the process . . . during which the ego . . . relinquishes its . . . identification with the Self."[86] It is after the appearance of his father in the fountain that Julian's behavior begins to be characterized by the ego-diminution necessary for the incarnation of the Self. Like Jesus, Julian takes the form of a servant: "he came upon the idea of using his life in the service of others" (III, 15).

The leper compels Julian to complete this process of ego-diminution through a series of "emptyings." Julian recognizes the necessity of obeying the leper and accedes to all his requests. Having taken all that Julian possesses, he orders him to undress so that he might be warmed by his body: "Julian took off his clothes; then, naked as on the day he was born, again took his place in the bed" (III, 53). The goal of the individuation process is the conscious recreation of the childhood state of unity. Julian, through ego-diminution and an acceptance of the authority of the Self (the leper), is approaching the goal. Jung writes that "adulthood is reached when the son reproduces his own childhood state by voluntarily submitting to a paternal authority."[87] The final configuration of the leper and Julian before the apotheosis reproduces that of the Original Uroboric Parents: "Julian stretched himself out on top, mouth against mouth, chest upon chest" (III, 56). The "hole" has finally disappeared—and from mouth to mouth, life-giving breath will pass.

At the moment that this "gap" between the conscious and unconscious mind is closed, the leper undergoes his miraculous transformation. The dynamic of diminution is now reversed,[88]

85. Philippians 2:5-6, quoted by Edinger, p. 138.
86. Edinger, p. 138.
87. Jung, "A Psychological Approach," p. 183.
88. The words of the prophet Jokanaan in *Herodias*, "In order that he [Jesus] grow, I must diminish" (translation is my own), could well serve as an epigraph for each one of the *Three Tales*. His words demonstrate the fundamental difference between Flaubert's novels and his short stories. In his article "La Mort et la rédemption dans les *Trois contes* de Flaubert," Frederic Shepler writes that "one of the themes that is at the center of the three stories is the progressive fall/decline that results in death" (*Neophilologus*, 56 [1972], 407). Death, however,

and the leper becomes larger and larger until he breaks out of the confines of the shack: "he... was growing, growing, touching with his head and his feet the two walls of the hut. The roof flew off" (III, 57). In his essay "Concerning Rebirth," Jung describes the psychic event of the "enlargement of the personality" (the birth of the Self) in terms that closely parallel the

---

paves the way for redemption. This "progressive fall/decline that results in death" corresponds to the "*progressive denuding toward zero*" which Per Nykrog maintains is the fundamental theme of all Flaubert's fiction (Per Nykrog, "Les 'Trois contes' dans l'évolution de la structure thématique chez Flaubert," *Romantisme*, no. 6 [1973], p. 64). Except for his inclusion of *The Temptation of Saint Anthony* with the *Three Tales*, I would agree with Nykrog that the short stories differ from the novels in that they contain an "ascending line" which prevails over the "descending line." According to Nykrog, the novels, lacking the "ascending line," "all end in total annihilation." We might compare Emma Bovary's lifetime of losses with the servant Felicity's (*A Simple Heart*) own dolorous existence, noting that Emma's culminates in a vision of darkness and damnation, while Felicity's leads to a vision of light and redemption. Both characters experience this "progressive denuding toward zero." In Emma's case it leads to a "total annihilation." For Felicity, the zero point is the moment in which a complete reversal takes place and the total personality is born. Diminution leads to an enlargement of the personality in *A Simple Heart*.

The structure at the end of Felicity's life corresponds exactly to Julian's experience of diminution/enlargement. Blind and deaf, the last survivor in a dilapidated house, she gives up her own breath (her lungs are diseased) in order to generate the breath of God (the vision of the giant parrot/Holy Ghost). This dynamic of diminution/enlargement corresponds to the *Kenosis* doctrine of incarnation by emptying discussed in relation to Julian's life. The leper has led Julian through a series of "emptyings" until he is left without even the clothes on his back. Even his naked body must be "given" to the leper. It is at this point of complete "denuding," the zero point of ego dominance, that the descending movement of diminution is reversed, becoming one of ascension and enlargement of the personality which culminates in the resolution of the ego-Self dichotomy. The diminution of ego dominance is necessary for the incarnation of the Self. In the novels, in spite of "decline" and "denuding," the pretense of ego dominance through ego-Self identification is never relinquished, and death (psychic or physical) is the result.

St. John's realization that "in order that I grow, I must diminish" now assumes its full significance. The ascending and descending axes in *Herodias* are embodied in two characters rather than one. Antipas, by saving his life, loses it. St. John, by losing his life, paves the way not only for his own redemption but for that of all persons. In *Herodias*, the association of individuation and "incarnation by emptying" is no longer a "symbolic" one. It points, rather, to the historical manifestation of God on earth. The search for redemption is revealed as the basic structure of Flaubert's fiction. This redemption, as a psychological phenomenon, can be understood as the creation of the individuated personality. An intense effort to actualize this process is evident in Flaubert's novels, which exemplify an arrested or aborted individuation, the failure of psychic integration. From this perspective, the final realization of individuation in the *Three Tales* marks them as the culmination of Flaubert's work.

apotheosis at the end of *The Legend:* "When a summit of life is reached, when the bud unfolds and from the lesser the greater emerges, then, as Nietzsche says, 'One becomes Two,' and the greater figure, which one always was but which remained invisible, appears to the lesser personality with the force of a revelation."[89] Julian, by recognizing "the least," has liberated the "immortal one" who also lived inside of him. Rather than trying to bring this "greater" down to the level of his own ego, he recognizes the authority of the Self and submits to it. This "greater" is projected in the person of Jesus Christ, "the perfect symbol of the hidden immortal within the mortal man."[90] This Christ figure is no longer the exiled Son, the suffering Christ, but the Christ of glory who ascends into Heaven to be reunited with his Father, who again lifts him up.[91]

The tension between Father and Son has been resolved. Although the Holy Ghost is not named as such in the text, his presence is readily apparent in the description of the transformation process: "a fullness of bliss, a superhuman joy flooded down into the soul of the swooning Julian" (III, 57). This flood of joy which descends into the soul of the believer has traditionally been the image used in the Christian religion to describe the experience of the descent of the Holy Ghost and the state of bliss and grace which it brings. For analytical psychologists, this descent of the Holy Ghost is consistently associated with the descent of the transpersonal into the realm of the ego and the establishment of the ego-Self axis. There is, however, a reciprocal movement on this ego-Self axis. At the same time that God descends, Julian rises toward Him ("Julian ascended toward the blue expanses," III, 57). Thus a dialectical relationship is established between ego and Self, and the process of individuation is complete.[92] Jung views this reciprocal movement and dialectical relationship as characteristic of the workings of the Holy Ghost: "the Holy Ghost, . . . a separate and incommensurable

---

89. C. G. Jung, "Concerning Rebirth," in *Four Archetypes* (from *C.W.*, vol. 9, pt. I), Princeton/Bollingen Paperback Edition (Princeton, 1970), p. 55.

90. *Ibid.*

91. See Chapter 1, note 47.

92. Berg points out that Sartre's psychoanalytical reading of Christ's sacrifice is "primarily from the father's point of view." He then suggests a reading from the son's point of view. I would suggest that both readings are simultaneous and interdependent.

'third,' . . . [is] the . . . unexpected resolution of tension between Father and Son. . . . The uniting 'third' is itself connected with the nature of . . . redemption, whereby God descends into the human realm and man mounts up to the realm of divinity."[93] This uniting "third" has enabled Julian to recreate the unity of childhood. Over the cradle of the infant Julian hung "a lamp in the shape of a dove" (I, 21), which burned continuously, like the eyes of the leper in the storm. An explosion of light first signals the leper's transformation: "his eyes suddenly began to shine like stars; his hair lengthened like sunbeams" (III, 57). It is in the end as it was in the beginning: there is no more darkness, for innocence has been restored.

The enlargement of the personality and the unification of its components which culminate in the apparition of Christ begin immediately following Julian's experience of the ego-Self axis. The Holy Ghost carries on the procreative work of the Father:

> The third step, finally, points beyond the "Son" into the future, to a continuing realization of the "spirit," i.e., a living activity proceeding from "Father" and "Son." . . . This extension of the *filiatio*, whereby men are made children of God, is a . . . projection of the psychic change that has taken place. . . . The son will transmit to his children the procreative spirit of life which he himself has received and from which he himself was begotten.[94]

The "spirit" has passed from "Father" to "Son," now become himself a "Father." The tension has been resolved, and the gap closed. Julian continues the procreative work of the "Father," giving birth to his "Son," Christ, out of his own body and mind. Julian's incarnation of Christ, made possible by the intervention of the "third" term (Holy Ghost, ego-Self axis), marks him as Creator.

93. Jung, "A Psychological Approach," p. 162.
94. *Ibid.*, p. 182.

3

A "Ferocious Heart": Love
and Parricide in *Saint Julian*

Michel Grimaud

●●●

The Plot and Its Literary Meaning

The original story of Saint Julian the Hospitaler evokes horror
and awe. Similarly, its impact in Gustave Flaubert's *Legend of
Saint Julian the Hospitaler* is due in part to the raw facts: the mass
murder of animals; the *mistaken* murder of the parents (reminiscent of the Oedipus myths and plays); the presence of predictions; and Julian's self-punishment, akin to repeated suicide and
culminating in the extreme self-denial of lying on top of a purulent leper—loathing transformed into religious ecstasy.

   Any narrator using such events should achieve powerful effects. But Flaubert's naïve narrator recounts the events with
surprising affectlessness.[1] Moralizing comments are conspicu-

---

1. The narrator's first, hardly noticeable, intrusion is the naming of the
beaver—an animal unknown to Julian (I, 55). The most obvious intrusion occurs
in II, 8: "It is he, *and no other*, who slew the serpent of Milan and the dragon of
Oberbirbach."

ously absent. The whole story, in fact, seems to be in a kind of moral and religious vacuum, in no way a justification of the ways of God to man. The tale's lack of didactic focus and information is perhaps its most striking characteristic. Readers do not know why Julian is a killer; they wonder why his parents do not share their secrets with each other; why they follow Julian; why Julian becomes a saint because of his repelling obedience to a leper. But it is perhaps the very nature of literary narratives to be built around gaps in understanding: Hamlet procrastinates, Julien Sorel "inexplicably" tries to kill Madame de Rênal, Alceste is in love with Célimène. The predictions further introduce an atmosphere of mystery which is enhanced by the lack of communication between the main characters and by Julian's own partial recognition of his parricidal wish.

Saint Julian, therefore, is not a simple retelling of the legend: there are too many apparently unintegrated facts. In this sense, no summary of the story would be felt as adequate, in contrast to the obvious ease in summarizing the hagiographic source. Yet the summarizing process itself probably is, from a psychological viewpoint, at the very core of reading, but particularly of literary reading.[2] A work, when it is read, has to be reconstructed according to certain "themes," that is, according to esthetic, personal, social, psychological clues in the text. But the literary text, when it is read as literature, appears to require a different mode of summarizing: events, words, must be categorized because they belong to the same semantic field despite their apparent, syntagmatic, unrelatedness in the manifest plot structure. The reality represented in the work of literature, to be read as literature, should be interpreted through the use of thematic series independent from plot structures as is made clear from our recognition of an author's work when we have read several of his or her books. Ideally, the critic's task is to facilitate reading by describing explicitly the main thematic series, relating them to

---

2. Much work needs to be done on the basic processes involved in reading. Since Gillian Cohen's survey of "The Psychology of Reading" (*New Literary History*, 4 [1972], 75–90), the best research has been interdisciplinary and, although written by poeticians, integrates cognitive psychology and artificial intelligence. See Teun van Dijk, *Macrostructures* (Hillsdale, N.J., 1980) and especially Robert de Beaugrande, *Text, Discourse, and Process* (Norwood, N.J., 1980).

each other, and showing how they are linked to some fundamental socioeconomic and psychological issues.[3]

Saint Julian deals with significant themes: the birth and
growth of a hero-saint and his relationship to animate nature
and society, family and God. But these categories are handled
through the medium of language in such a way that the experience of reading becomes not only a struggle for the communication of a certain reality, but a struggle toward establishing
another type of communication.

A Ferocious Society

A preliminary question is: Why is Julian a "ferocious heart," as
the stag says? "—'Accursed! accursed! accursed! One day, ferocious heart, thou shalt murder thy father and thy mother!'" (I,
68). The phrase itself is striking since it evokes the title of the
preceding story in *Three Tales* (*A Simple Heart*), as well as the
cruelty of Herodias and Salome in the following one.[4] In fact, all
three stories are about *society's cruelty:* Julian, then, is "ferocious" because he has been brought up in a cruel environment.
Certainly, Julian is crueler than many or most of his contem-
poraries. Yet the murder of his parents, though it is poetically
the high point of his ferocious behavior, is not to be adduced as
proof of his separateness from common humanity since Julian
did not know that he was killing his parents. This is a peculiar
point because we do, as readers, feel that this is the culmination
of Julian's cruelty and no chance fateful action. But if we are to
be consistent, we must first analyze the story on a realistic level:

3. Our method in this chapter may be compared to Dina Sherzer's in "Narrative Figures in *La Légende de Saint Julien l'Hospitalier*," *Genre,* 7 (1974), 54–70.
Background for our psychological and poetic approaches may be found in Algirdas Julien Greimas, *Sémantique structurale,* (Paris, 1966) and *Essais de sémiotique
poétique* (Paris, 1972) and in Norman N. Holland's *The Dynamics of Literary Response* (New York, 1968), pp. 28–30, and 5 *Readers Reading* (New Haven, 1975), p.
295. Jim Swan's "Giving New Depth to the Surface: Psychoanalysis, Literature,
and Society" (*Psychoanalytic Review,* 62 [1975], 5–28) provides a complementary
social perspective.
4. For further comments on "heart" in *Saint Julian* see "Poetics and Translation," p. 263. We use Edouard Maynial's edition of *Trois contes* (Paris, 1969).
Charles Carlut has published a concordance to Flaubert's *Trois contes* (New York,
1980).

at such a level, Julian commits voluntary murder but involuntary parricide. Nonetheless, there is no doubt about Julian's unusual cruelty, for which no psychiatrically sufficient reason is provided: this would be a flaw in a case history purporting to study the precise etiology of a patient's illness, but it is not so in a short story where it is only necessary to provide the reader with structural couplings. In this case, Julian's cruelty is satisfyingly linked to that of his parents and of the society of the time—in one word, to Julian's upbringing.[5]

The psychologically convincing power of society's cruelty is due to its being *underplayed* by the narrator. It is not presented as an explanation at all. The narrator shows aggression as past, he denies it or mentions it as an accepted social norm. Yet aggression is the constant backdrop of almost every scene in the story. The opening paragraphs present a picture of a curiously ambiguous nature. The first reinforces the title's legendary motif: it is a perfect beginning for a fairy tale—nameless parents, a hero known by his first name, a castle amidst the woods on a sloping hillside. But the castle is fortified (I, 2), its roofs are pointed, covered with lead scales, while the foundation rests upon what turns out to be an abrupt hillside. The gargoyles are called "dragons" (I, 3). There are several fences surrounding the cas-

5. Only very general hypotheses about Julian's psychological makeup can be made. One such assumption might be related to Gregory Bateson's "double-bind" theory ("Towards a Theory of Schizophrenia," in *Steps to an Ecology of Mind* [San Francisco, 1972]). This would fit well with an analysis of the hypocritical atmosphere concerning aggression, as the following passage implies—but there is no precise evidence that this is the mechanism involved: "A child may experience his mother as unresponsive to him and unloving and he may infer, correctly, that she had never wanted him and never loved him. Yet this mother may insist, in season and out, that she does love him. Furthermore, if there is friction between them, as there inevitably is, she may claim that it results from his having been born with a contrary temperament. When he seeks her attention, she dubs him insufferably demanding; when he interrupts her, he is intolerably selfish; when he becomes angry at her neglect he is held possessed of a bad temper or even an evil spirit. In some way, she claims, he was born bad" (John Bowlby, *Attachment and Loss*, vol. 2 [New York, 1973], pp. 317-318). Not the content, but the mechanism, described above is what we claim *might* have been one of the possible explanations for the etiology of Julian's mental organization—if one feels such a psychological explanation of a character's motivation to be needed. Other explanations would stress Julian's parents' clear lack of empathy for each other and for a Julian whom they almost venerate (I, 21). (See further comments in the Conclusion.)

tle. Methodologically, titles and first pages are important points of any analysis: they set the mood.[6] Here, the symbolic character of the page is emphasized by an element in the landscape itself: the flowers combine to compose "ciphers," or more probably "monograms": "A garden with *figures* wrought in flowers" (I, 4). This retrospectively confirms the oft-quoted symbolic role of plants in the preceding paragraph: the duality of basil and heliotrope corresponds thematically to the double character of Julian, an angry saint. As Dina Sherzer remarks: "We realize in retrospect that the three oppositions—basil/heliotrope, martyr's bone/carbuncle [I, 14], emperor/blood [I, 17]—are, at the outset of the story, *synecdoches* of Julien's life, since each of these oppositions stands for the whole of his life, which is about to be told."[7] This duality is immediately disavowed as being a thing of the past: "Life had been peaceful for so long that the portcullis could not be lowered anymore; the ditches were filled with grass; swallows built their nests in the cracks of the battlements" (I, 5).[8] Nowadays, even the archer goes to sleep "like a monk" (I, 5)!

Yet peace and wealth do not preclude memory of a glorious past of generalized warring and hunting: "In the armory could be seen, between banners and heads of wild beasts, weapons of all ages and of all nations, from the slings of the Amalekites and the javelins of the Garamantes to the broadswords of the Sara-

6. See Raymond Jean's "Ouvertures, phrases-seuils," *Critique*, no. 288 (1971), pp. 421–431, and Steven Kellman's "Grand Openings and Plain: The Poetics of First Lines," *Sub-Stance*, no. 17 (1977), pp. 139–148. In a similar manner final sentences or lines have typical closural features. At the end of each part of the story Julian vanishes from sight. Compare this, also, to the disappearance of the hermit, the beggar, and the partridges. Barbara Herrnstein Smith studies this phenomenon in *Poetic Closure* (Chicago, 1968), as does Philippe Hamon in "Clausules," *Poétique*, no. 24 (1975), pp. 495–526—a critique of Smith's analysis.

7. "Narrative Figures," p. 57. Note also that a homologous use of "flowers" and "figures" is not uncommon, as in the following passage taken from Chateaubriand: "The nasturtium flower . . . embroiders with its crimson figures the holy walls" (*Génie du Christianisme*, III, V, 2; quoted in the *Robert* dictionary).

8. Colin Duckworth notes: "Some editions give 'pleins d'eau,' which is nonsensical. One would expect a moat to be full of water only in times of danger, and overgrown with grass when not needed. The MS in Flaubert's handwriting gives 'herbe'; the mistake was subsequently made by the copyist" (*Trois contes* [London, 1959], p. 192, n. 9). This is confirmed by the episode of the pigeon in II, 32–33.

cens and the coats of mail of the Normans" (I, 7). There are quarrels in the present, but Julian's father succeeds in appeasing them. Indeed, the scene is too idyllic to last long: "During winter, he stared at the snowflakes falling, or had stories read to him" (I, 9). Surely our "good lord," as the narrator persists in calling him time and again, has not always been such a pacific soul. Though it seems difficult to pinpoint the uneasiness one feels in such a context, the very excess of food and revelry is disquieting—as is the passing mention of the lack of communication between Julian's parents. The father's fear of being thought overbearing on account of the prediction of his son's great future, his throwing alms for the Bohemian beggar *on the ground*—whether or not they are realistic historically—are essentially dysphoric notations which, moreover, stress the parents' dependence on the social order.

There are several other ambivalent notations. In particular, the dove over Julian's crib: it is a lamp which *burns constantly* and which thus evokes religion and violence, in keeping with the two predictions (I, 21). The context of the quasi virgin birth (I, 10) of a "little Jesus" (I, 21) suggests, of course, that the dove alludes to the Holy Ghost, as in *A Simple Heart*. Also puzzling is the ensuing reference to Julian as a "little Jesus" *with teeth.*

Despite narrative assurances to the contrary, the world around the castle is by no means safe: the traveling merchants need to be encouraged to visit the castle—a paradoxical situation when one considers that this is their normal way to ply their trade: "The foreigner, gaining confidence, would change direction; . . . in due time the good man took leave, with a handsome profit, having suffered no violence" (I, 25). The emphasis on the lack of violent behavior serves as a reminder of the impending dangers. The castle seems a haven of peace in a troubled world. The rhetorical insistence on lack of violence sensitizes the reader to the problem of violence and sets it up as an early potential organizer; it is such a reading strategy which gives weight to the ambivalent status of dove and teeth.[9]

9. "Teeth" are mentioned again in the final scene in the description of the Leper-*Christ* (III, 47). Compare the rhetorical device of paralepsis (or preterition) to Freud's famous remarks in "Negation" (XIX, 233–239), where he notes that a patient saying that he is *not* thinking about his mother cannot help but mention the fact that he had nonetheless thought of her even if only in a negative mode.

It certainly is a cruel world: pilgrims tell tales of the ferociousness of the pagans (I, 25), and these are followed by tales concerning the father's own feats about which he fondly reminisces with his old war cronies. The narrator adds that Julian would cry out so that "his father had no doubt that some day he would be a conqueror" (I, 26). This account is typical: the narrator only mentions Julian's reactions to pain or war. Julian cuts his teeth "without a whimper" (I, 21) and is said to smile "with delight" as he sits on a warhorse—not when he learns to sing with his mother (I, 22).

As he grows up, Julian's education is either infinitely tedious (I, 23-24) or about violence—or mingles both (I, 36-37). He learns how to hunt and kill with ease, but according to the *socially proper rules for the pastime of hunting.* "Déduit des chasses" (I, 36), which conveys this idea, is an obsolete and technical word which, as such, narratively downplays the coupling of killing and pleasure. Similarly, during the triumphal mass killing (I, 56), the French verb is not "tuer" but "occire," so that distancing occurs through the use of quaint language. Though one could assign such use to a wish to enhance the historical atmosphere, it is significant that these are two of the very few such cases in the tale. Obsolete language, therefore, stands out and must be interpreted.

Another typical event in Julian's education is his father's offer of a sword (I, 76)—with which Julian, accidentally, almost kills him. But the most serious indictment of society's casual view of killing is to be found in the description of polite family fun—that is, pouncing wildly on quails caught under a net. Dogs would bark, "quail took wing; and the neighborhood ladies invited along with their husbands, the children, the handmaids would all pounce, and capture them with ease" (I, 42). The thoughtless cruelty of a whole society is all the more significant as the scene will be repeated, unsuccessfully, by Julian in the second hunting scene (II, 69).

The society in which Julian lives believes in a special brand of cruelty, as should be clear from the above examples: bursts of killing are allowed (or required) at recurrent periods, but they are highly controlled. In this respect, law and order are repeatedly linked to religion from the start, and it is not surprising that the signs of Julian's boundless rage should appear in a mild and apparently controlled form in church. Obsessive orderliness also appears in the third paragraph: the courtyard is paved with the same care as the flagstones in a *church;* the household is run like a *monastery* (I, 10). Mass is an ordeal of self-restraint, as the narrator states by indirection: "[Julian's] seat in the chapel was next to his parents; and, no matter how long the services lasted, he remained kneeling on his prayer stool, his cap on the floor and his hands folded" (I, 27).[10] Order is such an obsession that the falcons are assembled "in order of size" on their perch (I, 40). The *pleasure of killing* with one's hounds is *required* of Julian, but it has to belong to an extraordinarily rigid world where the "rules of the quarry" (I, 36) are merely one instance of what must be learnt to become a man. Violence, then, has its own societally approved rules. Motionless hounds watch over the orderly setting up of the quail nets as a prelude to the beastlike behavior of the humans (I, 42). Even Julian's religious dreams are orderly: Paradise is a place where the new Adam need only extend his arm to see all the animals perish, or, later, see the animals assembled "in order of size" and paired as they were when entering Noah's ark; and then relentlessly killed with the same javelins with which Julian almost killed his mother (II, 20).

There are fewer allusions to society's violence in the middle section of *Saint Julian,* but Julian would not be a hero if there were not generalized warring to be miraculously ended by him. His earlier distaste for the "convenient contrivances" of social hunting (I, 44) now goes even further. Julian has become an outsider who turns his powers and those of other outcasts— "fugitive slaves, rebel peasants, penniless bastards" (II, 5)—to the service of the Establishment. He reintegrates the legitimate social order by remaining on its fringes, and by killing those who in many ways mirror him. As a consequence, it is not surprising that the double climax of the story will be Julian's renunciation of suicide as he realizes that he looks like his father (III, 13), and his suicide-like renunciation of self as he lies upon

10. See Heidi Culbertson Bart and Benjamin F. Bart, "Space, Time, and Reality in Flaubert's *Saint Julien," Romanic Review,* 59 (1968), 30–39. One of the notable time references in the story is the recurrent adverb "longtemps," which appears, in particular, at the beginning and end.

the leper in the final scene. But as far as the middle section of *Saint Julian* is concerned, his tale of violence ends when he saves the emperor of Occitania by cutting off the head of the latter's treacherous Moslem brother-in-law—a laudable deed indeed or, at least, one which is followed by the gift of the emperor's Christian daughter, although, ironically, one who was born out of wedlock (II, 9, 14).

In the third part, humanity—society—is shown in an openly bad light. People are hostile to Julian (III, 3). They seem "beastlike" to him (III, 6); they insult him and are blasphemous and thankless (III, 18). But this finally open aggressiveness can be seen as brought upon Julian by his own meek or self-deprecatory behavior, while, in any case, it is not of such magnitude as his own reckless killings.

Religion and Aggression

War and religion are associated as early as the fifth paragraph, through the use of a simile between the archer and a monk (I, 5). There is much talk about the ferociousness of the pagans, but the most noticeable linkage occurs when the old monk, *in the name of God*, orders Julian to bear arms, to practice swordsmanship or throw javelins: "In the end the old monk ordered him, in the name of God, of honor, and of forebears, to renew his gentlemanly pursuits" (I, 79). According to the narrator, God protects Julian because Julian protects the Church: "Thanks to divine favor, he always escaped; for he protected the clergy, orphans, widows, and foremost the aged" (II, 4). Finally, it is because of God's will that Julian has murdered his parents (see II, 82) and is taken up to heaven—is killed by the leper-Christ at the end.

The references to religion and violence are even more pervasive than may appear at first, but they are not present on the narrative level. "Little Jesus," the burning dove, teeth, the archer-monk, appear in seemingly descriptive passages. In one such case Julian is compared to a young dog (I, 33) just a few lines before the extensive listing of the various types of hounds in the pack his father has assembled for him. The first of the

hounds, greyhounds, are "liable to get out of temper" (I, 38)—a
trait reminiscent of the "basil" element in Julian's own character. The next race of dogs are "of faith unmovable," just as the
heliotrope was an emblem of Julian's saintliness. Benjamin F.
Bart has convincingly shown that this phrase is semantically
"ungrammatical," though not, one might suggest, meaningless.[11] A paraphrase might run as follows: the dogs *evoke* unmovable faith, both as hunting animals and as extensions of
Julian, the future saint. In fact, their colors are clearly emblem-
atic: white and red are linked to purity in Christian symbolism,[12]
reinforcing consequently the word "faith." Moreover, the two
colors can also function as opposites within the double thematic
code, first, of hunting, killing, or "blood" in the prediction made
to Julian's father (I, 17), and, second, of purity (white being
linked to the mother in I, 10, and elsewhere) as well as saintliness, both linked to the first prediction (I, 13). What is of interest
here is that the puzzling nature of the phrase "of faith unmovable" may be seen as serving as a marker toward symbolic reinterpretation.

The names of two of the falcons—sakers ("sacres," close to
"sacred" in French) and "pilgrim falcons"—enter into the same
thematic series. The presence of such a common breed as pilgrim falcons among supposedly rare birds of prey secured by
"paying great sums of money" and captured in "distant lands"
(I, 40) might further indicate that their semantic remotivation
takes precedence over their reference and that they function as
thematic reminders of Julian's dualism as well as that of the
society in which he lives.

Julian's fascination with aggression and cruelty follows the
practice of both his parents, of the Church in general, and of the
family monk in particular. What distinguishes Julian from this
milieu is not his aggressive behavior but his preference for an
asocial practice of it. The climactic scene where whole families
attack helpless quail is judged by Julian to be a mere instance of
"convenient contrivances" (I, 44). He prefers to hunt "loin du

11. Bart, "Flaubert and Hunting: *La Légende de Saint Julien l'Hospitalier*,"
Nineteenth-Century French Studies, 4 (1975–76), 43.
12. George Ferguson, *Signs and Symbols in Christian Art* (New York, 1966).

monde"—a phrase that connotes, since the seventeenth century, a religious weariness of the world. The narrator's choice of
words evokes, therefore, Julian's paradoxical destiny through
the use of polyvalent phrases. The description of Julian's favorite falcon is equally ambiguous. The falcon's role seems almost religious in view of the use of colors and the formalized
beauty of the descriptions: "It was almost always a large,
snow-white Scythian tartar. Its leather hood was crowned with
a plume, golden bells shivered at its blue feet... The falcon
would soon be back, tearing up some bird, and perched anew
on its master's gauntlet, with both wings trembling" (I, 44). The
focus is on the trembling of the bird of prey, on his flight into the
azure sky, and on his quivering wings—not on the unnamed
prey being torn to pieces ("*some* bird").

Denial of Affect

The narrator's matter-of-factness, his esthetic rather than realistic focus, as exemplified in the preceding quotation; his implicit
identification with the point of view of contemporary society; his
lack of ethical comment—all result in a lack of horror at most of
the killing that takes place in the first part of *Saint Julian* (I, 1–49).
In fact, the concluding paragraph before the first dream scene of
hunting retroactively seems to put Julian in the position of a
courageous hero killing only in self-defense: "He stabbed bears
to death, killed bulls with a hatchet, wild boars with a spear; and
once, with nothing left but a stick, even defended himself
against wolves which were gnawing corpses at the foot of a
gibbet" (I, 49). The position of this paragraph at the very
end of an important episode of Part I, and the mention of the
gibbet unexpectedly enforce a view of Julian as almost helpless
in the company of *rotting corpses*—in notable contrast to our
expectations at that point in the story but suggestive of the
grand finale of Part III. The tension between this type of conclusion and what must be our uneasy feeling about Julian's killings
is one of the striking features of the narrative: there is a constant
displacement of affects and meanings, an isolation of affect from
meanings, throughout the text. Society's cruelty is isolated from
Julian's. The *knowledge* of Julian's cruelty is dissociated from the

feeling of cruelty by the foregrounding of the attacker rather than the attacked or by summarizing techniques: "Julian flew in this fashion the heron, the kite, the crow, and the hawk. . . . On foggy days, he would go deep into a marsh to watch for geese, otters, and wild ducks" (I, 45 and 47). Each of these sentences is set out as an entire paragraph, thus emphasizing the facts, but being businesslike summaries, they are from a psychological and literary point of view divorced from any affect.

Even the original killings of mouse, pigeon, and small birds, because of the unreal ease with which they are achieved, because of the emphasis on Julian's surprise and quasi innocence and the lack of overt mention of suffering by the animals, do not allow us to react with strong emotion. In fact, because these killings remain *unexplained*, they take on a symbolic aspect: as readers of literature, we expect them to *mean* a reality, rather than be mimetic representations of reality; we therefore concentrate on the details of the description in an effort to understand their significance.[13] Finally, the factor of *chance* in the killing of the pigeon, the appositely childlike use of cake crumbs as bait for the mouse, and the use of the peashooter to kill the birds (I, 29–32), definitely distance us from the realities of death in order to foster a more general type of reminiscing or fantasizing about *childhood wishes of omnipotence.* The fantastic ease of infinite mass murders, their lack of precise locale, duration, or chronological setting ("He was hunting in some indeterminate land, for an indefinite time, solely because of his very existence, everything fulfilling itself with the ease which one experiences in dreams," I, 56), and Julian's distancing from his own acts and surroundings (depersonalization and derealization:[14] "Wild-eyed, he gazed at the magnitude of the slaughter, not comprehending how he might have done it" I, 62) lend to the scene the character of a *wish-fulfillment* in fantasy where death can be omnipo-

13. Holland makes a similar point about "puzzling movies," in which violence and sexuality are compensated by emotional distance in the characters themselves and uncertainty about plot structure for the viewer of Fellini, Antonioni, or Bertolucci (*Dynamics of Literary Response,* p. 166 and *passim*). The puzzlement itself also has an infantile correlate, as Holland shows (p. 169). His analysis applies to *Saint Julian.*

14. See the discussion of these concepts pp. 173–174 and 218–220. Berg deals at greater length with "dream or fact" (I, 15) in Chapter 1.

tently meted out without reality-oriented considerations. Because of its mimetic quality, literature can recreate this type of complex wishful thinking—a magic killing off of animals and parents— without any need for guilt in the reader.[15]

The co-occurrence of magic and a rule-ridden world has important psychological ramifications. The ritualistic aura of the Paradise murders (II, 20), for instance, squarely puts in psychological perspective the earlier hunting scene where the dream quality was obvious but unmentioned. This means that their status as miracles or as dreams, or as fantasies—like the duality of the mother's vision ("dream or fact," I, 15)—loses much of its relevance. What has to be understood is the textual reality of the scenes as *expressions* of desires (Julian is said to be sick from "a desire for love" [I, 73]). That we may differ in our interpretation of the likelihood of the reality of the scenes never detracts from their avowed psychological impact, from the fact that they are presented to us as significant for Julian.

Love, Religion, and Aggression

No aspect of life is more strongly denied than human love and human sexuality.[16] Without them the story of aggression is incomprehensible. Sexuality in *Saint Julian* is first and foremost linked to religion. As in all myths—and especially the Christian myth—the hero is born through a miracle, here that of virgin birth: in other words, without any previous encounter between Julian's father and mother.[17] This miracle is thematically prepared by the comparison of the future mother's household to a monastery and by her embroidering altar cloths (I, 10). In such a

15. On the importance of such self-oriented modes of thinking see Pinchas Noy, "A Revision of the Psychoanalytic Theory of the Primary Process," *International Journal of Psychoanalysis*, 50 (1969), 155–178, and "Symbolism and Mental Representation," *Annual of Psychoanalysis*, 1 (1973), 125–158, as well as Anne-Marie Sandler's "Comments on the Significance of Piaget's Work for Psychoanalysis," *International Review of Psychoanalysis*, 2 (1975), 365–378.

16. The psychoanalytic conception of sexuality includes all functions which are directed toward the obtainment of pleasure from whatever zone or organ of the body; it is not restricted to genitality (see, for instance, Freud's earliest discussion in the *Three Essays on the Theory of Sexuality*, VII, 177–178, 233).

17. On this topic see Edmund Leach's masterful essay "Virgin Birth" in *Genesis and Other Myths* (New York, 1969).

context, it would be an oversimplification to read the sentence "Through her fervent prayers to God, a son came unto her" (I, 10) merely as a naïve narrator's point of view or a Flaubertian ironic touch. Symbolically it establishes a "triangle" similar to the one between Joseph, Mary, and Jesus. This is confirmed by Julian's being called "a little Jesus." Among the many important dissimilarities evoked by the connection just established is the fact that father and mother hide their secrets from each other. The factual events related to the physical conception of Julian-Jesus are *made* irrelevant here. Whether Julian's birth is a miracle or simply the result of sexual relations willed by God, the reader cannot know; but the birth is made to seem independent of the father. The relations between father and mother are not so much between each other as to a *tertium quid:* God at first, then their son. Their keeping their secrets from each other points to their lack of relationships at all levels, including the sexual. Sexuality or its lack, then, is associated with religion.

As Moskos also points out in Chapter 2, Julian's aggressiveness is sexualized: "[The pigeon's] protracted life irritated the child. He began to strangle it; and the convulsions of the bird made his heart pound, filled his senses with a wild, tumultuous delight. With the final stiffening, he felt faint" (I, 35). The traditional connection between orgasm and death in many cultures (for example, in Elizabethan wordplay or in the French phrase "petite mort") rests on formal characteristics and on the diametrically opposed aspects of love and death in human experience, so that evoking one through the other as in "wild delight" ("volupté sauvage") unites rhetorically what cannot, in everyday life, be experienced in action. But here, too, Julian is in a peculiar situation: he does not enjoy a truly pure experience: he feels faint. The French phrase "il *se sentit* défaillir" puts him in the position of an observer, not totally involved in his acts. In fact, the strongest verb describing Julian's enjoyment of death is used when he can only be an observer: "He loved to sound his horn and follow his dogs... and when the stag began to moan under the bites, he killed it deftly, then relished the fury of the mastiffs as they gulped it down, cut into pieces on its reeking hide" (I, 46).

In a strange conclusion to a paragraph preceding Julian's

tender memories of his blond adolescent years (III, 20), food is suddenly associated with killing (as in "relish" ["se délectait"], above) for no apparent textual reason: "Next appalling frosts came, which gave things a stonelike rigidity, induced a mad craving for meat" (III, 19). Eating in the final scene will be one of the commands of the leper and is regularly associated with religion. This association is readily understandable in terms of the Eucharist, which is alluded to half-humorously at the end (wine, III, 42). In *Saint Julian*, animals (goats) are scapegoats linked to religion but killed mostly for the pleasure of killing, not for the purposes of nourishment. Nonetheless, Julian, who is soon to die, has the insane need for flesh at a point when he is about to meet with rotting yet live flesh and be reborn—a fact that brings us back to the events surrounding his birth, when a similar craving was present. Julian-Jesus is said to have three nurses (I, 21). We are not told whether they are wet nurses or not,[18] but the fact that they are three is deemed worthy of mention by the narrator. This fits well with Julian's parents' "*boundless* regard for his person" (I, 21) and with the semantic field of overabundance of food after Julian's birth—and with the allusion to Julian's teeth, usually associated with weaning and aggression from a developmental point of view. The Gargantuan meal which follows the delivery is characterized by metamorphoses and grotesque birth:

> So, there was great rejoicing, and a feast which lasted three days and four nights, under bright torchlight, to the sound of harps, over floors strewn with branches. The rarest spices were eaten, with hens as big as sheep; as entertainment, a dwarf popped out of a pie; and when the bowls were too few, for the crowd kept swelling, people had to drink out of hunting horns and helmets. [I, 11][19]

18. The wet-nurse episode in *Madame Bovary* is well known. A historical overview of this topic will be found in George D. Sussman's "The Wet-Nursing Business in Nineteenth-Century France, *French Historical Studies*, 9 (1975), 304–328.

19. Gargantua's birth is similarly accompanied by overabundant eating, but the function of eating in Rabelais is strikingly different. Oddly enough, the small world of *Gargantua* has psychological echoes in *Saint Julian*: the fantasylike quality of the former's war games and the latter's hunting scenes both correspond to the spatial feeling of an infinite world but finally show it up as being merely a child's dream during play in the family garden or neighborhood. At the end of

Julian's birth is not only accompanied by overabundance, it generates the main theme of the narrative: lack of restraint, a hyperbolic dreamlike growth (as in the first hunting scene), a release from the norms of everyday life. The implications of Julian's environment at birth can be summarized as continuous overstimulation connected with animal flesh and birth (the dwarf) where the only recourse is, if not war, at least the instruments of war: hunting horns and helmets.

Julian's textual milieu of overabundant feeding is unsurprisingly the triggering feature of his climactic act: he kills the *nursing* fawn (I, 64). If we were to explain this repetition in terms of Julian's specific psychological makeup, it would be dubious to say that the events surrounding his birth left a trace on his psyche. But for the reader this is an adequate coupling and justification because an event, in a literary text, is to be taken as a significant instance of a general trend. Further, the fact that it happened at Julian's birth is esthetically and psychologically essential in view of the cultural emphasis on the importance of beginnings. The murder of the father, mother, and nursing fawn also refers us back to the original nursing situation and is inseparable from the two sets of predictions—thus closing the circle of noncommunication between father, mother, *and son,* who at no point will reveal their secrets to one another.

The third major event repeats on another sociocultural and personal level the cluster of features connected with love, death, and religion. The opposition is casually and somewhat puzzlingly set up at the very beginning: "There was even... a Roman sweat room; but the good lord refrained from using it, deeming it to be a heathenish practice" (I, 8). The refusal to use the sweat room not only polarizes pagans and Christians but implies that in the past the castle had been the site of unchristian practices. Thematically, moreover, the sweat room emphasizes the feeling of stifling or more generally the physical analog of anxiety which will appear at all the crucial points in the story.[20] The opposition between pagans and Christians is not so clear

---

both hunting scenes, Julian finds himself far closer to his castle than he thought he was: Julian "chose a path at random, and found himself almost immediately at the gates of the castle" (I, 71; see II, 68).

20. See, for instance, I, 35, 57; II, 63, 67; III, 34, 56.

when the time axis is taken into account: the suppression of violence in the present as well as the displacement of guilt onto the pagans might in fact be seen as mediated by Julian, who shares tendencies that were historically present but had, *apparently*, only left traces at the very beginning of the story. The oppositions can be presented in the following way:

Present pagan "ferocity" (I, 25)	vs. Present Christian peacefulness (I, 5; I, 9)
Julian's "ferocity" toward animals (I, 68, etc.)	vs. Julian's appeasing of wars and killing only of dragons and other monstrous beasts (II, 6–10)
Pagan thirst for money (II, 9, etc.)	vs. Julian's parent's wealth and charity[21]

This series is mediated narratively by Julian, who manifestly, within the explicit plot structure, belongs to both worlds. Though, as we have shown, our underlying judgment of the Christian world does not establish a clear distinction between the violence of the two antithetical faiths, the text does emphasize this moral duality as a guiding principle. Within that framework, Julian is the only character who, in the present of the narration, roams both worlds and passes from violence loosely coupled with religion to a violence in the service of religion. Julian first kills in a church and then kills a pigeon—the realistic equivalent of the symbolic burning dove he had above his bed. Julian then kills pagans: he saves his Christian father-in-law by killing the Moslem and treacherous grandfather-in-law. Murder is still a family affair. The caliph's pretended *conversion* to Christianity is thus central to the plot and to Julian's being integrated as a mediator between the two worlds and his becoming part of the family of an emperor, as predicted. Violence, then, is a virtue: in effect, killing the pagan "king" *and* cutting his head off—a gratuitous deed (curiously reminiscent of the fall of the pigeon, also from ramparts)—is turned into a prerequisite to saving a father (the emperor) and being offered not riches or land but, at the end of the hyperbolic series of

21. The motif of money is one of the substructures of the text, which, like the many others (water, time, numbers, colors), characterizes it as rich and unique. It is in part because of the wealth of subcodes that the leading codes, by a kind of contamination through contiguity, take on their full range of affective and cognitive import.

offers, the emperor's own daughter. The apparent culmination of Julian's killing is marriage: *violence breeds love through religion*. One becomes interchangeable with the others. Yet that love seems only mildly erotic in the paragraph where Julian is shown to be in love at first sight (II, 13). The whole business is expedited in two paragraphs where the social aspects are stressed and the sexual ones mentioned in subordinate clauses (see pp. 265–266): "Julian was dazzled with love, all the more since he had till then led a very *chaste* life. *Thus*, the emperor's daughter was bestowed upon him, along with a castle she had inherited from her mother; and, when the wedding was over, leave was taken, after endless courtesies were exchanged" (II, 13–14). The narrator's brevity and *non sequiturs* are matched by Julian's previous lack of sensual freedom even with his mother: "Whenever his mother held him against her, he accepted her embrace coldly, as if dreaming of profound things" (I, 48). Julian's coldness seems linked to his obsession about killing animals, since this is mentioned in the following paragraph. But as the physicians say, it could well be "a desire for love"—in which case the contiguity of the two clauses in the sentence quoted would give the unconscious content of what is being warded off by aggression: love of the mother of too intense a nature to be coped with.

Sexuality is constantly denied: first between father and mother, then between mother and son, and finally between son and wife.[22] Julian's present situation is contrasted to his former one: *implicitly* with the description of the pagan castle ("in the Moorish style" II, 15) versus the earlier Christian one; *explicitly* in terms of war since Julian, now that he is in an Oriental setting, does not war anymore (II, 18; in clear opposition to expectations concerning the connotations of a pagan setting); *explicitly* in terms of hunting since he has ceased this activity too (II, 19). Julian's unnamed wife—her name is Basilissa in the legend—in this context plays the role of a consoling *motherly* figure rather than that of a wife. (Their marriage is, apparently, childless.) Finally, Julian is *still* very chaste:

---

22. As earlier, "sexuality" is not used here in the adultomorphic sense of genitality but in the broader psychoanalytic sense (see note 16).

She went out with him, in an open litter through the
countryside; at other times, . . . they watched the fish disport
themselves in the water, as clear as the sky. Often she tossed
flowers in his face . . . [and] inquired tremulously:—"What ails
you so, dear lord?"
He did not reply, or burst into tears. [II, 23–24]

When Julian finally tells his wife his horrible secret—thereby
breaking the wall of silence and noncommunication—she reasons *very convincingly* ("en raisonnant très bien," II, 25) that he
must be wrong. There is much obvious irony in this phrase, yet
its impact should not be reduced to dramatic irony. It functions
also as an explicit indicator of how not to read *Saint Julian:* If we
insist on reasoning and attributing chance events to chance
rather than to meaningful poetic "fate" (cf. the parricide), we are
missing the literary aspect of the narrative, its inclusion in a
world of meanings. It is only in exemplary works such as the
anonymous *Quête du Saint-Graal* (thirteenth century) that realistic adventures *can* be followed by their symbolic comment, as
Todorov notes: "This text contains, therefore, its own gloss.
Hardly has an adventure ended than its hero meets some hermit
who explains to him that what he has experienced is no simple
adventure but a sign of some other event."[23] The principle is
valid for all literary creations, but it is usually the task of reader
or critic to furnish the comment. Too rigorous reasoning, as in
the side-stepping of the wedding-scene material mentioned earlier, is at once a way to obfuscate meaning and, from a literary
standpoint, an almost blindingly obvious way to lead us to it, as
in the case of slips of the tongue: "In the case of the
psychopathology of everyday life . . . it is clear that every para-
praxis (slip) is a successful discourse—one might call it a nicely
turned 'phrase'—and that in the *lapsus* it is the muzzling effect
or gag which hinges on the Word and exactly from the right
angle for its word to be sufficient to the wise."[24]

23. Tzvetan Todorov, "La Quête du récit," in *Poétique de la prose* (Paris, 1972),
p. 131.
24. Jacques Lacan, "Fonction et champ de la parole et du language en
psychanalyse," in *Ecrits I* (Paris, 1971), p. 147. The translation is taken from
Anthony Wilden, *The Language of the Self* (1968; rpt. New York, 1975), pp. 31–32.
It is possible that literature can and should be analyzed in the way Freud does in
Jokes and Their Relation to the Unconscious (VIII) or *The Psychopathology of Everyday
Life* (VI).

Love and reference to women are patently absent from Julian's dreams: Adam is present but not Eve; the animals are by twos, but no mention of their being couples is to be found. Love of woman is not enough for Julian; his wife cannot satisfy him. Yet, she is described in a manner which provides a crucial link for the eye-and-light code of the tale.[25] Julian's first, symbolic, environment is the burning lamp in the shape of a dove. This is mentioned in the paragraph where the parents are said not to share each other's secrets (I, 21). The lamp reappears during Julian's illness, which follows the murder of the stag, doe, and fawn: "That night he could not sleep. By the flicker of the hanging lamp, he pictured again and again the great black stag" (I, 72). Whether the definite article indicates that the lamp is the same one or not, this is, in any case, the second mention of a lamp. Instead of its being accompanied by a reference to Jesus, we now meet with one to the Devil, and with Julian's obsession with the prediction: he wonders whether he does not in some way (unconsciously) want his parents' death. The following paragraph offers the incompatible suggestions of the physicians: "Julian's illness, they said, was due to some baleful wind, or to a desire for love" (I, 73). But, as logic was not to be trusted when Julian's wife spoke (II, 25), similarly here, the opposite seems relevant: chance and apparent incompatibilities might lead to a better understanding of Julian's predicament. Love and death will always be for him inextricably linked.

The third occurrence of the lamp is in a simile in the first sentence characterizing Julian's wife-to-be: "Her big black eyes shone like two very soft lamps" (II, 12). Such repetition is not haphazard: it appears at important points in the narrative in connection with love and death, and it will transform itself into the flickering (cf. I, 72) lantern present at the end—where it is freely interchangeable with the leper's *eyes* when *birds* hide it (III, 35; cf. burning dove, I, 21).

In short, love, religion, and aggression are associated not

25. The motif of looking is analyzed by Michael Issacharoff in " 'Trois contes' et le problème de la non-linéarité," *Littérature*, no. 15 (1974), pp. 27–40, and in Benjamin F. Bart's "Psyche into Myth: Humanity and Animality in Flaubert's *Saint-Julien*," *Kentucky Romance Quarterly*, 20 (1973), 321, as well as in the Introduction and Chapters 1 and 2 above.

only in the manifest plot but also on many different textual levels. Such thematic reinforcement is characteristic of the literary work.

Narration, Repetition, Rage

Julian's starting point is rage against a mouse whose innocent freedom enhances by contrast the endlessness of praying and of being motionless in church. Julian makes what might be termed an age-adequate response: not to get into a temper tantrum against his parents (a futile enterprise for a child) but to take revenge by displacement upon the mouse, who symbolizes all that Julian would wish to be but cannot be. Rage against the parents' strictness finds its natural outlet (see Tom Thumb!) in the cake-crumb trick. Once the outlet is discovered, more and more of Julian's pent-up feelings can be diverted through it. What is happening, however, is a kind of dissociation of sensibility: the very ease of using such an outlet turns it into a frightening projection of inner reality, one which in turn must be mastered. Julian kills, but his pleasure has become a compulsion which must be isolated:[26] "But Julian did not tire of killing ... and thought of nothing, remembered naught" (I, 56). Earlier, while being embraced by his mother he would seem to dream "of profound things" (I, 48). The following paragraph, by contiguity, links this with killing: "He stabbed bears to death, killed bulls with a hatchet, wild boars with a spear..." (I, 49).

How can the meaning of Julian's acts be understood? The narrative sequences, read paradigmatically, show them up as repetitive. The climactic embrace of the mother is followed by the killings. When Julian becomes an observer of a truly symbiotic and loving embrace of suckling fawn and mother at the end of the hunting "dream," the fawn is killed first, then the mother, whose voice is *human* (I, 65). This *exasperates* Julian,

26. See the definition of "isolation" in Ludwig Eidelberg's *Encyclopedia of Psychoanalysis* (New York, 1968): "Isolation involves a basic avoidance of contact, both libidinal and aggressive. It complies with the fundamental taboo of touching found in the obsessive compulsive; ultimately, the taboo against oedipal and preoedipal contact" (p. 207). See Anna Freud, *The Ego and the Mechanisms of Defense* (1936; rev. ed., New York, 1966).

possibly as a reminder of the original displacement of rage from mother and church onto mouse, and cannot be borne because it re-establishes the agony which killing animals had been supposed to alleviate. The prediction of the stag-father ("patriarch," I, 67) only formalizes this link, stressing its connection with the church through the tolling bell (to be repeated in the final death scene but not when the parricide is accomplished). Hunting was, at the time, linked to rage against the parents and possibly against the passive self (in the church scene). But the situation is still relatively unfocused: repetition involves the parents and the nursing situation—itself linked in *Saint Julian* to intake of food. The chance actions whereby Julian almost kills his father clarify the issue: use of weapons can only lead to murder since that is his secret desire ("supposing I wanted to?..." I, 72). Julian knows it, but cannot resist aiming at what he believes to be a stork. The fact that it is dusk and that Julian, though he cannot see distinctly "at the hour when haze lends an unclear cast to objects" (I, 81), has no "doubt" that it is a stork and not his mother's high headgear is a kind of double talk: although it unmistakably links desire for hunting to parricide from a magical point of view, textually the insistence on Julian's certainty that it is *not* his mother but a bird—who in folklore brings babies—emphasizes *a contrario* his obsession with the fact that it *might* be his mother and that he must make sure that it is not. Finally, birds are symbolically identified with the mother, a point which enables the reader to better appreciate the killing of the small birds and pigeon as thematic displacements.

After this accident, Julian flees the family castle but he still is obsessed with parricide: his constant fear is that he might kill his parents ("the aged," in II, 4). The important point here is that murder has become a quasi-automatic act for him: "Thanks to divine favor, he always escaped; for he protected the clergy, orphans, widows, and foremost the aged. Whenever he saw an aged person walking ahead of him, he would call out to know his face, as if he had feared to kill him by mistake" (II, 4). The contrast between the second and third sentences is astonishing: one does not kill all passers-by except one's parents—yet this is what Julian seems to do or want to do! Another interpretation of the sentence is that he at once wishes to kill his parents and not to kill them, and thus his calling out is an obsessive ritual destined to reassure himself.[27]

From a social point of view, however, the paradox is that Julian is now a *habitual murderer*, and that this has become a laudable occupation. Once more his rage has been turned to social use. Out-Heroding himself in the service of good is virtue indeed. Marriage intervenes. Julian's new virtue is of no use; constant brooding makes him return to an early situation in his life—hunting. Having given up killing humans, *he is obsessed with his earlier substitute gratification*. But "bad faith," rationalization, has interfered: he knows that symbolically (magically, psychologically), in his life, hunting and parricide are coupled. *He* believes in the stag's prediction. But his present thought is fuzzy despite the logical connective: "For he felt that murdering animals would determine the fate of his parents" (II, 21). It now merely *seems* to be the case. But a highly significant displacement has occurred which depicts Julian's state of mind (assuming the narrator is using free indirect speech to record Julian's thoughts): killing animals is no longer hunting, it is "meurtre," *murder*. Animals are human now.

The most ironic twist in the second hunting scene will be that the whole defensive structure, whereby *not* killing animals should prevent the death of the parents, crumbles and is reversed: *not* killing animals will result in parricide. The second hunting scene begins at night when Julian is kneeling down to *pray*—that is, in the same position as when the mouse came out of the hole in the church. The scene is marked by uncertainty: "he caught a glimpse in the dark of some animallike shadows" ("il entrevit dans l'ombre comme des apparences d'animaux," II, 27). The yelp of the fox defines the mood further since it refers us back to the mention of a fox as the first feature used to describe Julian's father (I, 9), who is always wrapped in fox skins. The return of Julian's parents coincides with the return of Julian's insurmountable temptation to hunt (II, 27). Since we had read, a few paragraphs before, that the two are linked (II, 21), it is poetic (esthetic, psychological) necessity and justice to

27. Both Moskos (Chapter 2, p. 98) and Sartre (Chapter 4, p. 182) insist on the importance of the mention of the aged in II, 4.

have the parents magically appear. Like the stone which happened to be next to Julian's hand when he wanted to kill the pigeon, and like Oedipus' chance killing of his father at a crossroads, chance here is the expression of a psychological wish omnipotently carried out in the world of literature. Chance, from such a standpoint, represents its disavowed opposite: it could be offered as a principle of literature that chance events mean events which are particularly wished for or feared and which chance magically presents to us as guiltlessly fulfilled in apparent independence from our secret but impossible dreams.

The arrival of Julian's parents is presented in the most naïve, traditional, and clichéd manner possible: this distancing may be interpreted as a sophisticated authorial defense against such an obvious contrivance. But, in context, it also shows us Julian's parents as completely dependent upon him, as cloyingly childish and admiring of their hero son whose *love* they seek. *It is the first and only time that a direct question concerning love is asked: its consequence is death* (II, 36). Like children, they are fed and put to bed, while small birds sing—ominously, if we remember the fate of the "little creatures" in Part I (I, 31).

Meanwhile, Julian finds himself paralyzed: "Then his soul collapsed with shame. Some higher power was destroying his strength; and, to find his way home, he went back into the forest" (II, 60). Temptation and defense against it are equalized—a fact which stands out because of the textual crux in II, 26 and 31, where it is unclear who, according to the narrator, is being irrational, Julian or his wife. First "Julian would listen and smile, but could not bring himself to yield to this [his and/or her] urge." Soon temptation prevails, however, and he decides to go hunting. He tries to reassure his worried wife, feeling "puzzled by this [his or her] change of mood." In both cases the masculine seems more probable, but both hypotheses ought to be kept in mind since there is no way to decide. For Julian's wife's surprise is, of course, perfectly normal from the point of view of common sense, and it serves to stress again the ominous import of Julian's quick decision and *new* lack of regard for his wife as compared with his behavior in the paragraphs immediately preceding (II, 23–26).

In the hunting scene the atmosphere is at once strongly

realistic in its detail, and allegorical. The whole episode gives an impression of *déjà vu*, although much of it had not previously occurred. The impression is due, at least in part, to the anxiety-dream structure (paralysis [II, 64], animal phobia) and to the attending concreteness of details linked with the hero's body. The forest is "a tangle of vines; and he was cutting them with his sword, when a weasel suddenly slid between his legs, a panther jumped over his shoulder, a snake wound up an ash" (II, 61).

A close study of this dreamlike scene (II, 59–67) would be required to prove in detail the link between rage, paralysis, and sexualization in passages such as this one.[28] Suffice it to say, in this context, that the mention of the snake provides a link to the story of Adam (II, 20) and to the final contact with the leper, which is the only other occasion when the word "snake" is used (III, 53). It should be noted that the other animals touch Julian while the snake encircles a tree, yet the effect of its climactic action is similar, and possibly reminiscent of the usual iconographic representations of the serpent in Genesis. The following paragraph confirms this feeling of paralysis through the typical anxiety-arousing staring of the "monstrous jackdaw"—the only other use of "monstrous" was in connection with the stag (I, 64)—so that Julian is transformed into a helpless being. That his impotence repeats that of the animals in Part I is made clear by the cluster of features mentioned in this context: eyes, looking, stars compared to rain (II, 62) remind us of the small birds raining down on Julian with unreal abundance (I, 31). For the first time the affects Julian had repressed are surfacing: "He cursed himself, longed to fight, howled imprecations, choked with rage" (II, 63). Julian had been cursed by the stag, now he curses himself; he had strangled a pigeon, now he himself is stifling and will later be choked by the animals breathing on him (II, 67). These reversals are accompanied by an awareness of his own

---

28. Benjamin F. Bart's "Psyche into Myth" contains an important analysis of a dream of Flaubert's, closely related to the second hunting scene, where the theme of sexuality is much more prominent. Kirsten Lund Hansen's "Saint Julien l'Hospitalier ou l'Oedipe de Flaubert, ou encore: Le bestiaire de 'Trois contes'" ([Pré]Publications [Aarhus], no. 1 [1973], pp. 7–18) is not psychoanalytic, as the use of the word "subconscient" and of the puzzling "phobie de la castration" amply shows.

body, whereas earlier when his mother embraced him he seemed to displace his attention to killing, and later attention to his own body will be transformed into attention to and acceptance of the repelling body of the leper. In short, understanding of Julian's rage would have to be undertaken through an analysis of what is absent in the first part of the narrative, rather than what is present. It is perhaps the highest paradox of a saint's life that his very lack of acknowledgment of his own physical being in the end permits him to accomplish what must be seen as an act of charity and self-abnegation. In a sense that seems compatible with Moskos's view of individuation in the conclusion of Chapter 2, *Julian's attitudes toward himself hardly change, but circumstances do.*

Strangely enough, at first sight, whereas Julian walks slowly so as not to "irritate" (II, 65) the animals, he suddenly becomes "exasperated" (II, 70) and wishes to kill human beings: "His thirst for carnage was taking over again; animals lacking, he longed to massacre men" (II, 70). Why did the unsuccessful attempt to catch the partridges cause this change of attitude? First, daybreak has canceled out much of the nightmarish quality of the scene (II, 68). The charm, as in folklore, seems partially lifted with the crow of the rooster. Moreover, Julian's attempt to net the red partridges with his coat is not a repetition of his earlier hunting; it reminds one of the socially regulated catching of the quails. The culmination of Julian's failure, then, is that he has come full circle: he cannot even succeed with the "convenient contrivances" which had prompted him to go "far from the crowd" (I, 44). All he has now is one long-rotten partridge. The catch is obviously symbolic and may point to the implicit author's (not the narrator's) ironic stance. Is Julian's soul not rotten too? One should also note, however, the linking of the central scene to the one previously mentioned and to the final encounter with the leper—living rotten flesh.

When Julian finally arrives inside the castle, he decides to "surprise" his wife (a parallel to her surprise as he left) by waking her suddenly. He makes suppositions about food (II, 73), reminding us that whenever someone reasons, he or she is wrong (cf. I, 81). He finally discovers a man in bed with "his" wife! The ambiguity of pronouns was already at issue in the episode that immediately precedes the hunting scene (and is therefore symmetrically placed). Now Julian makes a wrong assumption, and, forgetting that he has just murdered a partridge, forgetting that killing is fated to lead to parricide, he kills his "wife" and her "bearded lover." He then hears in their dying sounds the cries of the great black stag and hallucinates his wife standing in the doorway: but in this universe it is the hallucination which is real. As in earlier cases, Julian now understands his mistake but does not want to believe it (II, 79). May one conclude, then, that this parricide is the result of "pent-up rage" which has finally returned upon its original objects after a lengthy and circuitous route? This reading omits one chance detail: the motive for the murders. In everyday life, the mistake would have been meaningless bad luck—but, as frequently noted, literature, like religion, does not admit luck at the center of its plots. We must deal, consequently, with the outward meaning of the event: the murder of one's father and mother and its cause in the mother's unfaithfulness to her son with her husband. Clearly, whether we accept this as Julian's own motivation or not, its being carried out (even if desired) was due to chance. But Julian takes on the guilt since chance, to him too, is irrelevant: he *had* willed the act in his mind ("supposing I wanted to? . . ."). As in *Oedipus Rex*, the denial of the wish and its objective attribution to fate or chance make it easier to empathize with the hero's fate. In a sense, the reader has it both ways: the wished-for murder is accomplished; yet it is only a mistake; one is at once guilty and not guilty.

Parricide is the natural high point of a life of murder, but the way it is accomplished robs Julian of responsibility. Being robbed of it on the volitional level he can only—we can only—recover it on the symbolic or spiritual plane; we are encouraged to understand the act within a matrix of meanings rather than within a representational, mimetic context.

Let us now examine some of the details of the murder scene, trying to place them within the thematic codes of the story.[29] Julian's parents are in *bed* together, having committed "adul-

29. This method corresponds to what Freud recommended as a procedure in the analysis of dreams (*Interpretation of Dreams*, IV-V, 103–104) but also to Greimas's "isotopies" (*Sémantique structurale*). See my theoretical discussion of these problems in "La Rhétorique du rêve: Swann et la psychanalyse," *Poétique*, no. 33 (1978), pp. 90–106.

tery": this is what excites Julian's rage. The bed is first mentioned in connection with the hermit's prediction to Julian's mother immediately after she has given birth (I, 12–14). It occurs again as Julian's crib (I, 21) and does not reappear till he falls sick after the stag's prediction (I, 72–73). The next two occurrences involve, for the first time, the father and mother, who are in bed together (II, 51, 79). Each mention of the bed includes some religious object hanging over it: a martyr's bone and garnets, burning dove, and, in the crucial scene, an ivory crucifix bespattered with the parents' blood (II, 79). Metonymically, therefore, beds are linked to violence, to martyrdom, and more generally to suffering. If the story of *Saint Julian* ended here, one of the major themes linked to religion would not be adequately foregrounded, and the full significance of the parricide could not so readily be understood and correlated, for instance, to Julian's mother's immaculate conception. But once the end of the story is read, the central and final episodes can be seen as complementary reversals of each other with the missing theme of *love* taking precedence over death—through the recurrence of body contact and of death itself.

Love and sexuality, as indicated earlier, are replaced in Julian's miraculous birth by his mother's immaculate conception —the needs of the body being overabundantly catered to by displacement in the following paragraph on food and grotesque birth. (Note that this paragraph is surrounded by the only two mentions of pregnancy: end of I, 10, and beginning of I, 12.) Reread in the context of the murder scene, Julian's initial situation is therefore one where the father is absent. In the scene with the stag, it is the patriarchal, though impotent, father who is overwhelmingly present, leading to the slaughter of the whole family. The parricide is due to the father's enraging presence and his wished-for absence—while the final scene (preceded by an identification with the father in the fountain scene in III, 13) is a controlled coping with the image of the father/son, God/Jesus, leper/lover—*uniting all the features denied until then*.

The parricide is integrated into several of the thematic codes, but the meaning of the thematic patterns is unclear. Two types of psychoesthetic stances may be taken at this point:

(a) There is no deep intrinsic meaning to be pressed out of the plot: the horror of killing one's parents is interestingly linked to a story in the saint-sinner tradition of Saint Augustine with two hyperboles of violence at the center and end of the story. The final bed scene can be linked to the first one through the birth motif since Julian is symbolically said to be "naked as on the day he was born" (III, 53); violence here, at last, does mean rebirth in heaven. In this interpretation the horror of the leper's embrace and kiss is simply a reminder of and a contrast to Julian's early shunning of bodily contact or his enraged contact with the bodies of his parents. In short, the themes are closely linked by important characteristics, related to the senses and to the most basic facets of life: love, death, and bodily contact or horror of it. They are neatly reversed: Julian now approaches the leper; such a reversal of "natural" order can be felt as a sign of the *sacred*, as in the incest story of Lot's daughters or the prostitution of Tamar with her father-in-law in Genesis.

(b) The second psychoesthetic stance takes as its starting point the end of the preceding analysis. It posits that early experiences connected with the establishing of one's identity in terms of the outside world and the family constellation in particular—experiences which usually take their final shape during puberty—are what mold or structure our way of dealing with the world. The type of experience referred to is expressed in myths such as the Oedipus myths or in literature (*Oedipus Rex, Hamlet,* or *Saint Julian*), but it is transformed, retold in *adultomorphic* terms. Assuming, for instance, that a male child fantasizes that his mother belongs to him and not to that third party, the father—a natural feeling in view of the almost constant attention devoted to the child by the mother during early life—it will be easier to *represent* the child's feelings about his parents' being in bed together as adultery punishable by murder, than to attempt to cast a child as hero, if only because, as readers, we shall find it easier to understand what is closer to our present experience. But, as in *Saint Julian*, the link between the two will be stressed. In fact, the presence of the parents will be haunting to Julian and their death shining proof of the objective link between adultery and parenthood.

For the reader, another deep-seated fear is shown to be groundless. Fear of loss of parental love in this (gratifying) case, despite the child's hostile behavior, is proved to be pointless: the parents have followed their child to "the end of the world"—losing all their money in the process, as they themselves note in their usual money-conscious way (II, 45). But such extraordinary love is out of place: now the parents are like children to their own daughter-in-law. The reversal will be repeated with the fountain scene and solved through the mediation of the father-son-brother figure of the leper/Christ.

The present discussion rests on the assumption that a number of psychological concepts (Oedipus complex, primal scene, anxiety, fear of loss of love) adequately represent what is at work in our minds; and that when we read about parricide we connect it with our own feelings toward our parents: ambivalent love and hatred, jealousy, outdated knowledge and fantasies not quite relinquished despite our development, and so on. *If* this assumption is granted, the preceding discussion appears to hinge around the problem of the double interpretation of the parricide in terms of separation–individuation as well as of Oedipal jealousy and rage.[30] The remarkable characteristic of the literary rendering is that it deals with the whole situation on the level of lived thought, not action: both the adultery *and* the parricide are textually present; one need not, as in real life, choose between them or say that one is operant more than the other. It is all happening in our mental landscape, and we readers may alternately deal with each aspect, and need not feel that only one reading is permissible. Though one reading may be thought of as dominant, the basic trait of literature is to allow us nonetheless to tarry with the one that is not. It is of interest, however, that the final scene of *Saint Julian* might be read as relatively neutral sexually: though it concerns two males, it deals not only with a male's "negative Oedipal" conflicts but also with

---

30. Simon O. Lesser analyzes the "processes of response" in his *Fiction and the Unconscious* (Boston, 1957), where he develops the concept of "analogizing" (pp. 203 ff.). What is implied is that thinking, reading, memory are complex processes, only minute parts of which are ever conscious. Robert de Beaugrande, in his *Text, Discourse, and Process* (Norwood, N.J., 1980), provides a basic approach to some of the problems involved.

less sex-specific conflicts related to narcissism and separation-individuation (or the lack of separation-individuation).[31]

To sum up from our present vantage point: psychoanalysis posits the possibly traumatic effect of the child's observations or fantasies of parental intercourse, because they involve excitations which are overwhelming, especially when intercourse is interpreted by the child as a sadistic, destructive encounter—a view consonant with our summary of the underlying values in Julian's society. Under the impact of the Oedipal constellation, the repressed fantasies serve as organizing factors for previous fixations—especially deficits concerning the narcissistic organization of the self and separation-individuation.[32] In *Saint Julian* the original absence of intercourse in favor of a miraculous conception (I, 10) is striking: it corresponds to denial or to the common childhood fantasies on the topic, or to both. Such absence adds to the shock value of dealing for the first time in the manifest text with a man and woman together in bed. Assuming, then, the repression of sexuality (bodily contact) to be a motive force in the richly determined episode of parental embrace and "adultery," Julian's feeling of "separation" and consequent rage and murder are an apposite climax. Ironically, the scene which

31. The term "separation-individuation" refers to an early developmental stage of the child. The following passage from a *Festschrift* for Margaret S. Mahler edited by John B. McDevitt and Calvin F. Settlage will give an *aperçu* of its implications: "The infant's beginning capacity to perceive, at least fleetingly, a small part of external reality marks the transition, during the second month of life, from the normal autistic to the normal symbiotic phase. During the subsequent separation-individuation phase, which begins at the peak of the symbiotic phase, in the third quarter of the first year, the child slowly becomes able to separate out and to differentiate intrapsychically his primitive self and object representations from the hitherto fused symbiotic self-plus-object representation.... Intrapsychic separation consists of the child's emergence ('hatching') from the symbiotic fusion with the mother and centers primarily on the child's developing object representations. As for individuation, one consequence of the evolution and expansion of autonomous ego functions is that the actual self is differentiated from the object and comes to be represented internally as the self representation," (*Separation-Individuation* [New York, 1971], p. 4). See also Bowlby, *Attachment and Loss*. Further comments will be found in the Conclusion below.

32. The fantasies alluded to in the text concern the so-called primal scene in which the child fantasizes about what his parents do together at night. See Aaron H. Esman's survey of the concept in "The Primal Scene: A Review and Reconsideration," *Psychoanalytic Study of the Child*, 28 (1973), 49–81.

Julian thus interprets as proving his continued and final estrangement (after the frustrating hunt) and impotence is in fact the one where his symbiotic tie to his parents is shown to be strongest.

But the tangled web of fantasy and reality, assumptions about Julian's objective and subjective situation, the narrator's role, the reader's identification with Julian, and the sets of thematic systems as a whole make it difficult to write clearly about any one level without seeming to oversimplify the text. Such a problem is perhaps what makes *Saint Julian* a literary masterpiece, since it puts the reader-critic in a position where she or he must "work through"[33] the text, go back to all its details rather than be content with a superficial assessment. However, as far as our limited discussion is concerned, Julian's murder of his parents corresponds to a paradoxical denial of the parents' sexuality, a final refusal expressing his repressed rage against them. That an overstrong love (of the mother) should result in death (murder of both parents) not only is a commonplace in myth, literature, and fantasy life but is the very basis of the *Saint Julian* plot as actualized in the final scene.

The Leper/Christ in the Final Scene

The final scene naturally unites many thematic strands left loose in earlier sections or which can retrospectively be seen as preparing the last scene. It would be tedious to go over the third part in order to point out the way most of its notations are related to the first two; but though tedious, it is the relevance of this type of minute decoding which makes reading literature differ from reading the newspaper. Let us therefore mention without detailed discussion some of the textual couplings.

33. "Working-through" is perhaps the most fundamental concept in the theory of the psychoanalytic process; it is a kind of restructuring and reprogramming at all "levels" of the mind. We assume here that a homologous kind of learning is at work in the reading process in literature (whose modalities remain to be specified). See Ralph Greenson, *The Technique and Practice of Psychoanalysis* (New York, 1967), and Emanuel Peterfreund, *Information, Systems, and Psychoanalysis* (*Psychological Issues*, monograph 25/26, 1971), chapter 22.

FIRST TWO PARTS	LAST PART
Rotting partridge (II, 69); "worm-eaten crosses" (II, 58)	Putrid odor (III, 19) and leper's fetid breath (III, 37)
Coarse garments ("toile") of both parents (II, 33)	Leper's torn piece of linen ("toile," III, 31), to which Julian adds the sail made out of "toile" from his boat (III, 46); bed linen (III, 50)
Presence of leaves ("feuillage") at Julian's birth (I, 11); the doe is blond like "dead leaves" (I, 64); Julian is caught up in heaps of dead leaves (II, 54); his once deadly arrows alight on leaves like white butterflies (II, 63)	Julian's bed of dead leaves (III, 19); "And Julian, pulling the *cloth* up, lay down on the *dead leaves* (III, 50)
Julian is a "little Jesus" (I, 21);	The Leper-Christ (III, 35–57);
Julian falls over the he-goat, both arms spread out (I, 53);	Julian sprawled on the bed, flat on his belly (III, 20);
Julian's parricide is observed by Christ (the crucifix; II, 79);	Julian stretches himself out upon the leper (III, 56), who then becomes our Lord Jesus Christ.
Julian lies on his belly with arms "in the shape of a cross" ("en croix" [II, 84] is the phrase for "spread out" in French).	

Much of this and other incidental repetition strengthens our experience of the work as a unified, meaningful structure: there is no narrative link between the items, only the fact of a closely-knit world of meanings present in spite of the variations in situations. This may create for the reader a feeling of omnipotent control whereby a whole universe of experience (love, religion, parricide) is captured in a drastically reduced universe of discourse. Once this mode of reading is adopted, some of the apparently haphazard patterning can be seen to present significant ordering. The rotting partridge and the smell of rotting are hyperbolically metamorphosed into a rotting human being, the leper. The cloth imagery unites the parents, links them to the leper, and the latter to Julian himself, who disrobes to protect him. The leaves, a mere passing notation in the central paragraph concerning Julian's birth, become *dead* leaves in the striking simile used of the doe: "The doe, blond like dead leaves, browsed upon the grass" (I, 64). Leaves are henceforth always linked to death or associated with cloth and bedding. The references to Jesus, begun as a mere simile, are followed with crucifixion scenes associated with animals (in particular the traditionally lecherous he-goat) and with the parricide. The details vary but the common ground between all the occurrences is Julian's lying on his belly, with the opening simile with Jesus (I, 21) being replaced, in a perfect closural effect, by Jesus himself (III, 56).

The exhilarating effect of the ending is obviously connected to the number of thematic linkages and to the quite concrete uplift depicted in the last paragraphs. The ending reverses most of the expectations encoded in the earlier parts of the text:

FIRST TWO PARTS	LAST PART
Julian's lack of restraint	Julian's progressively greater, even hyperbolic, self-control
Julian's violence against others	Julian's lack of violence eventually turning against his self [34]
Julian's running away from his own violence	Julian's not running away from the progressively greater violence done to him by others
Julian's avoidance of bodily contact except when accompanied by rage and death (even with his wife)	Julian's acceptance of bodily contact leading to his (own death and) bliss
Julian's failures in his relationships with society, father, mother, wife (he has no children)	Paradoxical success of Julian's relationship with the leper-Christ.

There are many other oppositions: Julian finally allows someone to enter into his home ("hut") and share the basic human needs with him; the leper is at once the lowest point in society's opprobrious treatment of Julian and the beginning of the ascent of his fortune. Rejection by society and nature (cf. III, 1–7), failure in relationship with parents and wife are finally reversed. Na-

---

34. This is implied as early as II, 63, by the reflexives "*se* maudit" and "*se* battre." If one assumes an overly strong identification with the parents (lack of separation-individuation) the parricide already illustrates this self-destructive trend (see, however, Julian's non-suicide in III, 13). A classic instance of aggression turning against the self is described by Anna Freud in *The Ego and the Mechanisms of Defense.*

ture, which at first had been passive in accepting mass murder (first hunt) and then ironic (second hunt, II, 67) and unreachable, now is a "raging storm" (III, 29)—it is raging, while Julian is not; but he overcomes the storm. Julian, too, is changing, aging: seeing in himself the father he had once murdered, he does not commit suicide (III, 13). He has become a composite figure, a suffering son-father. He is, of course, killed by another son-father figure, Jesus, who has been allowed to die by the Father—thus reversing the process whereby Julian had killed his father. (The main features of the father identification of the leper have been dealt with in the Introduction and Chapter 1.) The leper's constant giving of orders, moreover, also puts him in this fatherlike position reminiscent of the initial rule-ridden state of Part I and in strong contrast with the childlike or subservient behavior of the helpless parents in Part II. Yet the contrast also enhances the profound similarity in their positions: the repetition of the situation of helplessness in the third part is a kind of undoing of the failure of the second. The undoing is concerned with saving a repulsive man's life as opposed to the killing of one. In both cases food and bed are provided, but in the latter case, Julian takes the place of the women, is both wife and mother. Julian, who has been chaste, even with his wife (within the framework of the story there is no allusion to eroticism, only to tenderness, if not solely motherliness, II, 23–25), and who was remote from his mother's love, finally reverses this trend in the revolting embrace with the leper. Sensual contact, till then foreborne or punished with death when viewed (witness especially the deer family and the parricide) appears at the end as the missing experience, the be-all and end-all which could not be assimilated into the story, yet one which retroactively was the sought after *primum mobile* constantly replaced by its opposite, murder. Its assimilation at the end re-establishes the equilibrium lost through the immaculate conception by erecting a new birth, as Moskos points out at the end of Chapter 2 (see also III, 53)—a birth where the "maculate" conception, with the originally absent father, replaces the mother's. Such a simple switching of roles is not sufficient. The lowliest on earth also becomes the spiritually highest: the leper is Jesus, the hut is greater than the castles. The assimilation of sensual contact is, in a sense, the height of its rejection. It is at once satisfied and denied by being carried over to the spiritual plane and accompanied by the swooning ecstasy of death (III, 57). This last trait clarifies God's role, making it cohere from the miraculous birth through the parricide (overseen by a crucifix) to the actual intervention of Christ at the close of the narrative.

If a religious story has power over readers, many of whom are not believers, it is because the plot combines basic elements of psychological import. The psychological and social need for separation from parents in the course of individuation runs full circle in the story: the price of individuation is heavy both for the parents and for the child. If one were to interpret Julian's relationship with his wife and parents as a fantasy, then his acts would reveal, on the mind's stage, an incapacity to deal with a spouse except in terms of earlier reactions with one's parents.[35] Julian's failure with his wife requires his trying again to reach individuation. Part II, appositely, ends with Julian's leaving his castle completely naked, ready for a new beginning (II, 81). Whether this nudity is "nuditas virtualis" or "nuditas criminalis" is not at issue—both being, in a sense, predicated by the duality of the sinner-saint. Though Julian is destitute, he is not yet symbolically reborn: nakedness does not yet imply symbolic rebirth, as it will at the end through the use of a simile (III, 53).

Is individuation attained at the end? The kind of individuation Julian achieves is in fact the opposite of separation from early ties: it is a relationship with a parental figure but this figure is difficult to distinguish from Julian's self. In short, the final word is a return to a symbiotic relationship similar to the child's earliest experience. If it were in the service of some kind of social, religious, or human activity, this symbiotic relationship could be called normal individuation. But, here, it is hardly a starting point; it is rather a grand finale.[36] The character's indi-

35. If the story is read as a fantasy one must establish in whose mind, from whose point of view, the fantasy is recounted.

36. In the opening pages of Chapter 1, Berg discusses the status of the literary character. In both Moskos's and the present chapter, it is assumed that readers are psychologically likely to think of Julian in the same way as they would of someone whose story they read in a newspaper. Such psychologizing would not

viduation, however, is less at issue than the whole situation surrounding it: we should deal above all with *The Legend of Saint Julian*, not Julian, with *Hamlet*, not Hamlet. Interpreted in this light the ending introduces new elements independently of any psychological interpretation of Julian: *he* is not responsible for the arrival of the leper except if we choose (a possible interpretation) to interpret the whole narrative as a fantasy of his; the narrative introduction of the leper and his outrageous demands bring into the text the hyperbolic horror of bodily contact: sensuality could not be more thoroughly disavowed. Yet its disavowal is immediately accompanied by its opposite, hyperbolic erethismic imagery displaced—as has been the case from the very beginning with the immaculate conception—from the sexual sphere to that of religion. The insistence on the repulsiveness of sexuality does not annul it but emphasizes it: the taboo quality of the leper's body is matched by its fascination and by Julian's acceptance of it. The power of the affect is not changed but its content is, in accordance with the dominant negative mode of the narrative. One might view repulsion not simply as a reversal but also as an expression of the ambivalence which the figure of the son-father leper can evoke, an ambivalence of feeling which now results not in Julian murdering but in his actively mothering. For, in that sense, Julian's becoming a saint implies his playing his mother's role to satisfy the prediction made to *her*—just as, in the central parts of the story, he played out the role assigned to him by the prediction made to the father. The predictions are accomplished in reverse order and not in the terms expected by either parent: the father saw his son as a "conqueror" (but what he conquers is his own aggressiveness), and the mother saw him as a worldly success, an archbishop (I, 26). Julian's refusal of a universe of archbishops, of rare expensive hounds, of condescending charity, is perhaps, after all, a genuine sign of progress if one looks back on the narrative from a critical viewpoint: the unrestrained, gratuitous pouncing on

---

preclude other readings, as Berg also points out (and see note 35). Despite Moskos's defense, individuation through purulence seems to us to be closer to the abnegation of a saint than to any mimetically appropriate individuation.

the quail (I, 42) is to be contrasted with the act of control that precedes Julian's double metamorphosis and ecstasy: his willingness to stretch himself out upon the purulent leper, "mouth against mouth, chest upon chest" (III, 56).

The Narrative Voice and Psychocriticism

The purpose of this chapter has been to present an intermediate level of psychoanalytic description. Such an undertaking seemed worthwhile inasmuch as psychoanalytic literary criticism, instead of progressing from surface analysis to deep analysis, often moves directly to the more abstract concepts. If our emphasis had been on the possible etiology of Julian's conflicts, reference would perhaps have been made to his narcissistic rage, to transformation of love into aggression because of defenses against incestuous strivings of an infantile oral and sadistic nature, as well as to his adolescentlike conceptions of sexuality. Evidence for the organizing impact of narcissistic rage on the story could then be found in passages such as the following:

> Before self-cohesion, aggression can be thought of as a pattern of diffuse discharge. With self-cohesion, aggression acquires the characteristic noted in narcissistic rage. It acquires its driving properties from the importance of self-cohesion. Restriction of narcissistic aims to *phallic- and gender-related* expansion restricts acute narcissistic vulnerability to those aims and conflicts, but also helps to give the characteristic coloring to infantile oedipal aggression.[37]

The italicized phrase would have to be related to a theoretical discussion of *Saint Julian* which would take us away from the more psycho*critical* aspects of our work. Further evidence in favor of the hypothesis of narcissistic rage could also be found in the focus on food, nursing, the mouth, and the purulent leper. The latter's very presence at the end is a witness to the hardly uncommon rejection of sexuality as initially repulsive, a reaction

---

37. David M. Terman, "Aggression and Narcissistic Rage: A Clinical Elaboration," *Annual of Psychoanalysis*, 3 (1975), 354. Ironically, one of Terman's patients tells him the story of Saint Julian—but neither one recognizes it as such (p. 243)! Further comments on narcissistic rage will be found in the Conclusion, below.

ultimately replaced by a realization of its attractiveness, as in the stories of Beauty and the Beast or the Frog King.[38] But though we assume such a framework and certain universal *modes* of elaboration, it is only the unique, minute aspects of the phenomena which will enable us to re-experience them within our selves and recreate what is only a universal *potential*.

This can be illustrated by a central passage toward the end of *Saint Julian* (III, 53–57) and by the use of direct speech throughout the story. Though obviously psychological, the problems involved will be seen to fuse with what is traditionally considered simply textual or literary. Indeed, on this level, it becomes clear that "stylistic" remarks are always dependent on psychological presuppositions and that networks of meanings are inseparably psycho/critical.

The sexual connotations of Julian's lying on top of the leper are emphasized by the choice of details: Julien is naked; his lips meet those of the leper; his thighs meet the latter's. There would be no compelling need to focus on the thigh here except if the notation is aimed at evoking an erotic situation. But, simultaneously, this meaning is disavowed: the narrator says: "il sent*ait*," where the imperfect defines the action as a continuous feeling and not as the sudden one which the logic of the paragraph would lead one to expect (III, 53).[39] This muted response is further accentuated by the displacement of attention from Julian's thigh to the skin of the leper: "Julian took off his clothes; then, naked as on the day he was born, again took his place in the bed; and he could feel against his thigh the leper's skin, colder than a snake and rough as a file" (III, 53). The matter-of-factness, the very length of the final clause, its cliché quality (snake and file are even associated in the title of a fable by La Fontaine), jar with any emotional involvement in the passage. Their presence five lines before the miraculous transformation and the explicit intrusion of the narrator in the last paragraph make the ending's physical elements less powerful than they

---

38. See studies of these fairy tales in Bruno Bettelheim, *The Uses of Enchantment* (New York, 1976), and in Morton Kaplan and Robert Kloss, *The Unconscious Motive* (New York, 1973), pp. 90 ff.

39. See also the imperfect of "le firmament se déploy*ait*" (III, 57).

might otherwise have been.[40] A small detail such as the *placing* of the reference to the mouth-to-mouth contact diminishes its impact: "Julian stretched himself out on top, mouth against mouth, chest upon chest" (III, 56). Had the notation ended the sentence and the paragraph, it would have taken on much more sensual significance. But the "mouth against mouth" would then have seemed to have an overly obvious triggering effect, since the very next paragraph describes the miraculous erethism and death of Julian. The effect is more subtle here: the anomalous placing of the phrase seems to imply a logic in the ordering of the two items other than a simple inversion. It is in fact possible to think of the description as a normal progression from head down. But the description stops with the top part of the body, though the lower part can be re-established by remembering the reference to the thigh four lines previously. Of the three possible placings of these concrete details, only the one actually used in the text downplays the sexual while at the same time acknowledging it. Because of this ambiguity, the collocation of the erotic notations (tempered, to be sure, by the age and health of the persons involved) with the religious ecstasy is not striking. Despite the similarity between sexual arousal and religious ecstasy as described here and by most saints, the narrator does not reveal his secret: affect and meaning are still isolated from each other. There has been a merging of two themes, the reli-

40. The narrator's use of periphrasis is reminiscent of Bossuet. "Celui dont les bras le serraient toujours" (III, 57) refers to Jesus. The periphrasis serves as an added clue to this new status of the Leper since the Bossuet phrase refers to God. There are remarkably few such direct (or indirect) references to belief, to the person of God, or to Heaven in *Saint Julian*. The use of "firmament," the abundance of stars and light in the penultimate paragraph, create a link with the only other use of "firmament" (in II, 62), which is also accompanied by references to abundant stars and light (and is in turn connected with the "shower" of small birds in I, 31). Finally, the mention of a "higher power" (II, 60) just before this use of "firmament" emphasizes for the first time since the conception of Julian and the two predictions—and for the first time *directly*, as far as Julian himself is concerned—the *active* involvement of God. After his possible involvement in the miraculously easy murders of the first hunt, his protection of Julian (II, 4), and his allowing the parricide (see Julian's comment in II, 82), there is at last a direct allusion to his role: "Some higher power [is] destroying [Julian's] strength" (II, 60). The fact that Julian manages to overcome his paralysis in II, 64, reinforces the parallel with the crucial efforts in III, 34, where Julian's powerlessness is overcome *consciously* because he knows that he is acting in the service of *Good* or *God*. This is the only case where such an insight is mentioned.

gious and the sexual, in terms of a third, the aggressive: leper and horror and sensuality do bring about erethism ("growing," III, 57), but Julian's "swooning" is religious. The final flood of emotion appositely expresses the utter confusion of concrete and figurative language: "a superhuman joy flooded down into the soul of the swooning Julian" (III, 57). As Sartre points out, flood waters are usually thought of as rising rather than descending.[41] Though the point is realistically arguable, dependent as it is on the physical location of a lake or river, the fact is that Julian, though on top of the leper, is touched by grace from above: the spiritual origin of the leper becomes more important than his physical position, while the interaction of the two creates a successful closural effect.

The absent element of sexuality in Julian's life has finally emerged—immediately to be taken over by a higher spiritual order: in the *Three Tales* physical love as such is doomed.

In view of the importance of secrecy, words, and communication in *Saint Julian*, an analysis of the rare instances of direct speech is also pertinent from a psychocritical standpoint. Not unexpectedly, the first use of it in the text confirms the title: "— Rejoice, O mother! Thy son shall be a saint!" (I, 13). But even such direct speech does not establish communication, since the hermit disappears. Curiously, Julian's mother's response is an unuttered cry, doubly establishing the pattern of nonspeech by a resort to wordless sounds, and by a refusal to utter even them. Julian's first use of language to communicate is through screams (I, 24). Indeed, Julian does not ask for religious salvation— although, paradoxically, the word "grâce" ("grace" or "mercy," II, 67) is in quotes but unuttered—a fact which finally closes the circle of noncommunication and makes the parricide inevitable. As the following list indicates, direct speech in *Saint Julian* appears at essential points in the narrative where it is a mark both of basic needs and motifs and of extraordinary personal relationships and ambiguity. This is vividly confirmed by the abundant typographical indicators of emotion. There are only two ques-

---

41. See Chapter 4, p. 189. For a discussion of some psychological aspects of Julian's experience, see Marian Tolpin's "The Daedalus Experience," *Annual of Psychoanalysis*, 2 (1974), 213–228, and the references in the Conclusion, below (e.g., note 32).

tion marks, which appear in successive and crucial quotations (I, 72, and II, 23); but, for an approximate total of twelve lines of text, one can count forty-one exclamation points. In addition, in the few other cases where question marks (II, 45) and exclamation points (II, 74; III, 36 and 42) are used, they stand out as instances of highly charged free indirect speech.

Each character's share of direct speech is also significant. Of the twenty-two direct quotations, the father utters only one (to himself) and shares one with his otherwise silent wife—the one which, being their triumphant avowal of parenthood, will be punished with death: "—'Well! here we are!'" (II, 39). Julian's wife, finally, is granted three direct utterances, including the first of Part II, the one which will paradoxically bring about an unhappy result through the *sharing* of a secret—the only occasion in the story in which such sharing occurs.

OCCURRENCES OF DIRECT SPEECH

I, 13	Rejoice, O mother! thy son shall be a saint! (The hermit to Julian's mother)
I, 17	Ah! Ah! thy son! much blood!... much glory!... ever fortunate! an emperor's family. (The Gypsy to Julian's father)
I, 20	If I mention this, people will laugh at me. (Julian's father to himself)
I, 68	Accursed! accursed! accursed! One day, ferocious heart, thou shalt murder thy father and thy mother! (The stag to Julian)
I, 72	No! no! no! I cannot murder them!... Still, supposing I wanted to?... (Julian to himself; ellipses points here and in II, 29, indicate the narrator's voice)
II, 23	What ails you so, dear lord? (Julian's wife to Julian)
II, 29	I am only obeying thee!... by sunrise, I shall be back. (Julian to his wife)
II, 37	Oh! yes! (Julian's wife to his parents)
II, 39	Well! here we are! (Julian's parents to his wife)
II, 48	He is my father! (Julian's wife to his parents, about the emperor of Occitania)
II, 67	(Julian does not even have the strength to cry out) mercy!
II, 73	Doubtless, she must have eaten... (Julian about his wife)
III, 21	Ah! poor father! poor mother! poor mother! (Julian about his parents)
III, 24	Julian! (the leper's voice to Julian)
III, 27	Julian! (the leper's voice to Julian)
III, 38	I am hungry! (the leper to Julian)

III, 41   I am thirsty! (the leper to Julian)
III, 43   I am cold! (the leper to Julian)
III, 45   Thy bed! (the leper to Julian)
III, 49   My bones feel like ice! Come near me! (the leper to Julian)
III, 52   Undress, I need the warmth of thy body! (the leper to Julian)
III, 55   Ah! I am about to die!... Come closer, warm me up! Not with the
           hands! no! thy whole person. (the leper to Julian)

The narrator seems to say that the stag's prediction is repeated three times (in which case "accursed" is said nine times).
Julian is quoted directly only four times if we exclude the unuttered "mercy!" II, 67). First, he refuses, then grudgingly acknowledges his murderous impulse: " 'No! no! no! I cannot
murder them!' next, he would reflect: 'Still, supposing I wanted
to?...' " (I, 72). His only words addressed to someone else are
hypocritical: "I am only obeying thee!"—as if he were going out
hunting to obey his wife. Just before the murder (II, 73), the appearance in Julian's quoted thoughts of the adverb "doubtless" is
notable since it had been mentioned only a few lines before
("Doubtless, she was asleep and he would surprise her," II, 71),
and it repeats the erroneous perceptions of the two almost fatal
accidents at the end of Part I (I, 77, 81). In this universe, reality
may need to be taken as hallucination (II, 76), and appearance
ought not to be trusted—as Julian seems to know from the way
he acts toward old people in II, 4. His last quoted words are the
only words of regret he ever pronounces in the story: "Ah! poor
father! poor mother! poor mother!" (III, 21).[42]
    The use of language must be considered important within
the explicit economy of the narrative, since Julian himself uses a
"different" voice to talk to his wife after the parricide (II, 80–82)
and since it is at that point that the narrator chooses to use what
is possibly the most effective "free indirect speech" in the whole
of the Three Tales.
    There are almost as many direct quotations in the last part of
the tale (ten) as in the first two combined (twelve), and nine of

42. The repetition of "poor mother!" is perhaps the only hint in the story of
Julian's love for her! For further details see Marc Bertrand's article "Parole et
silence dans les 'Trois contes' de Flaubert," Stanford French Review, 1, no. 2
(1977), 191–204.

them belong to the leper, whose direct speech dominates the last two pages. Julian himself is silent; the narrator merely says: "He tried to hearten [the leper]" (III, 54), leaving us with no further knowledge of Julian's inner reactions. Once more, therefore, the process of communication is one-sided. As in the case of the murdered beasts, the narrator does not insist upon the feelings of the passive actor. The only timid dialog to be found in the whole text is at once naïve in its content and lethal in what it leaves unsaid as well as in its consequences: Julian's secret, the parents' secrets, are not mentioned in the short conversation between Julian's wife and his parents. The narrator stresses the point twice in connection with all three characters: "She answered [their questions], but was careful not to refer to the ghastly idea that concerned them" (II, 44). And, a dozen lines later: "At that [the father] started, recalling the prediction of the Gypsy; and the old woman pondered upon the words of the Hermit. Doubtless her son's glory was but the dawn of eternal splendors" (II, 49). The last phrase highlights the commonplace quality of the parents' thoughts.

In the final episode of the story, direct speech seems to play an unusually significant role for Julian. There are only three occasions when Julian is addressed in direct speech. The first time is when the bells are tolling and the stag repeats his curse three times (I, 67–68). The second is a consequence of the first since, because of it, his wife repeatedly asks Julian, "What ails you so, dear lord?" (II, 23). Finally, the bells mentioned in connection with the stag's curse, although they toll no more, are present in the leper's voice, which is compared to a church bell. This is a significant progression: the realistic coupling is replaced by a fusion of the human and the spiritual worlds. Julian's name appears for the first and only times in direct speech: "Julian" is uttered three times by the leper, although, paradoxically, it is present only twice in the text (III, 22–27). In the same fashion, the stag's words appear only once, yet he seems to have said them three times. In a sense, then, Julian has at least reached psychotextual individuation. His name stands by itself: he is acknowledged by the leper-Christ—and the reader.

The task of combining discussions of what the psychoanalytic *experience* (not simply analytic concepts) implies with the careful literary analysis of texts is not easy. Just as analysts offer only vignettes of their infinitely lengthy clinical work,[43] so critics can at best offer sample studies of the wealth of thematic systems which make two plots on the same general theme ("the Oedipus complex") unique creations to which readers will respond in radically different ways. The ambitious attempts of Roland Barthes, Algirdas Julien Greimas, or Norman N. Holland, though they deal with relatively short texts, show to what extent this is the case.[44] But whereas a critic's practice is usually acceptable to literary scholars, the introduction of psychoanalytic concepts in a literary analysis seems alien, even though such concepts can be seen as clinical generalizations of the data of experience. Most psychoanalytic critics have attempted to alleviate this problem by quoting passages from Freud's unusually dense prose.[45] But this approach is not convincing because a whole theoretical framework is implicit but unavailable (our earlier reference to Terman's analysis of narcissistic rage would probably be a typical instance of this). What is perhaps needed is a kind of two-column text where clinical material would parallel extracts from the work under study. In the case of Julian's depersonalization and derealization, one might have quoted the following passage from Emanuel Peterfreund, where data homologous to those in *Saint Julian* appear in highly correlated fashion:

> Especially prominent is the absence of information processes corresponding to *touch* and *warmth*—modalities which are based on information from very *early infantile experiences*. In a typical case, seen not infrequently, the patient may be quite aware of the people in a room and of the general scene before his eyes; he can describe what he sees and even give a "high-level" cognitive report of the situation. . . . But the patient feels cold, *detached, out of contact* with himself and with others. He cannot seem to *touch* the world or get into the scene before him. He may feel dead

43. Two of the most complete case studies published to this day are the case of Carine in René Diatkine and Janine Simon's *La Psychanalyse précoce* (rev. ed., Paris, 1973) and Paul Dewald's *The Psychoanalytic Process* (New York, 1972). For further studies see the "Reader's Guide," section 5.

44. Roland Barthes, *S/Z* (Paris, 1970); A. J. Greimas, *Maupassant: La Sémiotique du texte* (Paris, 1976); N. N. Holland, *5 Readers Reading* (New Haven, 1975).

45. A felicitous example is G. D. Chaitin's *The Unhappy Few: The Psychological Novels of Stendhal* (Bloomington, Ind., 1972).

inside, only an *observer* both to the surrounding scene and *to himself*, and an *emotionless* observer who cannot genuinely participate. The full vividness and richness of experience are absent; *things seem unreal.* . . .

The programming that leads to depersonalization and derealization phenomena is unquestionably defensive. The deactivation of many affective systems, and the absence of certain touch and temperature modalities may be somewhat painful and distressing, but it protects the person from even greater pain and distress. When these patients attempt to "touch" the outer world, to make full emotional contact with *outer things* and with their *own bodies*, they may experience *violent rage*, confusion, pain, frightening *self-destructive* urges, and overwhelming anxiety, deprivation, and helplessness.[46]

The length of this passage shows that even cursory references to psychoanalysis may be unwieldy. Because of this we have attempted to follow the spirit of Charles Mauron's psychocriticism and have concentrated on explaining *Saint Julian* mostly in terms of the *Saint Julian* text.[47] The method implies de-emphasizing the theoretical background for much of what is being said; moreover, the method is not always possible, despite the common assumption that a literary text can furnish its own commentary: when what is *absent* is what is most significant, no amount of textual analysis can convincingly establish what is dependent on our knowledge of the world and our theories about it. In the case of *Saint Julian*, allusions such as the famous clue to Julian's unconscious wishes—" 'supposing I wanted to? . . .' " (I, 72)—are usually taken to furnish such a commentary. But its structural importance can only stand out if one assumes the existence of an unconscious Oedipal organization—that is, if one is already working within the psychoanalytic framework. Despite such a predicament, the following conclusion may, perhaps, be acceptable to psychoanalyst and literary critic alike.

Flaubert's *Legend of Saint Julian the Hospitaler* is a tale of violence where even love and redemption are acts of aggression.

46. Emanuel Peterfreund, *Information, Systems, and Psychoanalysis*, p. 176; italics added.

47. See, for instance, Charles Mauron, *Des Métaphores obsédantes au mythe personnel* (Paris, 1963) and the references in sections 11 and 12 of the "Reader's Guide."

Rage, displaced at first from the parents and their rule-ridden social and religious world onto animals and then onto evil, especially non-Christian, humans, returns to its familial origins with the act of parricide. When animals cannot be killed, one's creators must be. But this being accomplished, rage can only turn against the self—even if it is also, in part, in the service of others. Julian's "ferocious heart" eventually matches and is matched by society's own ferocity. But we are also faced with a ferocious God and a ferocious Flaubert. If love is always death in the religion of the *Three Tales*, was not Julian's parricide an adequate response to God's filicide?[48]

48. Further comments on psychocriticism and a psychological poetics will be found in my "Prosopopée de Sainte Sophie," *Poétique*, no. 43 (1980), pp. 372–392, and "Psychologie et littérature," chapter 12 of *Théorie de la littérature*, ed. Aron Kibédi Varga (Paris, 1981).

4

The Family Idiot:
Julian and Gustave

Jean-Paul Sartre

TRANSLATED BY WILLIAM J. BERG

Flaubert's Ailment as "Murder of the Father"[1]

... Of these three characteristic changes—declaring oneself cured, wanting to work, making love—only the first, the most important one in the evolution of Gustave's neurosis, will be considered here.[2] Indeed, as we noted earlier, the chief physi-

1. Sartre's *L'Idiot de la famille* [The Family Idiot] is a 2800-page psychobiography of Flaubert published by Gallimard in 1971–72. An English translation is currently being prepared by Carol Cosman for the University of Chicago Press. The two sections included here are from pp. 1897–1907 and 2106–2117 of the French edition, in volume 2. This English translation by William J. Berg is printed by permission of Editions Gallimard and the University of Chicago Press, and is © 1982 by The University of Chicago. All rights reserved. According to Sartre, the fact that Flaubert's father (Achille-Cléophas) and elder brother (Achille) were both medical doctors leaves Gustave without a destiny, a "family idiot." In particular, Sartre sees Flaubert's "ailment," originally diagnosed as apoplexy or cerebral congestion and later thought to be epilepsy, as a psychosomatic response to his family situation.——TRANS.

2. The second will be the subject of the next chapter. [Not included here.——TRANS.]

cian had scarcely been laid to rest, when Gustave took a deliberate stand on the side of recovery. This implies a complete reversal of his intentions. Certainly, for psychic facts as for social facts, the power of inertia is such that real deliverance can lag considerably behind the liberating event. The point is that Flaubert's condition improved notably. In the letter where he makes so lucid a confession, he partially explains his recovery by the whirlwind of activities in which his mourning had plunged him. He had to put everything back in order, worry about Caroline, who was ailing, and *especially* assure the passing of power from Achille-Cléophas to Achille. The latter's merits were being contested; a colleague was scheming; in short, his nomination to the post which his father had reserved for him was by no means secure, in spite of the last wishes of the chief surgeon. Fortunately, Gustave is there. He arranges everything, makes visits and takes measures. Thanks to him, Achille finds himself entrusted with the duties of his father—slightly diminished as a normal consequence of his youth. Let me repeat: Gustave *threw himself into action*; this sickly, sequestered quietist went of his own accord to see high administrators and learned physicians, and he knew how to talk to them—making use of the same practical parlance which ordinarily plunges him into stupor or appears like a foreign language to him. In short, Machiavellian and urbane, he had them eating out of his hand. All that to secure the usurped patrimony for the hated usurper. What can we make of this?

First, that the facts are probably accurate. Gustave did make visits. That goes without saying: who else could make them? Not Achille: that would have been offensive. Not Mme Flaubert, engulfed as she was in her grief. Not Hamard—who was unaware of the scheming. There remained only the younger son. This enterprise filled him with pride. He comes back to it later in his letters to Louise: it is to him, Gustave, that Achille owed his post. And this episode—practically unique in his life up to the period when he will take on the task of having the late Bouilhet's plays performed—permits him at times to present his passivity in the most flattering light. What he feels profoundly and what he admits willingly is that he is not made for action. What he repeats from time to time, when he recalls his role in the

"Flaubert succession," is that he is *above* petty human affairs: a quietist by excess not by default. But—a Flaubert adage—he who can do the most can do the least: if the circumstances require it, he rolls up his sleeves, routs the "men of action," carries off his coup in "record time," and returns to his hermitage with full military honors. Provided, he implies, that the enterprise is *gratuitous* and that he serves, by generosity, interests which remain alien to him. He is convinced, then, that he has placed his brother in the saddle. But what is the truth of the matter? He did make the visits, but is it he who won the day? Was there really resistance? Did he confront and conquer it? It is not possible to determine this, but, if we take into account the enormous prestige of Achille-Cléophas and the favor enjoyed by Achille, and if conversely we recall the awkwardness of the withdrawn younger son, more adept at sounding off with his friends than at maneuvering old administrators, it would seem more probable that the chips were already down. No doubt there were intrigues. But they *had to* fail; at the very most they worried the Flaubert family for a few days. In all probability, Gustave played the busybody. Not completely, however: etiquette required making certain contacts; he made them. If he didn't manage badly, it is because his action was merely a formality, hardly more than a role.

The fact remains that *he believes he is acting,* that he is serving to his own detriment the ends of a detested usurper. We should not be surprised by this. If he stood by passively at the transfer of power, he would feel disinherited. But if it is he who disdainfully leaves his monastic retreat to give his brother a secular power which was his own due, perhaps, but which he scorns today, the frustration disappears—along with the merits and rights of Achille. Two factors are involved—and only two: the glory of the dead father and the maneuvering skill of a younger son who remains submissive to him by a free allegiance. No more was required to win the day and change Achille—in Gustave's eyes—into an inert prebendary. A few whispered words, and here is water changing into wine and vice versa. Passivity acts, and the activism of Achille—an aping of the paternal *praxis*—reveals its true nature, the passive expectation of an undeserved gift. In any case, does the younger son not suffer by ratifying the unjust preference of the father? This question leads us to the essential point: no, Gustave does not suffer from it since, in this circumstance, he plays the role of head of the family and since, now at last, substituting himself for a father defaulted by death, he *is* the *pater familias* in flesh and blood. In his own eyes, naturally, and without anyone else noticing it: Achille does not seem to have been grateful to him for his interventions; he continued to take him for a *minus habens*, an "idiot" whom one does not invite to formal dinners; and Mme Flaubert noticed nothing. No matter: Gustave is free from the father only after replacing him for a few days. Is this a parricide? Yes, precisely. For the old warrior has bit the dust; he is—like his younger son in January '44[3]—no more than a corpse. The father's sadistic and savage wishes have no more importance than the whims of a newborn child: Gustave must *decide* to take responsibility for them and, in so doing, become his father's father. It depends on Gustave whether these "*last*" dying wishes are flouted or not. By replacing them with his own wishes, which are vital and effective, the young man carries them out, but degrades them in that his allegiance to the deceased, far from being submission, becomes an undeserved love, strongly resembling pity. And, when Gustave returns to his monastic life, the bypassed, surpassed *pater familias* will have life on earth only through Achille, his pitiful incarnation, the glaring and lasting punishment for his ill will, just as, according to Victor Hugo, "Little Napoleon" [Napoleon III] is the Great Napoleon's nemesis. Gustave, after his generous revenge, will turn away forever from the father and from the elder son.

Here he is—freed. If the objective reason for this deliverance resides in the abolition of a formidable, shrewd, and all-powerful Lord, he must also *live it out*, that is, interiorize it through subjective structures which, as such, will comprise liberating elements. Gustave could tear himself away from the hold of Achille-Cléophas, even dead, only by playing at dethroning and replacing him. In other words, this fundamental and long-awaited event had to be lived out by him as the ritual

3. It was in January 1844, at Pont-l'Evêque, that Flaubert suffered the attack which precipitated his ailment and which Sartre sees as a sort of nervous breakdown.——TRANS.

murder of the father. Like all the offspring of man, he had to kill his genitor and take his place for a moment in order to get rid of him. Stated simply, since the acts which he believed he accomplished were in fact only gestures, the sacred crime was no more than a criminal fantasy.[4]

It is for this reason, perhaps, that, from '45 on, parricidal intent is so self-conscious with Flaubert. Maxime [Du Camp] recounts in his *Souvenirs littéraires* that at that time he often came to keep his sick friend company. One day, the two young men went as far as Caudebec and entered the church; Flaubert, having noticed a stained-glass window tracing the life of Saint Julian the Hospitaler, "conceived the idea of his story."[5] After that, silence is absolute; until '56 there are no allusions to Julian in Flaubert's correspondence, not even to Maxime who nonetheless was aware of his project. This is somewhat puzzling, especially since he does not spare himself, at that time, from opening up to his friends about what he is writing, about what he counts on writing. However, the project is not abandoned; he must have mentioned it to Bouilhet, since he writes him, without other detail, *ten years later,* 1 June '56: ". . . I am preparing my *Legend* and correcting *Saint Anthony."*[6] He intended at that time to "return to Paris in the month of October with the *Saint Anthony* finished and *Saint Julian the Hospitaler* written." Why did he decide to take up this story again? In order to "furnish in '57 something modern, something medieval, and something from antiquity." This is not a superficial motivation: he always

---

4. I do not mean by this that others can *really* accomplish the murder of the father, with a gun or a knife. For practical agents what is *real* is the set of acts by which they dethrone their Moses and replace him . . . by founding their own family, by assuming his place as head of the business, or by rising higher than him in social status, etc. Thus homicidal intent is sustained by a symbolic yet true *praxis* which lends it solidity.

5. Maxime confuses everything, as is his wont. The stained-glass window was in Rouen, in the cathedral. At Caudebec there was only a statuette of Saint Julian. One can therefore venture the hypothesis that Gustave did not "conceive" his tale on that day—the statuette could hardly inspire him—but that, at Caudebec, he recounted the life of the Saint as it was on the Rouen window and confided to Maxime that he was thinking of making a short story out of it. The latter, as usual, overdramatized the episode.

6. *The Temptation of Saint Anthony:* Flaubert wrote several versions of this work in 1849, 1856, and 1874.——Trans.

dreamed of displaying simultaneously the three strings of his bow, and this same reason will lead him to write the three stories, between '75 and '77. The first one finished is in fact *Saint Julian*. However, in '56 it does not seem that he takes the *Legend* to heart; he especially sees it as a pretext for reading works on venery and for enchanting himself with archaic words. The proof is that he abandons everything outright and does not mention Saint Julian again before '75. One might say that he lacked some heartfelt reason for undertaking his tale. In fact, when he begins it for good, nearly twenty years later, the situation has changed: he is at Concarneau, alone with Pouchet; ruined, haggard, miserable, "the past devours" him; he stops thinking about "these cursed business affairs" only to "mull over his memories." It would seem that when he conceived *Saint Julian* and much later when he wrote it, he was a prey to misfortune, to anguish, and—we will return later to his frame of mind in '75—to his family. His *Legend* thrives on storms; he takes it profoundly to heart, since it reappears when this heart, a calm pond, stirs with the wind and when its "muck" surfaces; the rest of the time, it isn't even mentioned.

In any case, between '44 and '47, he is attracted by lyrical topics: he wants to see himself as a totality, sum up his life in one work, precisely what he had just done with the last pages of *L'Education sentimentale.*[7] What fascinates him in the story of Julian cannot be solely its medieval quaintness. The whole thing must have a *meaning* for him. Now, what does it tell of? Of a saint whose hard, daily penitence makes him the equal of Saint Anthony and who is bent on expiating the most unforgivable crime: in his youth he *killed his parents.* We have no idea of how Gustave would have presented the tale had he written it in '45: certainly the story would have differed profoundly from the '75 version.[8] What is certain is that the parricide-sainthood linking (long patience, anguish, exaltation) appeared to him on the spot in all its complexity. And, what is equally striking is that the

---

7. Sartre is referring here, as elsewhere, to the first version of *L'Education sentimentale,* written in 1845, rather than the later version, published in 1869.——TRANS.

8. I will take up this subject again in the following chapter. [Included here.——TRANS.]

murder of the mother—although Flaubert had often wished for the death of his own—appears to have secondary importance in the definitive text: she will die, like the genitor, so that a second murder will mask the ritual importance of the first one. Let us first look at the misunderstanding which explains the parricide: in Julian's absence his parents, from whom he had fled for so long, come to his castle and make themselves known to his wife; she honors them by giving them the nuptial bed, where they fall asleep; Julian returns late and half crazed from an infernal hunt, bends over in the shadows, and, believing he will meet his wife's lips, "felt... the touch of a beard" [II, 73]. Insane with rage, he seizes his dagger and strikes the two bodies with repeated blows. Thus the cause of the massacre is *adultery:* "a man lying with his wife!" [II, 74].[9] This adult cry is like the echo of a more distant fury, whose traces we found in many of Flaubert's early works, "a man lying in my mother's bed," a classical Oedipal configuration. It is the man in this case who is the criminal, it is the man who soiled the love relationship between Julian and his wife. It is he who must be slain; the mother is involved in turn, but as an afterthought. Or rather one might say that she expiates a real sin, initiated, however, by the man. Now, when Julian was fleeing the stag's curse—"'One day ... thou shalt murder thy father and thy mother!'" [I, 68]—and waging war throughout the world, half knight-errant, half mercenary, it was *his father* whom he feared wounding: "he protected... orphans, widows, and foremost the aged. Whenever he saw an aged person walking ahead of him, he would call out to know his face, as if he had feared to kill him by mistake" [II, 4].[10] Furthermore, when his heinous crime is accomplished and remorse pushes him toward suicide, it is the sudden appearance of his father's face which stops him: "while he was stooping over (the edge of a spring)... there appeared before him a very emaciated man, with a white beard and of such piteous aspect that he found it impossible to hold back his tears. The other also wept. Without recognizing his face, Julian

9. For further discussion of the motivation for this murder, see Chapter 1, p. 53.——Trans.

10. See the note on Poetics and Translation, p. 262; Chapter 2, p. 98; and Chapter 3, pp. 150–151, for additional discussion of this passage.——Trans.

had a blurred recollection of features resembling it. He cried out;
it was his father; and he gave up all thought of killing himself"
[III, 13]. In other words, Julian, aged by suffering and the hard
life he leads, bends over the water, sees his own image and
takes it for his father's. The genitor is dead, and here is Julian
resembling him; Gustave has transformed himself into
Achille-Cléophas by the very fact of having slain him. And, on
his own cheeks finally flow the very tears which he would have
so wanted to wrest from the chief physician—the very tears
which perhaps at least once during the terrible months of '44,
while pretending to sleep and stealthily observing Doctor
Flaubert, who was watching him, he saw spring from the terrifying "surgical" eyes. We should note that in '75 this remorse is
linked to the resurrection of his childhood. At the same time that
Gustave, who is at Concarneau, writes to all his correspondents
that memories are smothering him, that the "past is devouring
him," he writes in his *Legend*: "Months passed by when Julian
saw no one. He often closed his eyes, yearning, through memory, to come back to his youth;—and a castle courtyard would
appear, with . . . a blond youth between an old man wrapped in
furs and a lady with a high cap; suddenly, the two corpses were
there. Sprawled on the bed, flat on his belly, he would sob,
repeating:—'Ah! poor father! poor mother! poor mother!' And
would drop into a slumber while the ghastly visions continued"
[III, 20–21].[11]

It should be noted, incidentally, that this parricide is both a
crime and a punishment. If Julian's destiny is to kill his father
and expiate the deed—exactly like that of Oedipus—it is not
gratuitously, as in the Greek legend, but in order to punish his
pathological desire to massacre animals. If one recalls the numerous passages from his early works where Gustave speaks of

11. Madame Flaubert had died recently. Compare with the Concarneau letters
(*passim*): "I am having a great deal of trouble writing—physically—and my sob-
bing is smothering me. . . . The weakness of my nerves is astounding and
humiliating to me. . . . Many of the things which I see again here awaken
memories of my Britanny trip and are far from cheerful. I can only think about
bygone years and about people who are departed forever. I daydream, I feed on
my memories and sorrows, and the day whiles away. . . . Would you believe that
every night I dream about Croisset or one of my dead friends? Last night it was
Feydeau," etc., etc.

his *wickedness*, and if one also remembers the fascination which animals exert on Gustave, the respect which he has for "animality"—in himself as in so-called "wild" animals—and finally his love for dogs, one can see that this sanguinary taste for hunting represents the proud and spiteful hatred for men which he displayed in his twenties and the violent murderous impulses which he describes even up through *Novembre*. [12] Yes, a hundred times, a thousand times, Gustave, beside himself, at misery's and furor's end, wanted to kill. And it is precisely this criminal mood which made him desire the death of Achille-Cléophas. In a revealing passage from *Saint Julian*, a dying stag prophesies in a human voice: " 'thou shalt murder thy father and thy mother!' " [I, 68]. Julian returns home, and the following night he is haunted by this prediction: "By the flicker of the hanging lamp, he pictured again and again the great black stag. Its prediction haunted him; he struggled against it. 'No! no! no! I cannot murder them!' next, he would reflect: 'Still, supposing I wanted to?...' and he feared that the Devil might instill the urge in him" [I, 72]. These words elucidate the entire story: one might find it surprising that, after the catastrophe, Julian is bent on expiating a crime he did not even commit; it was after all only a regrettable misunderstanding. No doubt some will want to explain away his remorse by the objective magnitude of the event. A son has killed his father, which is impardonable, whatever might have been the murderer's intent. Thus Flaubert might have wanted to stress the pre-eminence of the actual deed for these primitive and absolute souls: self-examination would come later. Oedipus did not *want* to kill his father and fornicate with his mother. Should that keep him from gouging his eyes out for expiation? It might have been a question of showing the monumental quality of the ancient and medieval worlds, where everything is seen from the outside. But is this really the case? First, Gustave distinguishes perfectly between the Rome of the Caesars and the Middle Ages: "In the interval Christianity had prevailed." For him, that means a conscience, turning inward, self-examination. Indeed the modern Oedipus is not someone who becomes a parricide without knowing it, but someone who

12. *Novembre* is a short novel, written by Flaubert in 1842.——TRANS.

dreams of killing without going so far as the crime. Everything happens, in effect, as if, Freudian before the fact, Gustave understood the true sense of his hero's remorse. If he finds it perfectly intolerable to have killed his father accidentally, it is because he knows, deep down, that he is not innocent; yes, *this* crime has *all the appearances* of an accident; it is a case of mistaken identity. But had he not feared all his life that he might *want* to commit it? Had he not fled the paternal abode because he was not certain enough of conquering his evil thoughts? He chose to place himself in the physical impossibility of realizing the stag's prophecy because he did not have the love and the virtue necessary to create in himself the *moral impossibility* of accomplishing it. Of course, there are strokes of bad luck, which are multiplied by close contact: there is the sword which he takes down, which eludes him, and which nearly lops off the paternal head; there is the javelin which he throws at a bird and which spears the maternal bonnet. But who can affirm that these mishaps do not, quite simply, dissimulate ill will? The second incident is especially suspect: after the prophecy by the dying and furious stag, Julian "refused to hunt" [I, 75]; it's all for the best; it's a deal: I don't touch animals any more and my parents' lives are safe. But how then do we interpret the sudden resurrection of his murderous impulses: "One summer evening . . . he saw . . . two white wings fluttering about the espalier. He did not doubt but that it was a stork; and he threw his javelin. A rending scream rang out. It was his mother, whose cap and long streamers remained nailed to the wall" [I, 81–83]. Not for a moment did he doubt that it was a bird: we take his word for it. But since he now knows that parricide is indissolubly linked to his condemned hunter's instincts, isn't killing an animal, even once, accepting the murder of his parents? In effect, when he abandons the castle forever, it is himself whom he flees as much as his family—without getting away from himself, however. As the emperor's son-in-law he is steeped in melancholy; he refuses to hunt, "for he felt that murdering animals would determine the fate of his parents" [II, 21]. One day he confesses to his wife "his dreadful thought" [II, 24]. Things have become such that "his other urge" [II, 21], that of killing the beasts, becomes intolerable, but without causing his fear of parricide to diminish. Then one night, yielding once more to the desire to kill, he goes off, quite downhearted, feeling like a criminal already, yet incapable of resisting: it is upon his return from this hunt that his parents will be stabbed.

But Gustave goes even farther, since he attributes his breakdown in '44 to his sudden, terrified certainty of murdering Achille-Cléophas. In recounting the effects of the stag's prophecy, he showed us Julian who "struggled against it." It is night: "'Still, supposing I wanted to?. . .' and he feared that the Devil might instill the urge in him" [I, 72]. At which point he moves to a new paragraph and continues without any transition: "For three months, his mother in anguish prayed at his bedside, and his father, moaning, continually paced the halls. He summoned the most celebrated leeches, who prescribed much medicine. Julian's illness, they said, was due to some baleful wind, or to a desire for love. But the young man answered all their questions by shaking his head. His strength returned; and he was taken on strolls in the courtyard, the old monk and the good lord each holding him up on one side" [I, 73–74]. The reader will have recognized this mysterious nervous ailment; it gnawed at Flaubert after a night of horror; it was attributed to an ill wind, to a chance fit of apoplexy; and the good Phidias, in his study, had said: it's because he needs to have sex. But Gustave knew and dissimulated the causes of his languor; he knew—at the very moment when the entire household was assembled at his bedside and when his good Lord was pushing solicitude to the point of supporting him with all his strength, like a child attempting his first steps—the profound and unbearable resentment which would make of him the principal agent in the "Fall of the House of Flaubert."[13]

Of course these pages were written more than thirty years after his breakdown: the man has changed, his memories too. Tortured by the present, incapable—he repeats it incessantly to his niece—of "beginning his life anew" and of envisioning the future, he has taken refuge in the past and enjoys embellishing it. We will not find, in the Legend, the satanism of Doctor

13. For other readings of the significance of Julian's illness, see Chapter 1, p. 36, and Chapter 2, p. 88 and note 24.——TRANS.

Flaubert nor the haughty coldness of his wife; their son made them into sweet old people, tender-hearted, naïve, and slightly ridiculous. How they loved him![14] Julian, fleeing and lost, traveled thousands of leagues; and these good parents, aged and ever so weary, followed in his tracks. They *sought him out*. What would he not have given, our Gustave, for Achille-Cléophas to set out after him, if only a single day. In short, he lends to Julian's parents all the "feudal" virtues which he would have liked to find in his own parents. This is the period when he begins to feel sorry for himself, to sob in his room at Concarneau: no doubt this falsely naïve painting of loving parents— who, by a just reversal of fortune, find themselves dependent on their child—could not be finished without his bursting into tears. The consequence of this permanent tenderness is that the story is once again incomplete: hidden from us are the "beastly and boring" reasons behind the appetite for murder which is suddenly uncovered in Julian. The work does not suffer from this: it suits its naïveté to present us the facts without much commentary. One day the child killed a mouse; he took pleasure in it; he continued; that's that. Perhaps he was made that way; or else, it could well be that the Devil pushed him to it. No matter, when we find Julian again, an adult, a great captain, an Emperor's son-in-law, and perhaps his future successor; and when we see him, sad and solitary, "he leaned on his elbows in the recess of a window, recalling his past hunts" [II, 19], or dreaming that he is "like our father Adam in the midst of Paradise, among all the beasts" [II, 20], and that "by extending his arm, he made them die" [II, 20],[15] our modern sensitivity is disturbed by these obsessive and monstrous nightmares. Poor Julian; we still accept not knowing the origin of his troubles, but we cannot doubt that he is grievously afflicted. It is quite simply that the author, by switching childhoods, deprives us somewhat consciously of the key to the adventure. If Julian were in such fear of parricide, it is because he felt he had solid reasons for killing his father, of which certain go back to his earliest years.

14. It is to be noted, however, that his father does not understand him and wants to make him a warrior (a man of action *par excellence*), whereas his more sensitive mother would like him to become a saint (an artist).

15. These passages are also dealt with in Chapter 1, pp. 47–48.——TRANS.

Julian, at fifteen, is Garcia described in his blackness, but without allusion to his brother François.[16]

How would Gustave have portrayed the parents of the accursed hunter if he had written his *Legend* around '45, when he spoke about it to Maxime? Would the "good Lord" not have vaguely resembled Cosimo de' Medici or Doctor Mathurin?[17] This cannot be determined: Gustave, as we know, is skillful at stacking the deck. Besides, when he would gaze at the cathedral window, it was himself whom he was seeking and not Achille-Cléophas. Sainthood attracted him: sainthood conceived not as a native elevation of the soul, but as a terrifying conquest of all that is rotten. Better yet, what he liked in this story is that radical, original Evil is seen as a necessary condition of Good. Wicked and bloodthirsty, then ascetic and enraged at himself, Julian is never *good;* in no way does he possess this virtue which seemed so insipid to Flaubert. He saves lives, empires, and serves men, but for expiation, never for love. In the next chapter[18] we shall examine what is meant in this case by salvation. For this is the other sense of the *Legend* and, as we shall see, of the breakdown: showing how Gustave can be saved. For the moment, what is certain is that Julian, a new symbol of Flaubert, achieves his salvation not in spite of his parricide, but directly *because of it* and because of the cleansing effects which it has on his empassioned soul. Thus Gustave, confronting the stained-glass window in 1845, could not envision salvation without also thinking of Achille-Cléophas: the physician-philosopher had fashioned him so wickedly that the young rebel could rid himself of the paternal curse only by a symbolic murder. Julian's life served him marvelously: there had been a misunderstanding, an accident, a misdirected dagger—and, indeed, by collapsing at Pont-l'Evêque, Flaubert had not for one instant wanted to bring down the edifice of paternal will through a simulated breakdown. However, Julian in his horror and Gustave in his con-

16. Principal characters in Flaubert's short story *La Peste à Florence* (1836). Garcia murders his elder brother François, thus fulfilling the prophecy of a woman soothsayer. Garcia is later judged and killed by his father, Cosimo de' Medici.——Trans.

17. Titular character in Flaubert's *Les Funérailles du Docteur Mathurin* (1839).——Trans.

18. Included here.——Trans.

torted pride knew their guilt: before the crime there had been the dreams, the abominable temptations, the ruminated then rejected projects, which had become stratified at a "frightening depth" and which, unrecognizable and practically immovable, must have characterized the most fundamental levels of motivation. Innocent and responsible: it is thus that Gustave, nosediving toward the bottom of the carriage, meant to define himself. The fall itself, in '44, must have had the insignificance of an accident and the multiple meanings of a passive act, which, in any case, is *turned against his father*. It defines him in his own eyes as a demonic father, by seeming to result from his own curse. It also compels him to go back on his merciless acts and even to denounce them remorsefully as sins. Finally, it deprives him of his role as symbolic father and obliges him to give maternal care to his victim; and even this makes him ridiculous, since the "drugs," his specialty, remain ineffective and since his diagnosis is incorrect. All that is vaguely within Gustave's intent, but nothing must be *done:* everything, from the fall to the quiet disdain, must happen through necessity, so that when the father suffers ridicule, Gustave's voluptuous disappointment is *endured*. This is why parricide must be both an unforseeable accident and an act which is only manifest within the aura of meanings surrounding the opaque body of the event.

> "... Our Lord Jesus, who was carrying
> him into the heavens"[19]

"... a fullness of bliss, a superhuman joy *flooded* into the soul of the swooning Julian. . . . and Julian ascended toward the blue expanses, face to face with Our Lord Jesus, who was carrying him into the heavens" [III, 57]. Such are the final words of the *Legend*. We should note the permanence of the themes and the words: we are seeing them again after thirty-six years, just as they appeared in the *Mémoires d'un fou*.[20] First, absolute verticality: joy rushes *down* (curiously: "flooded" in fact implies—at least as concerns its cause—an *elevation* of the water level); Julian

---

19. At this point, we move from p. 1907 to p. 2106 of *L'Idiot de la famille*.
——Trans.
20. A novella written by Flaubert in 1838.——Trans.

ascends.[21] Next, passivity: the saint is *swooning*—like the young Flaubert when he was *"drowning"* at the edge of created worlds.[22] Finally, the assumption: Julian is carried into the heavens. This constancy can only underline the astonishing transformation of the basic idea and the change of signs which accompanies it: what descends is celestial joy; the saint himself ascends, with no mind for returning; he will remain on high forever. It is no longer Satan who carries him off and forces him to make a vertiginous ascent into the eternal void: Christ has taken him into his arms; "the expanses" are blue. One might say that the author wanted to paint the naïve faith of the high Middle Ages. That goes without saying: the fact remains that he used his own structures—the oldest and deepest—and them alone. They are also, one might object, those which the subject imposes upon him. Precisely: he chose the subject *for having recognized them in it* and because he wanted an objective law to impose them upon him from the outside. We must return to this tale.

In '45 or '46 he confides to Maxime his desire to recount the life of Julian as it appears on the cathedral window; in '75 he decides to begin the work. In short, the original conception goes back to the first years of his illness, the hardest ones; the drafting begins at the time of his financial ruin. Thirty years separate one from the other. Flaubert never abandoned his project, although he didn't open up very much about it to those closest to him, except to Bouilhet, and, even to him, rarely. Why did he choose to recount this story? Why did he temporarily abandon it for *The Temptation* [*of Saint Anthony*]? Why did the *Legend* remain in him for so long, always alive, like a task which he promised himself to fulfill? Why did he decide to write it when he was wandering around Concarneau, "deploring (his) wasted life"? If we can answer these questions, we will perhaps succeed in understanding how Flaubert *lived out* his original "loser wins"[23]

21. For an alternative reading of the "flood," see Chapter 3, p. 169.——TRANS.

22. Julian's passivity in this scene is further analyzed in Chapter 1, pp. 61–62.——TRANS.

23. "Qui perd gagne": the phrase "loser wins" is also the title of one English translation of Sartre's *Les Séquestrés d'Altona.*——TRANS.

and at the same time, the mode of existence which he assigned to it.

But we must first reread *Saint Julian*. Where does the sainthood of this slaughterer of man and beast, parricide to boot, come from? From his Charity? He has hardly any: his anomaly has excluded him from the society of his fellowmen: "In the spirit of humility, he would relate his story; then all would hurry away. . . . doors were bolted, threats were shouted, stones were thrown at him. . . . Rejected everywhere, he shunned his fellowmen" [III, 3–4]. How can we believe, after the insults and the bad treatment, that he doesn't hate them? Driven out of cities, the parricide sometimes sighs when he sees closed doors and windows. But, in truth, his love is only for nature, and one might say that in spilling his father's blood, he calmed the ardent, insane thirst he had for the beasts': he contemplates colts in their pastures, birds in their nests, even insects with "pangs of love" [III, 7]. But the animals themselves have forgotten nothing and flee, unreconciled. He saves children. Without warmth: the author is careful to tell us that it was *at peril to his life;* Julian cares less about returning these urchins to their mournful parents than about committing a useful suicide. This is so evident that the generous life-saver, having observed that "the abyss rejected him, flames spared him" [III, 11], resolves to kill himself with his own hands and, having no success, abruptly leaves his fellow beings to deal with their own danger. Are there indeed no more children at cliff's edge? in burning houses? If there are, Julian doesn't want to know about it. He settles by the side of a river, and "came upon the idea of using his life in the service of others" [III, 15]. This existence is at rock bottom; Julian is no more than trash in the eyes of men and, most of all, in his own. But since even death will not have his life, it might as well be of service. He will become a boatman. Gustave takes only a few words to describe the travelers who avail themselves of his services, but it is enough to shoot them down in flames. A few (the least objectionable ones) reward him for his troubles with the unwanted remains of food or rags. Others (the more brutal ones) vociferate—it is not known why—and curse him. Julian admonishes them meekly; then they abuse him; at which point, with the glacial detachment of his humility, he gives them his benediction: let them be hanged, let God take care of them. In short, contact with the human species is reduced to a *minimum*.

Will he at least be saved by faith? On this account he appears irreproachable: he has a childlike faith, never questioning anything: "He did not rebel against God who had inflicted this act upon him, and yet despaired that he should have committed it" [III, 10]. But this unshakable faith does not readily lend itself to mystical ecstasy, to the exquisite swooning where one loses oneself in the bosom of the Lord. This Christian is so filled with God that he never thinks about Him and does not even dare to pray. He even pushes absentmindedness to the point of forgetting to rely on the endless bounty of the Almighty and to ask for His pardon. We should note in particular that he takes pleasure in recounting his story—"In the spirit of humility" [III, 3]—to anyone and everyone, but *never* to a priest. This is not surprising if we recall in what esteem Gustave holds priests. It is surprising, however, that he did not hesitate to leave a great sinner of the Middle Ages alone under mute skies, *without intercession:* this is the most glaring anachronism of a story which pretends to be the faithful representation of a period when the Church was queen.

Julian, therefore, shines neither by bursts of faith nor by charity nor by hope. As for this last virtue, it is so lacking in him that after the murder he permanently commits the sin of despair. What then is his merit? It must be great indeed for this criminal to obtain not merely his salvation, but also his canonization. Yet it is nothing other than self-horror. Thus the fundamental trait of sainthood will be one of the prime constituent structures of the Flaubertian makeup, pushed to the extreme.

Julian has been evil since childhood. One fine day, while killing a mouse, he discovers in himself an inextinguishable urge for murder. Right after begins the systematic massacre of the surrounding fauna. This strange frenzy has all the characteristics of Flaubertian sadism. The future saint is still a child when, having located a pigeon which he had just felled and which is not completely dead, he is "irritated" by this persistence of life: "He began to strangle it; and the convulsions of the bird made his heart pound, filled his senses with a wild and tumultuous delight. With the final stiffening, he felt faint" [I, 35]. Later,

"Julian did not tire of killing" [I, 56]. When he sees stags filling "a valley . . . and huddling together" [I, 56], "the prospect of so great a carnage . . . made him choke with pleasure" [I, 57]. This murder wish clearly has a sexual origin, as is shown by the swooning and suffocation which precede or follow it.[24] But what is especially striking is the contrast between the violently *active* aspect of the "carnages" to which the hero surrenders and the *passivity* of the voluptuous pleasures which the hunt procures for him and which resemble fainting. It must be added that Gustave stressed the dreamlike character of these massacres. "Julian did not tire of killing . . . and thought of nothing, remembered naught. He was hunting in some indeterminate land, for an indefinite time, solely because of his very existence, everything fulfilling itself *with the ease which one experiences in dreams*" [I, 56].[25] The story itself, in its rhythm, retains certain qualities of a nightmare: things appear and disappear suddenly, in the nick of time. If we replace these beasts by human beings, we will have the masturbatory truth of this legend: the massacres are dreams.[26] Gustave, an adolescent, surrenders to onanism by imagining tortures; with him orgasm is accompanied by a blissful surrender to his native passivity; each time he is close to losing consciousness. This is how he saw himself around 1840: wicked but passive, dreaming about unheard of suffering but incapable of *inflicting* it. The death of Achille-Cléophas will be natural, but the young man will fear to have provoked it by his homicidal tendencies, magically, as if this murderous hatred which he bears for the human species were only a cover for that which he feels against his parents. The truth, as we know, is different. The fact remains that Gustave, having discovered in himself this arrogant wickedness— proudly confessed in his short stories and too often appeased by masturbatory fantasies—cannot keep from generalizing, as is his wont, and from making of it the *universal* and immediate consequence of original sin. It is in this ultra-Jansenist form that he

24. On the sexuality of this killing see Chapter 2, pp. 76–78, and Chapter 3, pp. 141–142.——TRANS.
25. My emphasis.
26. For discussions of the dreamlike nature of these scenes and the significance of dreaming, see the Introduction and Chapters 1 and 2.——TRANS.

conceives Adam's curse: we are all damned; all are vice-ridden to the core; all sexuality is haunted by the compelling desire to kill. In short, the species is done for from the start: living is not only an interminable and boring misfortune, it is a permanent crime. No one can escape it during life. Thus we can guess that Sainthood will not be characterized by the accession to a higher state or by an efficacious grace which would enable one to combat evil instincts: the saint is an earthbound creature who, barring countermand from on high, is fair game for hell. However, the stag's prophecy, so similar after so many years to that of the woman soothsayer in *La Peste à Florence*, [27] stimulates the beginnings of self-awareness in Julian. He does not discover his wickedness directly, but he grasps the horror of the homicidal wish through its magical consequence, the parricide. The urge to hunt does not cease to haunt him, but it now raises in him the terror of his own self. He no longer knows whether the awakening of his cynegetic yearnings and the way in which he accommodates them mark only the fact that he prefers the hunt to his parents or whether, on the contrary, he only wants to kill big game *in order* to be led, without having willed it, to commit the murder of the father. Whatever it may be, Julian's immediate wickedness is mediated. Denounced by others, known, accepted [28] and refused at the same time, it is consciously lived out *in the only way which is suitable:* in horror. For Gustave, this attitude is still not meritorious: it is simply *true;* human nature is such that it can only be lived out *authentically* in loathing.

The parricide happens by a convergence of *providential* circumstances (which will lead Julian to Sainthood just as the providential frustrations of Jules [29] push him to genius): it could not have been otherwise; it is Destiny. However, Julian recognizes his own part in it; there is no other fatality, in this affair, than his own nature. The latter, incidentally, has just become *reality:* his imaginary wickedness has reached its limits; Julian has become a true criminal. He had previously thought that he could flee from himself; now, all exits are blocked; a blinding light shines on his

27. And to those which mark the calvary of Emma Bovary.
28. Sartre's "assumé" is often translated as "assumed," in the sense that a responsibility is assumed.——TRANS.
29. The main character in the first *Education sentimentale* (1845).——TRANS.

act. Up to now Julian had seen himself as an unfortunate product of radical Evil; at present, radical Evil is his own product. What was virtual is irreversibly actualized, and Julian is beyond repair. His wickedness, formerly dreamed up and provoking loathsome dreams, has left its mark on the real world; he is a man through whom human nature is objectified. Pushed by vice to a paroxysm of being, he is no longer anything more than his essence, and yet his essence is outside himself, since it was affirmed through an act which was torn from his grasp by time. He *must* destroy it, and it is indestructible; his being is behind him, a past surpassed and insurpassable. In the beginning, Julian revolts against his act, as if he could still divorce himself from it, as if by denouncing *his* parricide publicly he could cease being *the* parricide. In vain: this self-criticism has no other effect than to universalize his crime by attracting universal reprobation to it; in fact—though unbeknownst to him—it procures him the isolation necessary for the terrible work which he must exert upon himself. On this point the author's intentions are undeniable; in the legend which inspired him, Julian goes off to beg on the road, *accompanied by his wife.* This is the true medieval conception; not only does the heinous crime not break the ties of holy matrimony, but moreover the spouse participates in it, in spite of her innocence, by a sharing of crimes which is the negative counterpart of a sharing of merits. Gustave eliminated this faithful companion in order to give Julian the high solitude in which he himself so suffered and so rejoiced. In any case, this penitent poverty appears as a first step, still quite easy, on the most uneasy of paths. The parricide, sequestered in nature, quickly perceives that his humility will never permit him to pay for his crime. He then persuades himself that his only recourse is in systematic self-destruction; since he *is* his own fault, he hopes to abolish it by annihilating himself. Nothing works: neither his pious deeds nor his mortifications will resuscitate the two aged parents or erase the stabbings. Moreover, death will not have him: here he is, condemned to remain on earth and to gaze in horror at his own past. This inevitably recalls the dichotomy in *Novembre,* which foreshadowed that of January '45: a child was dying, a turbulence of passion, yearning, and unhappiness, in order to give birth to an old man whose sole function was to rummage through the former's memory. As for Julian, his parricide is like a death; this seething and passionate man has lost even his vices; he is a pure horrified gaze[30] who does not cease to contemplate the last image in his dead memory. When he finally understands that the abyss rejects him and fire spares him, he discovers despair. That is, he sees clearly that he is seeking the *impossible:* one cannot erase what has been. His failure to commit suicide—the last of those which mark Flaubert's works, the most vivid one being recounted in *Novembre*—appears as the hasty and entirely subjective conclusion of this despair: Julian contemplates eliminating the unbearable harking back to an unforgivable transgression. We should note that at present he does not worry about Hell, any more than he used to care about Heaven. This member of medieval Christianity believes only in nothingness. Not for one second does he imagine that he will have to pay, in the other world, for his triple crime—parricide, suicide, despair. For Julian, as for Gustave, hell is on earth. He renounces killing himself when he mistakes his reflection in the fountain for his father's—an episode with a wealth of meanings. We will examine only one of these: the sight of this face steeped in tears makes him feel that his parricide has reappeared to bar the way to suicide. In other words, death settles nothing: it no doubt eliminates the vipers' nest of suffering that is Julian's subjectivity. But this wretch understands that his subjectivity has no more than an inessential reality; once annihilated, it would leave the statue of iniquity which his crime has sculpted forever untouched in the stone-cold of the past. In short, suicide is a useless act. Since death will not have Julian, and since he renounces taking his life—as if, all things considered, it were still better that a subjective consciousness remain to accept the infamous past and *suffer from it;* as if he were afraid, in disappearing, to leave this somber solitary figure in the hands of others, in a state of inexplicable objectivity—the life which he must lead seems to him a slow rotting process which, on its own, *cannot even* come to an end. It goes on; that is all that can be said for it, because it is deprived of

30. "Le regard" is a term frequently used by Sartre and often translated as "the look."——TRANS.

its own death. He cannot even *relive* his crime any longer, as he did at first, when he felt as if he were constantly perpetuating it: hardly does he ruminate it; seldom does the hallucinatory image of the two bleeding bodies suddenly emerge to crush him with its horror. But this ever growing distance of the cursed night, far from attenuating his despair, increases it with each day, because its objective essence, bit by bit, is escaping from him without ceasing to fundamentally control his subjective consciousness. In fact, it receives no new property from the present; it is nothing more than the unbearable and ever vaguer remembrance of a crime. From this standpoint the sin of despair is total: it is no longer even a question of living in order to hate himself; Julian lives and hates himself; that is all. What should be done, however, with this still vigorous body? Flaubert tells us that "Julian . . . came upon the idea of using his life in the service of others" (III, 15). One need only know Gustave slightly to understand to what extent this decision appears contemptible to him. Recall how he ranted, in the past, against philanthropists and how they swore to each other, Alfred and he, never to use their talents as lawyers "to defend widows and orphans." And the reader will not have forgotten the hatred Jules displays for his fellow creatures, nor the rejection of human goals and the disdain for action which appear on every page of the *Correspondence*. Besides, who are these brutal and ungrateful people whom Julian, in his old patched-up boat, transports from one side of the river to the other? Merchants who make the crossing to sell goods to the neighboring town; once in a while pilgrims who go from abbey to abbey. To serve the former is to alienate his working force in favor of *material interests*, which Gustave never ceased to disdain: it amounts to saying that Julian makes himself the tool of a utilitarian enterprise whose ignominy contaminates him. As for the pilgrims, true, they make an effort to secure their salvation: but, as painful as their path may be, how soft is the suffering which they inflict upon themselves and which will win them the benevolence of God, in comparison to the atrocious destitution, the moral tortures, and the physical pain which Julian imposes upon himself, knowing all the while that he will never be saved. In short, he willingly pursues his self-destruction, brutalizes himself by drudgery, and debases himself, not to expiate the inexpiable but to do himself harm, to slide down into the depths of degradation. He does not seek to punish his mortal remains in order to draw nearer to God, but on the contrary to draw even farther away from Him. Little by little, horror becomes familiar, corruption a daily affair: obstinate, insane, debased, living in self-hatred and disgust, but never thinking, Julian bent over his oars becomes like Gustave, a man condemned to repetition. He comes and goes from one bank to the other, his mind dulled by the fatigue of an unrewarding task; in the evening he collapses from exhaustion, only to begin again the next day. Let us salute in passing this appearance of calm in misfortune, which is created by eternal recurrence and which is worse than the storm.

Here, all of a sudden, is the leper, so heavy that the boat nearly goes adrift. Julian's first feeling is that of a weighty demand, stronger than those born of his hatred: "But, realizing that this was a matter of import, a command not to be disobeyed, he picked up his oars" (III, 34). We saw earlier that Beauty, if it is to visit Gustave, can assume no other form than that of a duty to be fulfilled, alien, frightening, and irresistible. But that is not yet the case with Julian: he will have to ferry the leper to the other bank, feed him, quench his thirst, and then finally, "naked as on the day he was born" (III, 53), "stretched himself out" (III, 56) on this rotting corpse covered with ulcers and with "blotches of scaly pustules" (III, 37). He clasps him, chest upon chest, and presses his mouth against "his bluish lips," from which "came breath thick like a fog, and foul" (III, 37). But why, might we ask, does he do this? For love? Certainly not: the leper has nothing lovable, even though the author noted that there was "in his demeanor something of a king's majesty" (III, 31). To be sure Julian is charitable—without warmth, as we know. But if he lies naked on the leper, it is not *primarily* to give him warmth: it is because these wounds, this running pus, fill him with a disgust never before experienced. Here is an opportunity to conquer the desperate resistance of his entire system and to inflict upon himself the most exquisite torture, whose intensity is measured by the repulsion which he must overcome. In short, it is an awesome opportunity which must not be wasted. Moreover, beyond this goal, there is another more distant and more important one: he seeks out contagion in order to catch leprosy, in order to become like this rotting body which provokes his loathing. Notice the verb which the author uses: Julian "*stretches himself out*" on the leper. Passive action: he lies down at full length on the living bed of leprosy; he *weighs down* upon the traveler's decaying system; he seems to be sinking into it. This horizontal "stretching out" is like the beginning of a fall, held back only by the purulent mass into which he sinks, that is, by the leprosy, as if the descent into Hell were to stop when it finally reached bottom. Julian experiences something like a hysterical vertigo in confronting the corruption of a living body, as in the past Gustave felt a fascination for the Nevers journalist.[31] *Contagion*, here, is reminiscent of the earlier *imitation*. The configuration is the same, since Gustave, on his father's word, thought that madness was catching and since he saw in it the lowest form of degradation. Logically, Julian's story should close with this tremendous loathing, so carefully sought like a forbidden pleasure: the leper would leave with the sun's first rays, having stuck him with his leprosy. The parricide would even abandon his work as boatman—proof that he cared little about helping others if it were not to mortify himself. Leprosy is the bodily acceptance of responsibility for the original blemishes on the soul and for Adam's curse. Might we not surmise, at least, that this somatic compliance would have cleansed Julian of his stain? In any case, when the latter holds the leper in his arms, he does not in any way think about his salvation: he wants to reach down into the depths of degradation and, since he cannot die, acquire a foul and lingering agony. Full of self-hatred, he wants to do himself in. At this moment, Jesus makes himself known and carries him off to heaven—in flagrant contradiction with the principles of Roman Catholicism: it is for having despaired of God that Julian will be saved.

For the Lord in His endless bounty had expressly willed all that had happened. He did not make man in His image: rather,

---

31. An epileptic beggar whom Flaubert had first seen and imitated around 1842. Flaubert's father had forbidden these imitations on the grounds that "madness was catching" (see *L'Idiot*, pp. 1734–1736).——TRANS.

He sought to realize in each one of us the fullest measure of vice, baseness, and suffering; and so He endowed all souls with an overpowering need for Him, which He can then frustrate by His absence. In this theological view, even an escape into Catharist asceticism is denied: we are in the world, and cannot get out of it, even by detaching ourselves from human ends. Try as we might to reach a higher roost, since our nature is evil, our intent will be vitiated from the outset, and the result can only be vice-ridden: the basic characteristic of Evil, if it is radical, is that one cannot work one's way out of it. Consequently, God's creatures can only struggle against themselves, and pursue, with hatred for themselves and the world, systematic self-destruction.[32] Ordinarily men hide their terrible mandate from themselves; they trick themselves, lie to themselves: such men are damned from the start. But he who, having recognized his True Self, rends his heart with both hands, he is God's chosen one, and his suffering is delectable to Him. Julian is canonized from the start. An old man predicted it at his birth: it is because his inexpiable sin will permit him to break through the shell of inauthenticity and to wreak hopeless self-hatred upon himself; thus he realizes the essence of Human Nature, which is none other than self-denial. God created him brutal and bloodthirsty. He led him by the hand to parricide—the author says clearly that He "inflicted" it upon him—then, the chips being down, He left him to his awesome sorrow. This *other* will decides and prophesies a Fate, then forces its victim to carry it out while feeling gently yet irresistibly led by that silent complicity with objects found only in dreams. And yet the victim feels responsible for his crime, or at least highly guilty, without the slightest notion of extenuating circumstances. It is easy to recognize here the old idea of the irresistible *Fatum*, that is, of the Father's curse and the savage will which the genitor employs to accomplish his designs. Let us suppose that in the *Legend* man is, as was the child Gustave, a monster placed on earth for the purpose of suffering. What has changed since *La Peste à Florence*? The fact that in 1875 a reconciliation with the father is achieved. The late Achille-Cléophas not only figures in the *Legend*, in the form of a gentle country squire

32. See also Chapter 2 at note 45.——TRANS.

who adores his only son; he is also God the Father: a God who is hidden but good.[33] The awful fate which He reserved for Julian, a prisoner of himself, is simply endured, without his discovering anything but calamity within it. But the author keeps at a distance; he sees the event from the outside, objectively, in all its dimensions, so he can declare with pious zeal: if Julian has suffered, I can testify that it was for his own good. Gustave has, of course, borrowed the ideas of trial and beneficial suffering. But he has transformed them for his personal use: the Roman Catholic does not remain without help in his quandary; the Church can bear witness to the fact that God wishes his eternal happiness; the intercessors—Jesus, Mary, and the Saints—and God Himself can deliver His grace unto him. Of course suffering can enter into purification, but at least a Christian is aware of the outcome, and there are other means of purification—confession and communion. Moreover, the Council of Trent had long ago decided that man was weak, but not naturally inclined toward evil. Flaubert disregards the Council and radicalizes everything: man is rotten, fallen, and this is God's doing: the rosy rosary of trials read by the Christian creature is a lie. Life is out there with its foul, disgraceful stench, and the human monster has to live it out, from one end to the other. God has extracted man from nothingness so that hatred shall exist in the universe. Here, by two different paths, Gustave and the Christian converge: since the Lord is good, He did not engender Evil for His mere delight; he sees human suffering only as a means. But to what end? On this point, Gustave is not very explicit. But we know him well enough to guess his reasons; already, in *Agonies*,[34] he acquainted us with them: most of man's misfortune stems from his *determinism*. *Reality* impoverishes the infinite set of possibilities; it is therefore finite and empty. But another change arises after 1844: Creation is no longer an irreparable error; it has become a necessary evil. Reality must exist to negate itself through hatred, to make the vain attempt to transcend itself—through that religious call to the infinite which can be born only in the finite—

33. For a complementary reading concerning the role of Julian's father in the final scene, see Chapter 1, note 45.——TRANS.

34. *Agonies* was a series of "skeptical meditations," written by Flaubert in 1838.——TRANS.

and to allow itself to be gnawed away by the imaginary, the ambiguous symbol of God. For Flaubert, the stage of reality— that of facticity[35] and isolation—is not the goal of Creation but on the contrary the first step in an ascent toward Being. Thus, when God bends over to hear Julian's despair, He pities him for suffering, but He appreciates, in this frantic negation of one's self, the protest of all *"beings"*[36]—in the name of an ontological truth which remains out of reach. In the desperate attempt of the parricide to destroy his inexpiable transgression, He is able to uncover and to love the bitter and frustrating search for the impossible, where, in His eyes, lies the sole grandeur of the Human Slave. Better yet, Julian is chosen because he has the obscure intuition that man *is* his own impossibility, since this creature refuses his finite determinism in the name of some infinite notion which he cannot begin to conceive. Since this is the case, our *heautontimoroumenos*[37] can do nothing more *on his own:* a self-conscious impossibility does not, *ipso facto,* destroy itself (contrary to what is said in *Novembre*); it continues to wal- low in the mires of time. After actualizing his essence by being perfectly wicked and in perfect despair at so being, the Almighty must intervene through a miracle in order to make possible what was impossible. Julian's crime is indelible, but by carrying the parricide off to heaven, the Lord does not modify the set-aside sin, does not eliminate one iota of it. By a logical and miraculous metamorphosis, He makes it the means which He has chosen in His wisdom to set Julian on the path to sainthood. Gustave has achieved the *tour de force* of preserving the black, accursed world of his adolescence intact, while integrating it into a calm, reli- gious universe.

35. "Facticité": a term used frequently by Sartre and which he defines as "the fact that things *are there* as they are without the necessity or the possibility of being otherwise and that I *am there* among them" (*Being and Nothingness,* trans. Hazel E. Barnes [New York, 1966], p. 671).——TRANS.

36. "Les étants": Sartre notes in an earlier reference (see *L'Idiot,* p. 2088) that he is. using this word in the sense of Heidegger's *Seiendes.*——TRANS.

37. From the Greek, meaning "self-punisher"; also the title of a play by Menander (342–292 A.D.).——TRANS.

CONCLUSION

Oedipus Sanctus: Psychology and Poetics

Michel Grimaud

••

—Julianus... "der katholische Ödipus."
　　　　　　　　　　　　　　　　—Otto Rank

"So *Hamlet* is about the Oedipus conflict"—thus runs the
argument—"But———"—and here some work of accepted
lightweight quality is named—"is also about the Oedipus
conflict. Obviously the fact that *Hamlet* deals with the
Oedipus conflict has nothing to do with its appeal."
　　　　　　　　　　　　　　　　—Simon O. Lesser[1]

••

1. Julian is called the "Catholic Oedipus" in the *Gestis Romanorum*, according
to Otto Rank, *Das Inzest-Motiv in Dichtung und Sage* (1926; rpt. Darmstadt, 1974).
Rank (pp. 330–334) provides a short summary of the traditional Oedipal interpretation of the Saint Julian legends. Simon O. Lesser's point is that the
hostile argument is a *non sequitur;* a necessary condition is not a sufficient one
(*Fiction and the Unconscious* [Boston, 1957], p. 74).

Saint Julian and *Oedipus Rex*

The choice of *Saint Julian* to illustrate the interest of a psychological approach might have seemed somewhat facile. The story is
about parricide and its prediction, as is *Oedipus Rex;* the narrator
of *Saint Julian* even stresses Julian's wish to kill his parents
(" 'still, supposing I wanted to?...' " I, 72). There does not seem
to be any need for an interpretation along psychoanalytic lines.
Yet one might suggest that this type of reading is *most* apposite
when it does not dig up repressed (dynamically unconscious)
material which can then be flaunted to the by now blasé reader
who can find manifest incestuous and parricidal acts
everywhere in contemporary literature (but incest was also
common in late-eighteenth-century French literature). It is not
the mere, crude content which is relevant, but the fine web of
details linked to what is a cross-culturally fundamental experience.

Even Sophocles' Oedipus is by no means a pure example of
the "Oedipus complex." No such "thing" exists: the Oedipus
complex is a working *concept* which includes a negative
component—the "negative Oedipus," which is not given as
much emphasis in Sophocles. Moreover, and this goes, for instance, against Jean Starobinski's analysis of the play,[2] Sophocles does *not* present us with a hero who *wishes* to accomplish
the acts he carries out, but one whom circumstances put into
such a position. In *Saint Julian,* on the contrary, chance (fate)
plays a smaller role inasmuch as we know about Julian's ambivalence toward his parents (I, 72). Reading the Sophocles play as a
paradigm of the Oedipus complex implies, therefore, turning
fate into a representative of the unconscious wish—a kind of
voice of conscience, a pre-diction and warning (this could also
apply to *Saint Julian*)—and turning the scene of the play into the
scene of dreams since the two sets of parents can then be interpreted as a splitting of the parent imagoes due to ambivalence.[3]

2. Starobinski, preface to the French translation of Ernest Jones's *Hamlet and
Oedipus* (Paris, 1967), p. xxvi. Among the numerous studies of *Oedipus Rex* see
André Green, *Un oeil en trop* (Paris, 1969), and Richard Caldwell, "The Blind-
ness of Oedipus," *International Review of Psychoanalysis*, 1 (1974), 207–218.
3. The best analyses of splitting are found in Robert Rogers, *The Double in
Literature* (Detroit, 1970). For a Jungian point of view, see Carl Francis Keppler,
The Literature of the Second Self (Tucson, Ariz., 1972).

Lack of knowledge, then, is an adequate representation for the lack of consciousness of Oedipal wishes. In short, a complex reconstruction of the whole action has to be accomplished before the play's fateful tragedy can be seen as an individual psychological event. The play is far from being an obvious case for the Oedipus complex and the family romance;[4] but nor are *Hamlet, The Brothers Karamazov,* or *Saint Julian.* If they were, *then,* we might as well call them crude fantasies or dreams rather than elaborate works of art.[5]

If we assume that *Saint Julian* is about "the Oedipus complex," we should be struck by the almost total absence of reference to incest wishes. It is a general principle of psychiatry that the patient will find it easier to talk about what is less important than about what is at the core of his or her problems. The very absence of certain facts, such as normal love or hatred for one's mother, will delineate just as clearly as direct discussion, the absent constellation of meanings. Further, a number of apparently discrepant aspects—non-sense—can direct the reader's attention toward absent motifs and motives. In *Saint Julian,* for instance, the anxious, eroticized atmosphere of the second hunt, Julian's puzzling passivity and failure, and the formal links to the first hunt can imply that the two scenes are thematically connected and that the *motives* present in either one should also be assumed to be at work in the other. Further, their being associated in textually unexplained ways to the parents, death, and adultery permits plausible reconstructions of another mode of discourse which will use the formal codes as further cues toward meaning.[6]

4. The family romance is the most common fantasy formation connected with the Oedipus complex. A general review of the concept can be found in Linda Joan Kaplan, "The Concept of the Family Romance," and Helen K. Gediman, "Narcissistic Trauma, Object Loss, and the Family Romance," *Psychoanalytic Review,* 61 (1974), 169–202, 203–216. Literary applications of the concept are found in Marthe Robert, *The Origins of the Novel* (Bloomington, 1980).

5. Fantasies and dreams need not be "crude." Only obsessive-compulsive thought will have such a character.

6. From a psychological and semiotic as well as a literary viewpoint, it would be preferable to avoid the opposition between the "form" and the "content" of communication: all coding systems *qua* systems are forms (structures) and contribute to meaning. See John Ellis, *The Theory of Literary Criticism* (Berkeley, 1974), pp. 155–183, and my "Préliminaires pour une psycholinguistique des discours: Le Champ de la poétique," *Langue française,* no. 49 (1981), pp. 14–29.

It must always be remembered, however, that mentioning the "Oedipus complex" or "repression" is merely saying that *Saint Julian* conforms to a traditional pattern found in countless forms from jokes and folklore to the most valued works in our culture. In a sense it might even be preferable to forgo the term "Oedipus complex," as Freud himself almost always did, and analyze the rich patterns of the text rather than *name* them. Especially in literary criticism, a description is worth a thousand concepts. In short, it seems worth repeating Simon O. Lesser's 1957 argument, which applies to *Saint Julian* as well as to *Hamlet*, and which is still largely ignored, though we hope that this book has followed it not only in theory but also in practice:

> To show the part the [Oedipal] theme does play in our response to *Hamlet*, we would have to proceed in precisely the opposite fashion [from using reduction, synopsis, concepts as labels]: we would have to do justice to the theme *in its fulness*. We would have to suggest the infinite cunning with which it is orchestrated in nearly all the play's key relationships and in innumerable actions and speeches.[7]

Intertextual Approaches

Excepting the essay by Jean-Paul Sartre, the studies included in this book have avoided what we may call "intertextual readings"—the comparing of different texts to the master text in order to support or supplement interpretation. Intertextuality is particularly liable to result in a neglect of the specificity of the texts in order to reach generalizations applicable to several works or to Flaubert and his works as a whole. This approach, then, tends to neglect the unique qualities of a work in order to emphasize a broader thematic unity. It would, theoretically, be possible to take a work as a starting point *and* an end point, using intertextual readings to underline differences and, particu-

---

Similarly, the metaphors describing the unconscious (the repressed) as deep or hidden have long made psychoanalysis appealing to those prone to the treasure-hunt theory of true meaning. Jacques Lacan's "Seminar on [Poe's] 'Purloined Letter'" (*Yale French Studies*, no. 48 [1972], pp. 38–72) neatly shows how underlying "latent" meanings are just as "manifest" as the supposedly superficial ones. What is at work is not the uncovering of the hidden but the construction of meanings through the use of different decoding strategies.

7. *Fiction and the Unconscious*, p. 74.

larly, to uncover the series of transformations which a theme undergoes from real life and early attempts to masterpiece; but this is rarely done as it still implies, at each stage, close analysis of each single work. In other words, in order to carry out a useful intertextual reading, it is desirable to have available separate structural studies of each work so as to appreciate the significance of the items compared within their separate frameworks, since their functions may otherwise be misunderstood through the imposition of an essentially unrelated pattern.[8] This is the essence of the structuralist position, as the following passages from Benveniste will make clear:

> One cannot determine the place of a word in a lexical system until one has studied the structure of the said system. . . .
> The fundamental principle is that a language constitutes a system whose parts are all united in a relationship of solidarity and dependence. This system organizes units, which are the articulated signs, mutually differentiating and delimiting themselves. *The structuralist doctrine teaches the predominance of the system over the elements,* and aims to define the structure of the system through *the relationships among the elements,* in the spoken chain as well as in formal paradigms, and shows the organic character of the changes to which language is subject.[9]

The italicized phrases show that what is essential is the system and that an intertextual reading must compare intertextual systems, not items—an important but difficult task.

It might seem nonetheless revealing to note that in a preface to an early work, "Un Parfum à sentir" (April 1836), Flaubert talks of God's "ferocity," of his "bizarre" and "bitter" handling of life, and denies the guilt of his characters, preferring to attribute it to society and nature: "Responsibility lies in circumstances, prejudices, society, and nature who has become a bad mother."[10] In a slightly later story dated December 15, 1836, Flaubert tells another bizarre tale about a man named Ohmlin

8. On intertextuality see, for instance, Michael Riffaterre, "The Poetic Functions of Intertextual Humor," *Romanic Review,* 65 (1974), 278–293, and also his seminal "The Stylistic Approach to Literary History," *New Literary History,* 2 (1970), 39–55.
9. Emile Benveniste, " 'Structure' in Linguistics," chapter 8 of *Problems in General Linguistics,* trans. Mary E. Meek (Coral Gables, Fla., 1971), pp. 81, 83 (italics added). See also Jean Piaget, *Structuralism* (New York, 1970).
10. Gustave Flaubert, *Oeuvres de jeunesse inédites,* I (*183..-1838*) (Paris, 1910), pp. 69, 70. My translation.

(manikin) buried alive and almost saved by his dog named Fox. The story is entitled "Rage et impuissance,"[11] a striking title when one thinks of the similarity with the unfolding plot of *Saint Julian*, as exemplified by the two hunting scenes, while the name of the dog might be connected with the fox skin which functions as a synecdoche for Julian's father (who always wore one; see I, 9, and II, 27). How fragile this type of coupling can be is made clear by the fact that only recourse to Flaubert the person will make this *sort* of linking worth mentioning. It does not otherwise enrich our understanding of the *works* in question except on the greatest level of generality.

The significance of leprosy, sensuality, and death might also be read differently if seen in terms of the death of the homosexual mercenaries in *Salammbô*, which is almost immediately followed by that of Hannon, who is covered with "ulcers" and is crucified.[12] But such loose parallels underscore the magnitude of the task to be undertaken, since the differences between the two story systems are blatant.

Similarly, if Benjamin F. Bart's striking analysis of a dream of Flaubert's corresponding to the hunting scenes in *Saint Julian* is to be used in a study of the latter, the presupposition that the elements have parallel functions must be proved.[13] In particular, the strong sexual undercurrent which Bart finds by comparing the various texts where aspects of the dream appear is hardly foregrounded to the same extent in *Saint Julian*. The references to parts of the *Temptation of Saint Anthony* are especially probing in this respect. But, independently of Bart's main thesis (pantheism), what becomes intertextually obvious is not in any way easy to extract from *Saint Julian* alone. What is most significant about sexuality in *Saint Julian* is its absence: the effect of this peculiarity, therefore, is what has to be analyzed in order to understand the literary achievement of the story. But Bart is not concerned with what the reader can understand; rather, he would reconstruct the meaning of *Saint Julian* for Flaubert. His study would then furnish an excellent starting point for an analysis of the *transformations of sexual motifs* in this and other

11. *Ibid.*, pp. 148–161.
12. Flaubert, *Salammbô*, ed. Edouard Maynial (Paris, 1961), pp. 320–321, 328.
13. Benjamin F. Bart, "Psyche into Myth: Humanity and Animality in Flaubert's *Saint-Julien*," *Kentucky Romance Quarterly*, 20 (1973), 317—342.

works of Flaubert, and, in this context, intertextual reference to texts where Julian's wife embraces the leper would be most appropriate:

> The curiously bisexual detail "bouche contre bouche" [III, 56] can be accounted for more easily if we assume Flaubert's *point de départ* for the scene as being the *Prose Tale* episode, in which it is the wife who offers her warmth; now, the *Prose Tale* also describes Julian's parents as sleeping in his bed "bouche à bouche." The parallel between the two bed-scenes would have been obvious to Flaubert, especially after reading in the *Prose Tale* that Julian and his wife die "in the same way as Julian killed his father and mother, with one blow."[14]

Two problems remain: why Flaubert chose to modify the story; and why such a modification is a *literary* success.

Another closely related critical presupposition is that an intertextual reading is preferable to one that analyzes the work on its own terms, because the former encompasses a broader range of data. Yet what can be recovered from an intertextual analysis is often different from what is foregrounded by the structure of the *specific master text to which the reader is responding* and which is the basis of our interest in the work in the first place. The critic's overly broad knowledge of an author's life and works usually succeeds in blurring this distinction: what is "true" (what forms a structurally meaningful pattern) on one level need not be so on another. The unusual value of Sartre's *L'Idiot de la famille* is that it makes this problem stand out in paradoxical light. The book, in spite of its nearly three thousand pages, seems too short. *Because* Sartre goes into great detail and because he does not conceal his theoretical assumptions, the reader becomes aware of how much is missing when one attempts to reconstruct a complex series of texts through exhaustive analysis. Sartre's perceptive study, like Eissler's fifteen-hundred-page analysis of ten years in the life of Goethe, enables one to grasp the overwhelming difficulty of intertextual interpretation.[15]

14. Colin Duckworth, introduction to *Trois contes* (London, 1959), p. 59. See also Berg's Introduction and note 1, above.

15. Kurt R. Eissler, *Goethe: A Psychoanalytic Study (1775–1786)* (Detroit, 1963). Jean-Paul Sartre's Chapter 4, above, provides at once a corrective to our downplaying of intertextuality and a justification of our belief that intertextual readings are most appropriate as part of pluralistic approaches.

Psychoanalytic readings of an author's works furnish another example of the biographical predicament. Psychoanalytically-oriented critics, but especially psychoanalysts writing on literature, have been accused of distorting the works of art they analyze. Their point of view usually is a special one: they try to understand how or why a writer wrote a certain piece. They are, consequently, interested in elucidating the meaning of one text in terms of the complex relationships it has with another: the life of the author as we know it. Alain Costes, in his analysis of Camus' works, sees a certain anal motif which explains the stone imagery in the *Myth of Sisyphus* or in a short story from the *Exile and the Kingdom* ("La Pierre qui pousse"). Yet, when the latter story is read, the anal theme seems remote from reader-oriented interpretations. Its irrelevance (not to mention its shocking aspect for anyone not cognizant of psychoanalytic thinking) is not a criticism if one realizes that Costes is not dealing with "La Pierre qui pousse" as a work of art destined to be enjoyed as literary communication, but is furnishing an explanation of the underlying motive force for the choice of certain themes which—in their new literary context—may (or may not: this has to be investigated as a separate issue) take on new general meanings both conscious and unconscious.[16]

This distinction can be further illustrated with vignettes from *Saint Julian*. A psychoanalytically-minded critic might associate the killing of the mouse coming out of its hole with a primal-scene fantasy or with the connected idea of anal birth. Our psychoanalyst might note that Flaubert often calls his sister "rat":

16. Alain Costes, *Albert Camus ou la parole manquante* (Paris, 1973). Because of his biographical interests this is an issue Charles Mauron never confronted. Mauron was a pioneer of both psychoanalytic criticism and the study of the semiotic patterns of texts. Unfortunately he did not see the need for poetics, psychology, or the expanded and systematic study of semiosis: his "psychocriticism" was not broadly psychological but only psychoanalytic and was directed toward the text and the author more than the reader. This fact might be of merely historical interest were it not that the excellence of his literary criticism and the vogue of the label "psychocriticism" have resulted in a de-emphasis of his methodological weaknesses. For further comments see my "Psychologie et littérature," Chapter 12 of *Théorie de la littérature*, ed. Aron Kibédi Varga (Paris, 1981). Sections 9 and 10 of the "Reader's Guide," below, provides references to works on and by Mauron.

What a nice letter, sister dear, as nice and unassuming as you are, my little mouse [*rat*]. I could almost see you with your curly, disheveled hair and that little dimple [*trou*] in your cheek; by the way, I certainly hope to see you again with your *papillotes*. I don't have anyone anymore to strangle with my own two hands while saying: you old mouse! you old mouse! . . . You'll roll again on my bed as the dog used to, and I'll play the black man: "Yes, me love mistress, me love mistress" (p. 245).[17]

We would be reminded of the psychological importance of sibling love and rivalry and note that it will be especially strong when the sibling is born only two years and seven months after oneself. Moreover, the sister and mother are both named Caroline, which can facilitate a symbolic displacement of Oedipal conflicts onto the sister. The killing of the animals might then be a displacement from a wish to kill the sibling. The three nurses, the stress on food in the first two killings and before the parricide, the climactic murder of the nursing fawn, and the reference to the mother as a stork all point in that direction. A reading of *Saint Julian* taking these ideas into account might (if further evidence were adduced) provide an explanation for Flaubert's *not* detailing the genesis of Julian's rage. It might even be possible to assume that the many readers who have lived through similar situations will focus on these details during their unconscious interpretative thematic reorganization of the narrative or that they will be easily convinced of its relevance. But the point is that these are isolated details insufficiently foregrounded and linked to the main textual patterns: they do not furnish a satisfactory answer to why readers will find *Saint Julian* a profound experience. This does not mean that an interpretation which is appropriate for the writer will never be appropriate for the reader, but the parallelism is in no way necessary since a work of art is not only a personal statement, even from the point of view of its creator: details which are focusable when placed in the context of the writer's known life-obsessions need not be focused in the economy of the text as literature. Encoding is not decoding.

17. Letter to his sister Caroline (July 10, 1845) in *Correspondance I* (*janvier 1830 à avril 1851*), ed. Jean Bruneau (Paris, 1973). "Rat" being a term of endearment in French, the translation "mouse" has been preferred here. The reference to strangling can evoke the episode with the pigeon in I, 35.

The homosexual aspect of the end of *Saint Julian* can readily be related to several aspects of Flaubert's psychology (witness his *Correspondance*), but it is hardly mentioned in our discussions of the scene in Chapters 1–3. Though the episode can be read as homosexual, the use of an adult, abstract concept tends to hide the specific features involved. The terms would be clear to a psychoanalyst, for whom it would evoke a cluster of related concepts and phenomena; but using the language of the psychoanalyst is, to some extent, giving up one's function as a literary critic in the same way as it would be a failure of the analyst as clinician to say to a patient, "You have an Oedipus complex":

> These words or concepts are appropriate to the theoretical model currently in use; they are not the language of persons. We never tell a patient about his ego or his id, about psychic energy and neutralization, or about the positive and negative oedipus complex. We speak the language of persons, and we talk about the patient's love and hate for his parents, the sexual urges that he feels, and so on.[18]

Emanuel Peterfreund goes on to describe his technique, stressing the fact that one must remain as close as possible to one's "text":

> When the ideas "oedipus complex" and "sibling rivalry" occurred to me I was much too remote from the clinical material. I was temporarily "resisting." I was at a level of advanced clinical generalizations. This level is much too abstract to enable one to understand the specific observables in a given case. I had to make more immediate contact with the clinical material and find the simpler generalizations embodied therein.[19]

It is only in a published summary of research that the analyst will be right to conclude in conceptual terms. The experience of

---

18. Emanuel Peterfreund, *Information, Systems, and Psychoanalysis* (*Psychological Issues*, monograph 25/26, 1971), pp. 34–35. See also André Green, "Surface Analysis, Deep Analysis," *International Review of Psychoanalysis*, 1 (1974), 415–424. It should be pointed out that Julian's *manifestly* homoerotic acts do not necessarily imply *latent* (unconscious) homosexuality, though sloppy psychoanalytic published practice often seems to negate this prime principle of psychoanalysis. As noted in the following section the manifest Oedipal data might more properly be seen as a problem in differentiation between self and object rather than from an Oedipal, conflictual standpoint.

19. Peterfreund, pp. 294–295.

literature and the critic's contribution to focusing the reader's experience should similarly take advantage of knowledge from seminal concepts; but they should be presented as late as possible in the text, when they will function as synopses or as discovery procedures—not as replacements for the working-through of a unique textual mesh of associations.

A few words must finally be said in this concluding chapter about the one intertextual system whose relevance is *textually* averred. Indeed, it is probably rare to find a collection of short stories like *Three Tales* where intertextual reading reveals that they truly form a whole. Because this book deals only with *Saint Julian*, a whole aspect of its art cannot be discussed.[20] Yet there is no doubt that each story is the greater for its being embedded in the trinity of *A Simple Heart, Saint Julian,* and *Herodias.* The stories are in antichronological sequence, a masterly stroke since it establishes a progression whereby the first two closing religious ecstasies are unexpectedly contrasted to the heaviness of the horizontal imagery of the last lines of the last story, which announce the coming of Christ. There is also an apparent reverse progression in sanctity from Felicity to Julian to the quite unsaintly Herodias, accompanied by an obvious progression in cruelty from the first woman to the second.

Through Julian's "rage" then "impuissance," *Saint Julian,* at the center, seems to mediate between Felicity's lack of "rage" but "impuissance," and Herodias' "rage" and "puissance"—her apparent victory being in truth a defeat, while the first two heroes' defeat is a spiritual victory. Significant details reappear from one story to the next. The dove in *A Simple Heart* (III, 3) is

20. Among the more recent studies of *Trois contes* one might mention the following: Raymonde Debray-Genette, "Du mode narratif dans les *Trois contes,*" *Littérature,* no. 2 (1971), 39–62; Marie-Julie Hanoulle, "Quelques manifestations du discours dans *Trois contes,*" *Poétique,* no. 9 (1972), pp. 41–49; Michael Issacharoff, "'Trois contes' et le problème de la non-linéarité," *Littérature,* no. 15 (1974), pp. 27–40; Per Nykrog, "Les 'Trois contes' dans l'évolution de la structure thématique chez Flaubert," *Romantisme,* no. 6 (1973), pp. 54–66; and Frederic J. Shepler, "La Mort et la rédemption dans les *Trois contes* de Flaubert," *Neophilologus,* 56 (1972), 407–416. See also Michael Rengstorf's remarkable dissertation, "Les 'Trois contes' de Flaubert: Essai de sémiotique narrative" (State University of New York, Buffalo, 1976) and the *Festschrift* for Don Demorest edited by Charles Carlut, *Essais sur Flaubert* (Paris, 1979).

explicitly identified with the Holy Ghost, whereas it might be taken simply as a realistic detail in *Saint Julian*. But, in Chapter 3, through independent analysis of the second story, we did arrive at its religious meaning, thereby establishing the basis for an intertextual reading of that detail. Its appearance in both stories, as well as the similarity of the endings and the common obsession with animals, would require careful analysis: strangely enough, animals are not linked only to religion and violence in *A Simple Heart*, but also, most emphatically, to sexuality in a stylistically foregrounded aside: Felicity "was not innocent in the way young ladies are—animals had been her teachers—..." (II, 10).[21] This original learning from animals will eventually result in a turning to animals for religious and other solace in the "person" of Loulou, the parrot.

In *Saint Julian* a pagan's head is cut off; this needless cruelty is implicitly lauded by a Christian emperor who gives Julian his daughter in marriage. In *Herodias*, Jokanaan's head is cut off—an act which has become a byword of extraordinary cruelty; it is linked not only to a woman but also to sexual desire and incest. If we are to understand *Three Tales* as a whole, such recurrent events and their apparently contradictory valuations in different stories must be accounted for.

It is curious, finally, that two quotations from *Herodias* could serve as epigraphs for both *A Simple Heart* and *Saint Julian*: "Nec crescit, nec post mortem durare videtur [The body does not increase, nor does it seem to subsist after death]" (III, 46)—a fact in ironic contrast not only with the whole Christian dogma but also with the ending of *Saint Julian* and the state of the Holy-Ghost-as-parrot in the last paragraph of part four of *A Simple Heart* ("Although the parrot was not a corpse [it is stuffed], worms were eating it"). In *Herodias*, Jokanaan himself looks like a sick beast; he repeats "What does it matter? If he [Jesus] is to wax, I must wane" (I, 26).[22] The phrase is repeated in the last four lines of *Herodias*—and of *Trois contes*: in a paradoxical reversal of Christ's suffering on the Cross for the love of humankind, Jokanaan, to exalt Him, must bear his cross.

---

21. "Un coeur simple," *Trois contes* (Paris, 1969), p. 9. My translation.
22. "Hérodias," *Trois contes* (Paris, 1969), p. 145. My translation.

Anti-Oedipus and the Individual Reader

One important aspect of Oedipal interpretations is their partial irrelevance. The traditional psychoanalytic point of view is that

> limitations in living could, if found to occur in conjunction with evidence of disavowed ties to parental figures, be attributed to the effects of those ties.... But again, it makes equal sense to consider, for example, how a longing for the ideal caretaker-beauty (mother) of childhood might be fostered by a current life style which excludes fully satisfying experiences of intimacy and sensual satisfaction.[23]

Paul Wachtel goes on to emphasize that the "lure of Oedipal imagery is strengthened each time the person has a frustrating or disappointing encounter. And in the course of growing up, many experiences accrue which keep this pattern going." He concludes:

> In this view, then, Oedipal longings, while "real," need not be the primary motor of the patient's current difficulties. One can acknowledge the evidence for their existence, and even intensity, without necessarily viewing them as the crucial center. Instead one sees the conflicts generated in the family leading to a continuing series of experiences which develop their own momentum and of which the Oedipal yearnings of the adult years are themselves a function.[24]

Wachtel's insistence that by "de-emphasizing the longing as a simple perpetuation of the past, we may see how it is brought about in the present, both by the patient's own behavior and by the behavior he evokes in others" can help us understand the parricide as a kind of self-fulfilling prophecy: Julian's self-abnegating behavior may originally have been motivated by the need to cover up his strong aggressive urges, but such a life style *now* generates rage. As Wachtel says of a patient who sounds like a psychological brother of Julian's: "Disavowed anger may be a continuing feature of his life from childhood, but the angry

---

23. Paul Wachtel, "Structure or Transaction? A Critique of the Historical and Intrapsychic Emphasis in Psychoanalytic Thought," *Psychoanalysis and Contemporary Science*, 5 (1976), 134. In view of their condensation, the formulations of this paper are used here rather than those from Wachtel's book *Psychoanalysis and Behavior Therapy* (New York, 1977).

24. "Structure or Transaction?" pp. 134–135.

thoughts which disturb his dreams tonight can be understood by what he let happen to him today." In a formulation Sartre would not disavow, Wachtel also emphasizes that the patient "perpetuates his personal myth that there resides within him an untouchable kernel of rage which is part of the essence of who he is."[25] The reader, like the analyst, is often tempted to return to the first occurrence of the rage while neglecting the continuity in its development so clearly depicted in Flaubert's tale. Consequently, the critic is also tempted to attribute great weight to the Oedipal constellation, even though Wachtel clearly shows that the Oedipus complex is not necessarily the prime mover but can be the result of longings similar to those of Julian in III, 20.

But if, for instance, the final scene should not be read as a "negative or positive Oedipal" union with the son-parent figure (father *and* mother) of the leper who is symbolically playing all the roles, why should our book and this final chapter hark back to Oedipus? Because the lure of Oedipus is real. Longings, fantasies that turn us toward the past, though they might not always point to the psychological *causes* of our present state of being, point to the reality of our illusions about ourselves. Such illusions, especially reinforced in our sociocultural setting, are also the stuff much of our mental life is made on. As such they are well worth studying in literature—the only medium in which our society allows us to ponder them reflexively and empathically.

At one level of analysis, then, *Saint Julian is* about Oedipal fantasies. This narrative content of the tale can hardly be disputed in a general way. The predictions and facts of parricide or of assumed adultery, the importance of the parent-child relationship, cannot fail to unconsciously evoke, in readers with a psychologically predominant Oedipal fantasy structure, the whole complex including the incest fantasies almost entirely absent from the text. But one must note that this formulation does not imply that all "normal" human beings must go through true Oedipal structuralization of the mind. It is equally possible to be

25. *Ibid.*, pp. 119–120.

"normal" (that is, functional in our society) with a predominantly schizophrenic organization.[26] The point that even male readers do not necessarily identify strongly with Julian's predicament, since it implies a nonuniversal homologous Oedipal configuration, has to be further restricted by stressing that female readers are likely to enjoy the story even less. Mere lip service is usually paid to these facts while emphasis is placed on the psychoesthetically satisfying potential of other aspects of the literary text. Certainly. But the *strongest* pleasures of literature, the true loves, are not dependent to such an extent on the "poetry" of a text as on its psychological fit with our own mental organization and fantasies. It is only to the extent that there is at least a rough ready-made fit that we can significantly process the text in any detail and talk of literary enjoyment.

From this viewpoint, students or teachers who must read a novel or a poem are in a special situation where the element of obligation changes the relationship between the elements of appreciation. The cultural coercion of prepackaged "great literature" also conceals the fact that, for any one individual, genuine psychoesthetic greatness (as opposed to adherence to the cultural hierarchies) is not only a function of the text and the culture but equally of this preset fit, which will *then* allow infinite mental reweaving of the text in personal terms. We must underline how rare such an event is: lasting love affairs with one book or poem or play are *not* everyday occurrences even among the literate. Consequently, the ecosystems of psychological fits as opposed to the isolated class of "great books" will imply that any general high or low valuation of a work will, for any one individual, be a poor predictor of this person's enjoyment.

In other words, criticism and poetics do not—and perhaps should not—deal with literary enjoyment. They describe seman-

---

26. See Jean Bergeret's careful distinctions on this topic in *La Personnalité normale et pathologique* (Paris, 1974), pp. 15–16. Though the Chicago school of psychoanalysis would analyze the situation in a different frame of reference (self psychology), it would also stress the irrelevance of an Oedipal (conflictual) viewpoint. See Heinz Kohut, *The Analysis of the Self* (New York, 1971) and *The Restoration of the Self* (New York, 1977), e.g., p. 241.

tic and semiotic structures. Such structures can then be specified as more or less complex and universal from sociological, cultural, political, and other points of view. If it was felt necessary, a composite picture of ideal readers (perfect fit) could also be drawn. Each text could then be matched with its ideal readers—after appropriate psychological testing!

Narrative content is only part of what a text provides its reader. Even if they are central to the story of *Saint Julian*, its Oedipal variations—which can be interpreted as fantasies and defenses, or more simply as elaborate fantasies[27]—still require a complementary set of data: in literary terms, those which are connected with *atmosphere* and, in the language of the Chicago school of psychoanalysis, with phases of self development.

In *Saint Julian*, the vagueness or loss of references to time and place in the key hunting scenes;

the insecure sense of self which accompanies them;

the lack of definite object-directedness and purposiveness in all the killings;

the lack of differentiation between animals and human beings in relation to the parents (father, fox, and stag; mother, dove, bird, and stork) and in relation to Julian himself (stag's curse; animals of the second hunt);

the erotization of the animals of the second hunt, ending in the rotting partridge;

the erotization of Julian's relation to the rotting leper, ending in fusion;

the fusion with the father in the fountain scene and the general merging of roles in the final episode;

the lack of sexual maturity of the parents (I, 10); their infantile dependence on Julian, as illustrated by the central scene;

the same asexual quality in the relationship between Julian and his slightly plump, motherly wife (II, 12);

Julian's general inability to relate to anyone;

27. The concept of "defense" is usually used to imply defense against conflicts rather than a habitual mode of processing events. Defense mechanisms are much more probably "plans" *sometimes* used for defensive purposes. Since all fantasies need not deal with conflicts and defenses, it is preferable to avoid the term (see a more detailed discussion in my "Psychologie et littérature").

Julian's parents' inability to relate to each other or to Julian in an empathic way (secrets; double standards concerning aggression and religion) as well as their overprotectiveness (*three nurses, I, 21*) and obsession with order (see Chapter 3);

these and other motifs in the text create an atmosphere consonant with what we earlier called aspects of the separation-individuation phase, according to Margaret Mahler (Chapter 3, last section), or which, with Kohut, one could term deficiencies in the development of the self.

Since this type of undervaluation of Oedipal and, generally, psychosexual (pregenital, preoedipal) aspects is not usually known to form a vital part of current psychoanalytic thinking, we shall quote at some length a passage from a recent paper in an official journal of the International Psychoanalytic Association. Stanley I. Greenspan writes:

> If the clinician determines . . . that the individual has not achieved [libidinal, rather than simply cognitive] object constancy and the processes that accompany it, and therefore did not clearly have a capacity for entering into triangular [Oedipal] patterns of relating, it is likely that the drive derivatives manifested are in the context of dyadic object relationship patterns. The lack of a relatively complete separation from the dyadic partner, the maintenance of symbiotic issues and various aspects of the separation-individuation process will likely emerge. The clinician would not be misled if fantasy material appeared to have phallic, oedipal content (e.g. dreams and fantasies are filled with themes of three people, competition and castration) because it would be clearly understood that the individual had not matured enough, from an object relations point of view, to be fully capable of maintaining triangular styles of relating. The drives may have developed to the point of phallic or even genital strivings, and it may appear that there are oedipal wishes, feelings and fears towards both mother and father, but it is likely that these wishes, feelings and fears are in the context of dyadic object relationships and can be viewed most usefully in the context of partially unresolved symbiotic relationship patterns.[28]

28. Stanley I. Greenspan, "The Oedipal-Pre-Oedipal Dilemma: A Reformulation according to Object Relations Theory," *International Review of Psychoanalysis*, 4 (1977), 384. There are four main trends in psychoanalysis today. Only in the still dominant ego-psychological school originating in the work of Heinz Hartmann and David Rapaport does the Oedipus complex have the importance traditionally assumed to be the essence of psychoanalysis. The other

It is conceivable, then, that *Saint Julian* is not so much about the Oedipus complex—that is, about triangular conflicts—as about types of self representation and development. Heinz Kohut and the Chicago school of psychoanalysis, from the point of view of the psychology of the self, in this instance can be seen as dealing with data in a way compatible with those of Mahler's more traditional ego-psychological separation-individuation concept and Greenspan's object-relation point of view of the English school. They would see Julian's acts of destructive rage not as jealousy and hatred of the parents (usually deflected onto animals) and as a symbolic repetition of infantile Oedipal conflicts, but as *narcissistic* rage, that is, as rage due to a feeling of injury to the self, to a sense of loss or of fragmentation of one's world.[29] From this standpoint one could make a good case for the rebuilding of the self image after the murders. Julian begins with utter rejection of his self (body-self and mind-self), continues through reckless enterprises that are obvious forms of attempted suicide, and ends at last with a settling down, which, though

---

three schools are the English object-relations movement closely associated with the works of Melanie Klein; the Chicago school of self psychology whose leader is Heinz Kohut; and the isolated research of those who like Peterfreund (*Information, Systems, and Psychoanalysis*) or Alan Rosenblatt and James Thickstun (*Modern Psychoanalytic Concepts in a General Psychology* [*Psychological Issues*, monograph 42-43, 1977) are attempting to reformulate psychoanalysis in epistemologically acceptable terms.

French psychoanalysis, taken as a whole, reflects the first three trends—although psychoanalytic *critics*, today, are predominantly Lacanian. The Lacanian and structuralist trends within French psychoanalysis share some of the epistemological concerns of the fourth trend mentioned above. For instance, Jacques Lacan's early interest (1954–1955) in artificial intelligence and information processing (*Le Séminaire, Livre II* [Paris, 1978]) and his views on semiosis make his work surprisingly close not only to the best in semiotics but also to the cognitive psychology paradigm (see Peter H. Lindsay and Donald A. Norman, *Human Information Processing* [New York, 1977]). His impact on psychoanalytic thought and literary criticism in France has been due to his unrelenting questioning of the referential theory of meaning. As a consequence, his contributions to psychoanalysis *per se* are meager, whereas his insistence on epistemological issues has influenced recent French thought in a way comparable to Jacques Derrida's directly philosophical writings. See Lacan in section 8 and Ragland-Sullivan in section 12 of Reader's Guide.

29. See, for instance, Kohut's *The Restoration of the Self*, pp. 115–118. On the relation of the Oedipus complex to self psychology, see his chapters 4 and 5, "The Bipolar Self" and "The Oedipus Complex and the Psychology of the Self."

self-denying and self-deprecating, is at least a minimal, non-reckless form of sustained esteem of his own person. As mentioned in Chapter 3, he can now show *control* in the face of "wondrous" events,[30] instead of his previous bouts of overwhelming undifferentiated rage accompanied by a loss of sense of self which was sexualized at least as early as the killing of the pigeon.

But what of the reader? In this case the differences do not cut along the male-female line; they fit, rather, aspects of self development. An ideal reader would not be, as one might suppose, a person whose development closely paralleled Julian's, for such a person would, very probably, suffer unbearable anxiety in reading the story, or would defend against anxiety by not freely analogizing to it and recreating it in his or her own mental terms: that is, by reading it merely "cognitively" rather than also "affectively" (according to secondary, reality-oriented rather than primary, self-oriented modes of mentation). The ideal reader would probably be a person who, from the point of view of self psychology, has not established overly firm self boundaries but has relatively strong Oedipal fantasies. He or she would be very different from Julian himself. Further, social and cultural factors would also come into play, as would the immediate reasons which brought one to read the story.[31]

Finally, to call Julian a Catholic Oedipus, an "Oedipus *sanctus*," implies that apart from the Oedipal psychology one must consider the psychology of mysticism, which, as is known from numerous accounts, is directly related to fantasies of merging with the deity and with flying fantasies or with what Freud and Romain Rolland called the oceanic feeling, in which the self

30. *Wondrous* events occur at three turning points of the story (though not at the parricide): when Julian first talks ("wondrous wounds," I, 26); when he meets the stag ("wondrous animal," I, 67); and when he meets the leper (the boat sinks down "wondrously," III, 32).

31. Colin Martindale sums up the reader's role in the following terms: "What is attended to and remembered is a function not only of the text and of universal schemata but also, in large part, of the particular receiver's unique cognitive and motivational traits, his current concerns, and his ongoing flow of thought ("Preface: Psychological Contributions to Poetics," *Poetics*, 7 [1978], p. 130). For an introduction to contemporary views on the affective component of cognition, see Carroll E. Izard's *Human Emotions* (New York, 1977).

expands and fuses with the universe.[32] Understood in this manner, the erethism of the last episode and the image of the "flood" are closer to the general theme of a tale in which abundance and growth (as in I, 11, or in the first hunt) are diffuse experiences more than object-directed ones.

The questions raised in this section cannot be solved within the limits of this book. Inasmuch as they imply a heavy, direct use of psychoanalytic theory, discussion of alternative formulations, justification of hypotheses that have not yet been fully worked out by psychoanalysts, it was felt that it would not be in keeping with our role as psycho*critics* to insist on these aspects while other equally important ones were still unexplored.

To summarize briefly:

(a) From the standpoint of a traditional reading in terms of Julian's character, a diagnosis of Oedipally based psychology would be wrong. Julian's personality only *seems* Oedipal.[33]

(b) But from the standpoint of a male reader's reading strategy, it is likely that positive (especially Parts I and II) and negative (Part III) Oedipal features would be construed from the text and form the basis of a reading.

(c) From the viewpoint of male or female readers whose personalities are in tune with issues of separation-individuation and the definition of the self in terms of self-objects, the Oedipal aspects would not be processed in much detail, whereas elements such as the boundlessness of the parricidal rage would be empathically understood and the story would be assimilated in this mode.

32. In *Civilization and Its Discontents,* Freud stresses "the part played by the oceanic feeling, which might seek something like the restoration of limitless narcissism." He adds that the oceanic feeling becomes connected with religion and that "the 'oneness with the universe' which constitutes its ideational content sounds like a first attempt at a religious consolation" (XXI, 72). Although Freud's formulation would require considerable elaboration in view of the current theory of narcissism (Paul Ornstein, "On Narcissism: Beyond the Introduction," *Annual of Psychoanalysis,* 2 [1974], 127–149), its essentials seem, in this case, to be still acceptable.

33. Of at least anecdotal interest is the fact that Marvin Margolis, in his study of a case that almost leads to matricide ("Preliminary Report of a Case of Consummated Mother-Son Incest," *Annual of Psychoanalysis,* 5 [1977], 267–293), finds that the son's pathology is *not* Oedipal. One is reminded of the fact that the Oedipus *complex* is about unconscious fantasies, not acts.

(d) Though readers will be able cognitively to understand items a–c, their own affective and cognitive understanding and enjoyment will not usually involve the processing of *all three* categories; moreover

(e) their knowledge of negative Oedipal aspects of Flaubert's biography, even if they can be related to the final scene, will play only a minor role in their enjoyment of the text—unless these readers are morally outraged or pleased by those aspects.

(f) Finally, intertextual readings will perhaps be pleasing but they will belong to a *logically* different set from the processes involved in a reading of *Saint Julian;* and psychologically, they are not likely to play much of a role until the texts have been studied countless times—a situation rarely achieved except by critics.

Interpreting Literature

Reading *Saint Julien* in the French—along with the new English translation which we provide—is perhaps one of the best ways of reading in the literary mode. Flaubert's attention to detail can be matched only with difficulty by the reader; yet, as the remarks in "Poetics and Translation" suggest, treating this short story as if it were the bilingual edition of a poem enables one to compare, enjoy, and understand.

Our two common goals were to make some of those comparisons—the micro- and macronetworks of meanings— explicit and to relate them to psychological frameworks. For structures, however interesting or significant in isolation, ought to be related to our minds' modes of functioning and to what intimate motivations affect us, lest we be left with the puzzling look of Julian's dead parents (II, 79): they seem happy, but why? Our aim, then, was never to lose sight of this psychocritical *why?*

Berg insisted on the associations between Julian, his father, the stag, and the leper by paying close attention to the wording of the text and to the parallels between the two main hunting episodes. He thus provided us with an organizing principle in our study of the problems of fantasy, reality, and the odd mimetic status of Julian.

Moskos saw those same events as being played on a stage of dreams, which provides a psychologically appropriate setting for the kind of spiritual development toward adult individuation he describes. As does Grimaud, he discusses society's violence, its relation to the family unit, and its relation to Julian himself.

Grimaud further stresses the surprisingly subdued affective perspective of the narrator and some of the difficulties involved in interpreting *Saint Julian* within what seems to be a manifestly Oedipal framework.

Sartre takes the Oedipal interpretation for granted, but this is due to his vantage point: he is concerned with the psychology of creation and wants to explain the process leading from Flaubert's life experiences to Julian's.

The close reading of *Saint Julian* leads each critic to different psychological conclusions. Berg and Grimaud stress the importance of the oral merger, the former as a disturbing regression that might explain the need for the narrator's final intervention, the latter as part of a recurrent pattern in the story which can be shared by all readers because of its link to continuing basic experiences that are particularly clear in the early development of the self. Moskos sees the merger as an allegorical representation of the processes involved in reaching an adult identity. Sartre relates Julian's "passive activity" to his desire for suicide (an oral wish according to psychoanalysts), to Flaubert's own life, and also to the attending distortions in the depiction of medieval society and religion.

Thus each chapter emphasizes the importance of non-Oedipal as well as Oedipal elements in the *Saint Julian* story. As we noted, Julian is "Oedipus *sanctus*," so it is not surprising that the oral elements throughout the narrative will be associated with religion. This conclusion is further confirmed by a study of the narrative structures themselves. Michael Rengstorf, a semiotician, and Colin Martindale, a psychologist, both suggest, through their narrative analyses, that *Saint Julian* is clearly organized as a saint's story.[34] Martindale shows—through a

---

34. The research reported here is unpublished. Martindale's work was carried out at my request. For details on his methods see his *Romantic Progression: The Psychology of Literary History* (New York, 1975); Rengstorf's dissertation, "Les 'Trois contes' de Flaubert," has not been published.

computer-assisted study of the relative proportion of primary-process to secondary-process words in each of the forty-eight two-hundred-word segments of *Saint Julian*—that the story has a double inverted U pattern, which he had previously described as typical of narratives of salvation like Dante's *Divine Comedy*. Rengstorf, in his Greimasian study, goes beyond an analysis of recurrent semiotic patterns as developed by Dina Sherzer or, here, by Berg, in order to show the striking regularity of the plot itself:

> Julian has a home;
> He leaves it temporarily;
> There is a peripetia;
> He then leaves his home permanently;
> He is homeless (he wanders);
> He settles down in a new home.

This narrative program is carried out twice completely: first in the parental castle, then in the mother-in-law's palace. The third home is Julian's first home of his very own (he even builds it himself, III, 17). He leaves it temporarily to cross the river during the storm and experiences the sudden swooning ecstasy (peripetia) which leads to his final departure from his hut. The narrator's naming of the leper as Our Lord Jesus (III, 57) and his reference in the coda (last paragraph) to Julian's story being visible on his hometown church window confirm the appropriateness of the tale's title, *Saint* Julian the hospitaler. The twice-repeated six-part sequence of events is broken, and there is now no wandering—suggesting that we should supply the last term of the sequence but that, this time, Julian is settled permanently.

Rengstorf's and Martindale's work point to psychological aspects of the reading process, and of literary enjoyment, which we hardly touched upon: how does one construct a narrative as one reads? Why do stories about redemption have the patterning of primary processing discussed by Martindale? Do the structures discussed by Rengstorf correspond to a conscious or unconscious process of plot understanding? Do all recurrent patterns function in similar ways in providing literary pleasure?

Because of the multiplicity of perspectives from which one might approach any single text, even our psychological focus reveals itself to be incomplete: but readers interested in further modes of psychoanalytic criticism will find numerous examples in our "Reader's Guide to Psychoanalysis."[35]

However, since the hermeneutic act is essentially an infinite one, it is perhaps a relief to realize that at least one aspect of literary pleasure does not come so much from the interpretations one arrives at as from the *process* of interpretation itself. In short, a psychological reading of *Saint Julian*, as of any mental product, implies a thematic working-through in which reclassification is an experience in itself, a self-oriented learning process corresponding to modes of thought constantly operational in our lives but to which we rarely give pride of place in our daily, reality-oriented activities. The role of such processes in literature is what constitutes art's uniqueness, as implied by Pinchas Noy's words, even though his stress is on the impact of primary processes:

> In prevailing theory, the primary processes are regarded as more primitive than the secondary ones. This seems like a very one-sided judgement. One can say that operating with word presentations, using abstract concepts, or considering the time factor is a more developed function than operating without them is regarded to be. But this is a "superiority" only if the function is evaluated from the viewpoint of reality. If the viewpoint is shifted to the self and its needs, then the contrary is true: the ability to represent a full experience, including all the feelings and ideas involved, is a higher achievement than merely operating with abstract concepts and words, and the ability to transcend time limits and organize past experiences with present ones is a higher ability than being confined to the limitations of time and space.[36]

35. For an introduction to narrative studies see chapter 2 of Mary-Louise Pratt's *Toward a Speech-Act Theory of Literary Discourse* (Bloomington, Ind., 1977) and Robert de Beaugrande and Benjamin Colby's "Narrative Models of Action and Interaction," *Cognitive Science*, 3 (1979), 43–66. There have been several dissertations on Flaubert in recent years, including psychoanalytically oriented studies of the *Three Tales*.

36. Pinchas Noy, "A Revision of the Psychoanalytic Theory of the Primary Process," *International Journal of Psychoanalysis*, 50 (1969), 176.

The impact of art lies in its power to transmit the reality- *and* self-oriented information corresponding to the primary-mode structures of basic experiences. For Noy the experience of art is between free play or fantasizing and mathematics or geometry: the former is without a specific formal-esthetic structure while the latter is without content but with a structure and organization. For better or for worse, reading in the esthetic mode partakes of both:

> The value of any work of art does not depend exclusively on either the specific meaning embedded in it or on its formal structure. It depends on the specific meaning presented in a specific structural vessel. The most sublime idea is far from being art as long as it remains without the specific structure in which it is presented. The ideational value of a work of art may be indisputable (perhaps superior material for a philosophical essay), but as an idea per se it has not yet anything to do with art. To the same extent, every artistic gratification is an integrated gratification. It is experienced when certain psychic contents are challenged and gratified by corresponding meanings, and when the mental act of perceiving, transforming, and understanding these meanings is being felt as pleasurable.[37]

The pleasures of the literary text are in those particular modes of access to particular meanings; psychocriticism explicates them; *Saint Julian* exemplifies them.

37. Pinchas Noy, "A Theory of Art and Esthetic Experience," *Psychoanalytic Review*, 55 (1968), 643. See also "About Art and Artistic Talent," *International Journal of Psychoanalysis*, 53 (1972), 243–249.

PART TWO

The Legend of Saint Julian
the Hospitaler

Translator's Note

La Légende de Saint Julien l'Hospitalier was first published in *Le Bien Public* from 19 to 22 April 1877. A few days later—along with *Un coeur simple* and *Hérodias*—it appeared as the central story in *Trois contes*, published in Paris by G. Charpentier.

With one exception (in I, 5; see Chapter 3, note 8), our text of *The Legend of Saint Julian the Hospitaler* follows the fifth printing of the original edition, the last one published before Flaubert's death in 1880.

The Legend of Saint Julian the Hospitaler

BY GUSTAVE FLAUBERT

Translated by Michel Grimaud

••

I

[1]   Julian's father and mother dwelt in a castle, in the midst of the woods, on the slope of a hill.

[2]   The four towers at the corners had pointed roofs covered with lead scales, and the base of the walls rested upon the blocks of rock, which dropped abruptly to the bottom of the moat.

[3]   The stones of the courtyard were as smooth as the paving in a church. Long spouts, representing dragons with yawning jaws, spewed rain water toward the cistern; and on the windowsills, at every story, in a painted earthenware pot, a basil or a heliotrope bloomed.

[4]   A second enclosure, made with stakes, included first a fruit orchard, next a garden with figures wrought in flowers, then a vine-covered arbor for taking the air, and a game of mall for the entertainment of the pages. On the other side were the kennels, the stables, the bakery, the winepress, and the barns. A pasture of green grass spread all around, itself enclosed by a thick thorn hedge.

[5]   Life had been peaceful for so long that the portcullis could not be lowered anymore; the ditches were filled with grass; swallows built their nests in the cracks of the battlements; and the archer, who all day long strolled on the curtain, as soon as the sun shone too bright withdrew to the watchtower, and fell asleep like a monk.

[6]   Inside, the ironwork everywhere gleamed; arras hangings in the rooms kept out the cold; and the armoires overflowed with linen, the casks of wine were piled up in the cellars, the oak chests groaned under the weight of the bags of money.

[7]   In the armory could be seen, between banners and heads of wild beasts, weapons of all ages and of all nations, from the slings of the Amalekites and the javelins of the Garamantes to the broadswords of the Saracens and the coats of mail of the Normans.

[8]   The master spit in the kitchen could turn an ox, the chapel was as gorgeous as a king's oratory. There was even, in a secluded part, a Roman sweat room; but the good lord refrained from using it, deeming it to be a heathenish practice.

[9]   Always wrapped in a foxskin cape, he strolled about his estate, rendered justice among his vassals, quieted his neighbors' quarrels. During winter, he stared at the snowflakes falling, or had stories read to him. As soon as the fine weather came, he would ride away on his mule along narrow paths, beside greening fields of grain, and talk with the peasants, giving them advice. After many adventures he had taken himself a wife of high lineage.

[10]   She was very white, a trifle haughty and earnest. The horns of her headdress brushed the tops of the doors; the train of her cloth gown trailed three paces behind her. Her household was ruled like the inside of a monastery; every morning she assigned work to her maids, watched over the preserves and unguents, spun at her distaff, or embroidered altar cloths. Through her fervent prayers to God, a son came unto her.

[11]   So, there was great rejoicing, and a feast which lasted three days and four nights, under bright torchlight, to the sound of harps, over floors strewn with branches. The rarest spices were eaten, with hens as big as sheep; as entertainment, a dwarf popped out of a pie; and when the bowls were too few, for the

crowd kept swelling, people had to drink out of hunting horns and helmets.

[12]   The new mother was not present at the festivities. She kept to her bed, quietly. One evening, she awoke, and she noticed, under a moonbeam that crept through the window, a kind of moving shadow. It was an old man clad in sackcloth, with a rosary dangling at his side, a scrip on his shoulder, to all appearances a hermit. He approached the foot of her bed and said to her, without opening his lips:

[13]   —"Rejoice, O mother! thy son shall be a saint!"

[14]   She was about to cry out; but, gliding along the moonray, he rose slowly through the air, then disappeared. The singing at the banquet rang out louder. She heard the angels' voices; and her head sank back onto the pillow, which was crowned by a martyr's bone framed in garnets.

[15]   The following day, all the servants questioned declared that they had seen no hermit. Whether dream or fact, this must be a message from heaven; but she was careful not to speak of it, lest she be accused of pride.

[16]   The guests departed at daybreak; and Julian's father stood outside the castle gate, where he had just bidden farewell to the last one, when a beggar suddenly rose up before him, in the fog. He was a Gypsy with braided beard, with silver bracelets on both arms and burning eyes. He stammered in an inspired manner these incoherent words:

[17]   —"Ah! Ah! thy son! . . . much blood! . . . much glory! . . . ever fortunate! an emperor's family."

[18]   And, stooping to pick up his alms, he disappeared in the grass, vanished.

[19]   The good lord of the manor looked to the right and to the left, called out with all his strength. No one! The wind howled, the morning mists were lifting.

[20]   He attributed the vision to a head weary from too little sleep. "If I mention this, people will laugh at me," he thought. Still, the splendors meant for his son bedazzled him, although the promise was not clear, and he even doubted having heard it.

[21]   The couple kept their secret from each other. But both cherished the child with equal love; and since they respected him as marked by God, they showed boundless regard for his

person. His cradle was lined with the softest down; a lamp in the shape of a dove burned over it, continually; three nurses rocked him; and securely wrapped in his swaddling clothes, with his pink cheeks and blue eyes, with his brocaded cloak and his pearl-laden cap, he looked like a little Jesus. He cut all his teeth without even a whimper.

[22]   When he turned seven, his mother taught him to sing. To make him brave, his father lifted him onto a big horse. The child smiled with delight, and soon became familiar with everything pertaining to chargers.

[23]   An old and very learned monk taught him the Holy Scriptures, Arabic numerals, Latin letters, and how to paint daintily on vellum. They worked together, in the very top of a tower, away from the noise.

[24]   When the lesson was over, they would go down into the garden where, strolling slowly, they studied the flowers.

[25]   Sometimes one could see, filing through the valley below, a train of pack animals, led by a pedestrian, in Oriental garb. The lord of the manor, recognizing him as a merchant, would dispatch a servant after him. The foreigner, gaining confidence, would change direction; and once ushered into the castle hall, would take out of his trunks pieces of velvet and silk, jewelry, spices, unwonted items of unknown use; in due time the good man took leave, with a handsome profit, having suffered no violence. At other times, a band of pilgrims would knock at the door. Their wet garments steamed in front of the hearth; and after they were well fed, they related their journeys: the roving vessels on the foamy seas, their travels on foot across burning sands, the ferocity of the pagans, the caves of Syria, the Manger and the Sepulcher. Then they gave shells from their cloaks to the young lord.

[26]   Often the lord of the manor feasted his old brothers-at-arms. While drinking, they recalled their battles, the storming of fortresses with the beating war machines and the wondrous wounds. Julian, listening to them, would cry out; then his father had no doubt that some day he would be a conqueror. But in the evening, after the Angelus, as he passed among the bowing paupers, he would dip into his purse with such modesty and with such a look of nobility, that his mother fully expected him to become an archbishop.

[27]   His seat in the chapel was next to his parents; and, no matter how long the services lasted, he remained kneeling on his prayer stool, his cap on the floor and his hands folded.

[28]   One day, during mass, he raised his head, and noticed a little white mouse scurrying out of a hole, in the wall. It trotted on the first altar step, and after two or three gambols right and left, ran back in the same direction. On the following Sunday, the idea of seeing the mouse again worried him. It returned; and every Sunday, he would watch for it, was annoyed by it, felt hatred toward it, and resolved to do away with it.

[29]   So, having closed the door, and scattered some cake crumbs on the steps, he stationed himself in front of the hole, with a stick in his hand.

[30]   After a very long while a pink snout appeared, then the whole mouse. He struck lightly, and stood stunned before this little body which no longer moved. A drop of blood stained the flagstone. He wiped it away with much haste using his sleeve, threw the mouse out, and said not a word about it to anyone.

[31]   All kinds of small birds pecked at the seeds in the garden. It occurred to him to put some peas into a hollow reed. Whenever he heard chirping in a tree, he would approach softly, then lift the tube, swell his cheeks; and the little creatures rained down on his shoulders in such abundance that he could not help but laugh, delighted with his mischief.

[32]   One morning, as he came back by way of the curtain, he noticed on top of the ramparts a large pigeon preening itself in the sun. Julian paused to gaze at it; the wall being cracked where he stood, his fingers happened upon a loose stone. He swung his arm, and the stone squarely hit the bird which fell straight into the ditch.

[33]   He rushed down toward it, tearing himself on the brambles, ferreting on all sides, nimbler than a young dog.

[34]   The pigeon, its wings broken, throbbing, hung in the branches of a privet.

[35]   Its protracted life irritated the child. He began to strangle it; and the convulsions of the bird made his heart pound, filled his senses with a wild and tumultuous delight. With the final stiffening, he felt faint.

[36]   That evening, during supper, his father announced that at his age one must learn venery; and he fetched an old writing

book which contained, in question and answer form, the whole pastime of hunting. In it, a master showed his pupil the art of training dogs and taming falcons, of laying traps, how to recognize the stag by its droppings, the fox by its footprints, the wolf by its claw marks, the right way of discovering their tracks, how to start them, where their lairs are usually found, what winds are the most favorable, with a listing of cries and the rules of the quarry.

[37]   When Julian was able to recite all this by heart, his father put together a pack of hounds for him.

[38]   First there were twenty-four Barbary greyhounds, speedier than gazelles, but liable to get out of temper; then seventeen couples of Breton dogs, flecked with white on a russet background, of faith unmovable, broadchested and loud-baying. For wild-boar hunting and perilous doublings, there were forty boarhounds, hairy as bears. Mastiffs of Tartary, almost as high as asses, flame-colored, with broad backs and straight legs, were intended for the pursuit of wild bulls. The black coats of the spaniels shone like satin; the yelps of the setters equaled the singing of the beagles. In a separate enclosure, tossing their chains and rolling their eyes, growled eight bloodhounds, formidable beasts who fly at horsemen's bellies and have no fear of lions.

[39]   They all ate wheat bread, drank out of stone troughs, and bore high-sounding names.

[40]   The Falconry, perhaps, surpassed the pack; the good lord, spending money unstintingly, had secured Caucasian hawks, Babylonian sakers, German gerfalcons, and pilgrim falcons, captured on cliffs, bordering the cold seas, in far-off lands. They were housed in a thatched shed and chained in order of size to the perch, with a strip of turf in front of them, upon which from time to time they were placed to let them exercise.

[41]   Bag nets, baits, traps, all manner of snares, were prepared.

[42]   Often pointers were taken out into the countryside, and they would set almost immediately. Then whippers-in, taking one step at a time, cautiously spread over their motionless bodies a huge net. At a command they barked; quail took wing; and the neighborhood ladies invited along with their husbands, the children, the handmaids would all pounce, and capture them with ease.

43]   At other times, to start hares, a drum was used; foxes fell into pits, or a trap, as it sprang, would catch a wolf by the paw.

44]   But Julian scorned such convenient contrivances; he preferred hunting far from the crowd, with his horse and his falcon. It was almost always a large, snow-white Scythian tartar. Its leather hood was crowned with a plume, golden bells shivered at its blue feet; and it perched firmly on its master's arm while the horse galloped, and the plains rolled by. Julian, undoing its tether, suddenly let it go; the bold bird would shoot straight up into the air like an arrow; and one could see two unequal spots circle around, unite, then disappear in the blue heights. The falcon would soon be back, tearing up some bird, and perched anew on its master's gauntlet, with both wings trembling.

45]   Julian flew in this fashion the heron, the kite, the crow, and the hawk.

46]   He loved to sound his horn and follow his dogs along the hillsides, over the streams, into the woods; and when the stag began to moan under the bites, he killed it deftly, then relished the fury of the mastiffs as they gulped it down, cut into pieces on its reeking hide.

47]   On foggy days, he would go deep into a marsh to watch for geese, otters, and wild ducks.

48]   At daybreak, three equerries waited for him at the foot of the steps; and the old monk, leaning out of his high window, vainly beckoned him to return, Julian would not look back. He heeded neither the broiling sun, the rain, nor the storm, drank spring water out of his hands, munched on crab apples as he trotted along, if he was tired lay down under an oak; and he would come home in the dark of the night, covered with blood and mud, with thorns in his hair and smelling of wild beasts. He grew to be like them. Whenever his mother held him against her, he accepted her embrace coldly, as if dreaming of profound things.

49]   He stabbed bears to death, killed bulls with a hatchet, wild boars with a spear; and once, with nothing left but a stick, even defended himself against wolves which were gnawing corpses at the foot of a gibbet.

50]   One winter morning, he set out before daybreak, well equipped, with a crossbow on his shoulder and a quiver of arrows in the saddlebag.

[51]   His Danish jennet, with two basset hounds close behind, under its even tread made the ground ring. Icicles clung to his cloak, a violent breeze was blowing. The horizon cleared on one side; and in the white light of dawn, he noticed rabbits hopping near their burrows. The two bassets, instantly, were upon them; and, at random, quickly, broke their backs.

[52]   Soon, he came to a wood. On the end of a branch, a grouse numb with cold was asleep with its head under its wing. Julian, with a sweep of the sword, cut off both its feet, and without picking it up rode on.

[53]   Three hours later, he found himself on the tip of a mountain so high that the sky seemed almost black. In front of him, a long, wall-like rock hung down, over a precipice; and at the far end, two wild goats stood gazing into the abyss. Having none of his arrows (for he had left his horse behind), he reckoned he would climb down to where they stood; half bending, with bare feet, he at last reached the first male goat, and thrust a dagger below its ribs. The second one, in its terror, sprang into the void. Julian threw himself forward to strike it, his right foot slipped and he fell over the corpse of the other goat, face downward above the abyss and both arms spread out.

[54]   Having come back down to the plain, he followed a line of willows along a river. Low-flying cranes, from time to time passed over his head. Julian struck them down with his whip, and never missed one.

[55]   Meanwhile the milder air had melted the hoarfrost away, patches of haze were floating, and the sun came out. He could see glistening far away a frigid lake, which looked like lead. At the center of the lake, there was an animal that Julian did not know, a black-nosed beaver. Despite the distance, an arrow hit it; and he was chagrined that he could not take the skin with him.

[56]   Next he entered an avenue of tall trees, the tops of which seemed to form a triumphal arch, at the edge of a forest. A roe deer sprang out of a thicket, a fallow deer appeared at a cross-roads, a badger crawled out of a hole, a peacock on the grass spread its tail;—and once he had slain them all, other roe deer came forth, other fallow deer, other badgers, other peacocks,

and blackbirds, jays, polecats, foxes, porcupines, lynxes, a host of beasts, with every step more numerous. They circled around him, trembling, with a meek and beseeching look in their eyes. But Julian did not tire of killing, in turn stretching his crossbow, drawing his sword, thrusting with his knife, and thought of nothing, remembered naught. He was hunting in some indeterminate land, for an indefinite time, solely because of his very existence, everything fulfilling itself with the ease which one experiences in dreams. An extraordinary sight stopped him. Stags filled a valley shaped like an arena; and huddling together, they were warming one another with their breaths which could be seen steaming in the fog.

[57]   The prospect of so great a carnage, for a few minutes, made him choke with pleasure. Then he dismounted, rolled up his sleeves, and began shooting.

[58]   With the whistling of the first arrow, all the stags turned their heads simultaneously. Gaps appeared in their mass; plaintive voices could be heard, and a great agitation seized the herd.

[59]   The rim of the valley was too high to climb. They leaped around the enclosure, trying to escape. Julian aimed, shot; and the arrows fell like shafts of rain in a storm. Maddened with terror the stags fought, were rearing, clambering over one another; and their bodies with their interlocked antlers formed a mound, which tumbled down, as it moved.

[60]   Finally they expired, lying on the sand, their nostrils frothing, bowels protruding, and the heaving of their bellies gradually subsiding. Then all was still.

[61]   Night was about to fall; and behind the wood, between the branches, the sky was red like a sheet of blood.

[62]   Julian leaned back against a tree. Wide-eyed, he gazed at the magnitude of the slaughter, not understanding how he might have done it.

[63]   On the opposite side of the valley, on the outskirts of the forest, he noticed a stag, a doe, and her fawn.

[64]   The stag, which was black and of monstrous size, bore sixteen points with a white beard. The doe, blond like dead leaves, browsed upon the grass; and the spotted fawn, without hindering her progress, sucked at her dug.

[65]   The crossbow again twanged. The fawn, immediately, was killed. Then its mother, looking up at the sky, uttered a deep,

rending, human wail. Julian exasperated, with a shot right in the breast, laid her down on the ground.

[66]   The great stag had seen him, made a leap. Julian aimed his last arrow at him. It hit his brow, and remained stuck there.

[67]   The great stag did not appear to feel it; striding over the dead bodies, he was coming nearer and nearer, was about to charge, rip him open; and Julian recoiled with unspeakable terror. The wondrous animal halted; and with eyes aflame, solemn like a patriarch and like a justicer, while a bell in the distance tolled, he repeated three times:

[68]   —"Accursed! accursed! accursed! One day, ferocious heart, thou shalt murder thy father and thy mother!"

[69]   He sank to his knees, gently closed his eyelids, and died.

[70]   Julian was stunned, then overcome with a sudden weariness; and a disgust, an immense sadness assailed him. Holding his brow between his two hands, he wept for a long time.

[71]   His horse was lost; his dogs had forsaken him; the solitude all about him seemed fraught with ill-defined perils. Then, impelled by terror, he started running across the countryside, chose a path at random, and found himself almost immediately at the gates of the castle.

[72]   That night, he could not sleep. By the flicker of the hanging lamp, he pictured again and again the great black stag. Its prediction haunted him; he struggled against it. "No! no! no! I cannot murder them!" next, he would reflect: "Still, supposing I wanted to?..." and he feared that the Devil might instill the urge in him.

[73]   For three months, his mother in anguish prayed at his bedside, and his father, moaning, continually paced the halls. He summoned the most celebrated leeches, who prescribed much medicine. Julian's illness, they said, was due to some baleful wind, or to a desire for love. But the young man answered all their questions by shaking his head.

[74]   His strength returned; and he was taken on strolls in the courtyard, the old monk and the good lord each holding him up on one side.

[75]   After he had completely recovered, he stubbornly refused to hunt.

[76]   His father, hoping to cheer him, made him a gift of a large Saracen sword.

[77]   It was high on a pillar, as part of a panoply. To reach it, a ladder had to be brought. Julian climbed up. The sword being too heavy slipped from his grasp, and as it fell came so close to the good lord that his cloak was torn; Julian imagined he had killed his father, and fainted.

[78]   Thereafter, he was fearful of weaponry. The sight of a bare blade made him turn pale. This weakness caused great sorrow to his family.

[79]   In the end the old monk ordered him, in the name of God, of honor, and of forebears, to renew his gentlemanly pursuits.

[80]   The equerries, every day, enjoyed javelin practice. Julian readily excelled. He could send his into the neck of a bottle, break the teeth of a weather vane, hit doornails at a hundred paces.

[81]   One summer evening, at the hour when haze lends an unclear cast to objects, while under the arbor in the garden, he saw at its far end two white wings fluttering about the espalier. He did not doubt but that it was a stork; and he threw his javelin.

[82]   A rending scream rang out.

[83]   It was his mother, whose cap and long streamers remained nailed to the wall.

[84]   Julian fled from the castle, and was seen no more.

II

[1]   He joined a troop of adventurers who were passing by.

[2]   He experienced hunger, thirst, fevers, and vermin. He grew accustomed to the din of melees, to the sight of dying men. The wind tanned his skin. His limbs became hardened through contact with armors; and as he was very strong, brave, temperate, judicious, he easily obtained command of a company.

[3]   At the outset of battles, he would urge his soldiers on with a great flourish of his sword. With a knotted rope, he climbed citadel walls, at night, rocked by the storm, while the sparks of wildfire clung to his cuirass, and the boiling tar and molten lead poured from the battlements. A stone often hit, shattering his shield. Bridges overladen with men gave way under him. By swinging his mace, he got rid of fourteen horsemen. In the lists, he threw all those who came forward. More than a score of times, he was given up for dead.

[4]   Thanks to divine favor, he always escaped; for he protected the clergy, orphans, widows, and foremost the aged. Whenever he saw an aged person walking ahead of him, he would call out to know his face, as if he had feared to kill him by mistake.

[5]   Fugitive slaves, rebel peasants, penniless bastards, all kinds of bold men rallied to his banner, and he put together his own army.

[6]   It grew. He became famous. He was in demand.

[7]   He gave assistance in turn to the Dauphin of France and the king of England, the templars of Jerusalem, the surena of the Parths, the negus of Abyssinia, and the emperor of Calicut. He fought against Scandinavians covered with fish scales, against Negroes bearing bucklers of hippopotamus hide and mounted on red asses, gold-skinned Indians who, above their diadems, wielded great swords brighter than mirrors. He defeated the Troglodytes and the Anthropophagi. He traveled through regions so torrid that under the sun's heat hair burst into flames like pitch; and through others so icy, that arms, separating from the body, would fall to the ground; and through countries where the fogs were such that one walked surrounded by ghosts.

[8]   Republics in disarray consulted him. When he conferred with ambassadors, he obtained unhoped-for terms. If a monarch behaved too badly, he would suddenly appear, and rebuked him. He freed nations. He rescued queens sequestered in towers. It is he, and no other, who slew the serpent of Milan and the dragon of Oberbirbach.

[9]   Now, the emperor of Occitania, having triumphed over the Spanish Moslems, had taken the sister of the Caliph of Cordova as a concubine; and he had had a daughter, whom he brought up as a Christian. But the Caliph, feigning a wish to be converted, paid him a visit, with a large escort, slaughtered his entire garrison, and thrust him into a deep dungeon, where he used him harshly, in order to exact treasures from him.

[10]   Julian ran to his aid, destroyed the heathen army, laid siege to the city, killed the Caliph, chopped off his head, and threw it like a ball over the ramparts. Next he took the emperor out of his prison, and set him back on his throne, in the presence of his entire court.

[11]   The emperor, to reward so great a service, presented him with basketfuls of money; Julian would not hear of it. Thinking that he wanted more, he offered him three quarters of his wealth; another refusal; then to share his kingdom; Julian declined; and the emperor wept with vexation, not knowing how to show his gratitude, then tapped his forehead, spoke a word in the ear of a courtier; arras curtains lifted, and a maiden appeared.

[12]   Her big dark eyes shone like two very soft lamps. A charming smile parted her lips. The ringlets of her hair were caught among the jewels of her half-opened bodice; and her translucid tunic revealed the youthfulness of her body. She was so dainty and plump, with a slender waist.

[13]   Julian was dazzled with love, all the more since he had till then led a very chaste life.

[14]   Thus, the emperor's daughter was bestowed upon him, along with a castle she had inherited from her mother; and, when the wedding was over, leave was taken, after endless courtesies were exchanged.

[15]   It was a white marble palace, built in the Moorish style, on a promontory, in an orange grove. Flower terraces sloped down to the shores of a bay, where pink shells crunched underfoot. Behind the castle, spread a fan-shaped forest. The sky unceasingly was blue, and the trees were swayed in turn by the ocean breeze and the wind from the distant mountains that closed the horizon.

[16]   The dusky rooms drew light from the inlayings on the walls. High columns, as thin as reeds, held up the arches of the cupolas, embossed to imitate stalactites in caves.

[17]   There were fountains in the halls, mosaics in the courts, festooned partitions, hundreds of architectural niceties, and everywhere such silence that one could hear the rustle of a scarf or the echo of a sigh.

[18]   Julian no longer made war. He rested, surrounded by a peaceful people; and every day, throngs came before him, kneeling and kissing his hand in Oriental fashion.

[19]   Dressed in crimson, he leaned on his elbows in the recess of a window, recalling his past hunts; and he longed to scour the desert after gazelles and ostriches, remain hidden among the

bamboos in wait for leopards, travel through forests filled with rhinoceroses, reach the most inaccessible peaks to aim better at eagles, and on icefloes fight polar bears.

[20]   Sometimes, in a dream, he fancied himself like our father Adam in the midst of Paradise, among all the beasts; by extending his arm, he made them die; or else, they filed past, by pairs, in order of size, from the elephants and the lions to the ermines and the ducks, as on the day they entered Noah's ark. From the darkness of a cave, he aimed unerring javelins at them; others would appear; there was no end to it; and he awakened, wild-eyed.

[21]   Princes, friends of his, invited him to hunt. He always demurred, believing that, by this sort of penance, he might ward off his misfortune; for he felt that murdering animals would determine the fate of his parents. But he suffered from not seeing them, and his other urge was growing unbearable.

[22]   His wife, to amuse him, sent for jugglers and dancers.

[23]   She went out with him, in an open litter, through the countryside; at other times, stretching on the side of a boat, they watched the fish disport themselves in the water, as clear as the sky. Often she tossed flowers in his face; crouching in front of his feet, she drew melodies from a three-string mandolin; then, laying her two clasped hands on his shoulder, inquired tremulously:—"What ails you so, dear lord?"

[24]   He did not reply, or burst into tears; at last, one day, he confessed his dreadful thought.

[25]   She fought against it, arguing very well: his father and his mother, probably, were dead; should he ever see them again, what accident, what purpose, could lead him to this abomination? Thus, his fear was groundless, and he must take up hunting again.

[26]   Julian smiled as he listened to her, but could not bring himself to yield to this urge.

[27]   One evening in the month of August while in their bedroom, she had just gone to bed and he was about to kneel in prayer when he heard the yelping of a fox, then light footsteps under the window; and he caught a glimpse in the dark of some animallike shadows. Temptation was too strong. He took down his quiver.

[28]   She showed surprise.

[29]   —"I am only obeying thee!" he said, "by sunrise, I shall be back."

[30]   Yet she dreaded some calamity.

[31]   He reassured her, then departed, puzzled by this change of mood.

[32]   A short time afterward, a page came to announce that two strangers, in the absence of the lord, begged to see her ladyship at once.

[33]   And presently an old man and an old woman plodded into the room, stooped, dusty, dressed in coarse linen, and each leaning on a stick.

[34]   They plucked up their courage and said that they brought Julian news of his parents.

[35]   She bent forward to hear them.

[36]   But, after glancing at each other, they asked her whether he still loved them, whether he spoke of them sometimes.

[37]   —"Oh! yes!" she said.

[38]   So they cried out:

[39]   —"Well! here we are!" and they sat down, for they were quite exhausted and spent with fatigue.

[40]   There was nothing to convince the young woman that her husband was their son.

[41]   They proved it, by describing birthmarks he had on his skin.

[42]   She jumped out of bed, called her page, and a meal was served to them.

[43]   Though they were very hungry, they could scarcely eat; and she observed obliquely the unsteadiness of their bony hands, as they grasped the goblets.

[44]   They asked hundreds of questions about Julian. She answered each one of them, but was careful not to refer to the ghastly idea that concerned them.

[45]   When he failed to return, they left their castle; and had been wandering for several years, following vague clues, without losing hope. So much money had been needed for river tolls and in the inns, for the dues of princes and the demands of highwaymen, that their purse was quite empty, and that they had to beg now. No matter, for soon they would embrace their son? They extolled his good fortune in having such a nice wife, and did not tire of staring at her and kissing her.

[46]   The luxury of the apartments surprised them greatly; and the

old man, after examining the walls, inquired why they bore the coat-of-arms of the emperor of Occitania.

[47]   She replied:

[48]   —"He is my father!"

[49]   At that he started, recalling the prediction of the Gypsy; and the old woman pondered upon the words of the Hermit. Doubtless her son's glory was but the dawn of eternal splendors; and the two of them sat in awe, under the shining candelabrum which lit up the table.

[50]   They must have been very handsome in their youth. The mother had kept all her hair, whose fine plaits, like drifts of snow, hung down along her cheeks; and the father, with his stalwart figure and his long beard, looked like a statue in a church.

[51]   Julian's wife suggested that they not wait for him. She put them herself into her bed, then closed the windows; they fell asleep. Daybreak was near and, behind the panes, the small birds were beginning to chirp.

[52]   Julian had left the grounds; and he was walking in the forest at a fast clip, enjoying the soft grass and the balmy air.

[53]   The shadows of the trees lay upon the moss. At times the moon made white patches in the glades, and he proceeded gingerly, imagining he could see a pool, or else the calm surface of the ponds blended with the color of the grass. A great stillness was everywhere; and he failed to discover any of the beasts that, only a few minutes before, were wandering round his castle.

[54]   The woods grew thicker, darkness deep. Warm gusts of wind wafted by, heavy with enervating scents. He sank into piles of dead leaves, and he leaned against an oak tree to catch his breath a little.

[55]   Suddenly, behind his back, sprang a darker mass, a wild boar. Julian had no time to seize his bow, and he grieved over it as if it were a misfortune.

[56]   Next, having left the wood, he saw a wolf running by the side of a hedge.

[57]   Julian shot an arrow at it. The wolf paused, turned its head to see him and went on. It trotted along always keeping at the same distance, paused now and then, and as soon as it was aimed at, resumed its flight.

[58] Julian traveled in this way over an endless plain, then mounds of sand, and at last found himself on a plateau overlooking a great stretch of land. Flat stones were interspersed among crumbling burial vaults. One kept stumbling over dead men's bones; here and there, worm-eaten crosses leaned mournfully. But shapes moved in the uncertain darkness of the tombs; and out came hyenas, quite frightened, panting. Their claws clattering on the stones, they approached and sniffed him with a yawn that bared their gums. He drew his sword. They scattered at once and, continuing their swift, limping gallop, disappeared in the distance with a flood of dust.

[59] One hour later, he encountered in a ravine a raging bull, with threatening horns, pawing the sand with its hoof. Julian thrust his spear under its dewlaps. It snapped, as if the beast were made of bronze; he closed his eyes, awaiting his death. When he opened them again, the bull had vanished.

[60] Then his soul collapsed with shame. Some higher power was destroying his strength; and, to find his way home, he went back into the forest.

[61] It was a tangle of vines; and he was cutting them with his sword when a weasel suddenly slid between his legs, a panther jumped over his shoulder, a snake wound up an ash.

[62] Among its leaves was a monstrous jackdaw that watched Julian; and, here and there, between the branches great numbers of large sparks appeared, as if the firmament had showered all its stars down into the forest. It was the eyes of animals, wildcats, squirrels, owls, parrots, monkeys.

[63] Julian shot away at them with his arrows; the arrows, with their feathers, lighted on the leaves like white butterflies. He hurled stones at them; the stones fell, without touching anything. He cursed himself, longed to fight, howled imprecations, choked with rage.

[64] And all the beasts he had pursued reappeared, forming a narrow circle around him. Some sat on their haunches, others stood at full height. He remained in their midst, numb with terror, incapable of the slightest movement. By a supreme effort of his will, he took a step; those that perched in trees opened their wings, those that trod the earth moved their limbs; and all came along with him.

[65] The hyenas strode in front of him, the wolf and the wild boar

in the rear. The bull, on his right, swung its head; and, on his left, the snake slithered through the grass, while the panther, arching its back, moved with muffled footfalls and long strides. He proceeded as slowly as possible so as not to irritate them; and he could see emerging from the depths of the bushes porcupines, foxes, vipers, jackals, and bears.

[66]   Julian broke into a run; they ran. The snake hissed, the foul beasts slavered. The wild boar rubbed its tusks against his heels, the wolf the inside of his hands with the bristles of its muzzle. The monkeys pinched him and made faces, the weasel rolled over his feet. A bear, with its paw, knocked off his cap; and the panther, disdainfully, dropped an arrow it was carrying in its mouth.

[67]   A kind of irony was apparent in their devious manner. As they watched him out of the corners of their eyes, they seemed to ponder a plan for revenge; and deafened by the buzzing of the insects, bruised by birds' tails, choked by their breaths, he walked with outstretched arms and closed eyes like a blind man, without even the strength to cry out "mercy!"

[68]   The crowing of a cock rang through the air. Others answered; it was day; and he recognized, beyond the orange trees, the top of his palace.

[69]   Next, at the edge of a field, he saw, three paces away, some red partridges fluttering around in the stubble. He unfastened his cloak and flung it over them like a net. When they were uncovered, he found only one, and long since dead, rotten.

[70]   This disappointment exasperated him more than all the others. His thirst for carnage was taking over again; animals lacking, he longed to massacre men.

[71]   He climbed the three terraces, burst open the door with his fist; but, at the foot of the stairs, the memory of his beloved wife soothed his heart. Doubtless, she was asleep and he would surprise her.

[72]   Having removed his sandals, he unlocked the door softly, and entered.

[73]   The lead-lined panes dimmed the pallor of dawn. Julian stumbled over some garments, on the floor; a little farther on, he knocked against a credence still laden with dishes. "Doubtless, she must have eaten," he thought; and he made his way toward

the bed, lost in the darkness at the back of the room. When he reached the edge, in order to kiss his wife, he leaned over the pillow where the two heads were resting close together. Then, he felt against his mouth the touch of a beard.

[74]   He drew back, thinking he was going mad; but he returned to the bed, and his groping fingers encountered hair, which was very long. In order to prove himself wrong, again he passed his hand slowly over the pillow. It *was* a beard, this time, and a man! a man lying with his wife!

[75]   Bursting into boundless rage, he sprang upon them thrusting his dagger; and he stamped, foamed, with howls like a wild beast. Then he stopped. The dead, pierced through their hearts, had not even budged. He listened closely to the two almost equal death rattles, and, as they grew weaker, another one, very far away, prolonged them. Faint at first, this long-drawn, plaintive voice, drew nearer, grew louder, turned cruel; and he recognized, with terror, the bellowing of the great black stag.

[76]   And as he turned round, he imagined seeing, framed in the doorway, his wife's ghost, a light in her hand.

[77]   The noise of the murder had brought her there. In one full glance, she understood everything, and fleeing in horror let the torch drop.

[78]   He picked it up.

[79]   His father and his mother lay before him, on their backs, with a hole in their breasts; and the majestic softness of their faces seemed to cherish some eternal secret. Splashes and blotches of blood spread over their white skin, on the bedclothes, on the floor, down an ivory Christ that hung in the alcove. The scarlet reflection of the window, just then hit by the sun, threw light upon the red spots, and splattered even more of them throughout the room. Julian walked toward the two corpses, telling himself, trying to believe, that this was not possible, that he had made a mistake, that there are sometimes inexplicable likenesses. At last, he bent over lightly to get a close look at the old man; and he saw, between his half-closed lids, a lifeless eye that scorched him like fire. Then he proceeded to the other side of the bed, occupied by the other body, whose white hair hid part of the face. Julian slipped his fingers beneath her plaits, raised her head;—and he gazed, holding it stiffly at arm's

length, while with his other hand he held up the torch. Drops, oozing from the mattress, fell one by one upon the floor.

[80]   At the close of day, he appeared before his wife; and, in a voice different from his own, he commanded her first not to answer him, not to come near him, not even to look at him anymore, and that she follow, under pain of damnation, every one of his orders which were irrevocable.

[81]   The funeral was to be held in accordance with the written instructions he had left, on a prayer stool, in the death chamber. He surrendered to her his castle, his vassals, all his possessions, without even withholding the clothes on his body, and his sandals, which could be found at the top of the stairs.

[82]   She had obeyed the will of God, in bringing about his crime, and must pray for his soul, since henceforth he had ceased to exist.

[83]   The dead were buried sumptuously, in the chapel of a monastery three days' journey from the castle. A monk with a cowl pulled over his head followed the procession, apart from everyone else, with no one daring to address him.

[84]   During the mass, he lay flat on his belly, in the middle of the entranceway, his arms spread out, and his forehead in the dust.

[85]   After the burial, he was seen to take the road leading into the mountains. He looked back several times, and finally passed out of sight.

III

[1]   He left, begging his way through many lands.

[2]   He held out his hand to horsemen on the roads, would bend his knee as he approached harvesters, or remained motionless in front of courtyard fences; and his face was so sad that no one ever refused him alms.

[3]   In the spirit of humility, he would relate his story; then all would hurry away, crossing themselves. In villages through which he had passed before, as soon as he was recognized, doors were bolted, threats were shouted, stones were thrown at him. The more charitable people placed a bowl on their windowsill, then closed up to avoid seeing him.

[4]   Rejected everywhere, he shunned his fellowmen; and he nourished himself with roots, plants, stray fruits, and with shellfish which he sought along the shores.

[5]   Sometimes, as he came round a hill, he could see below a jumble of crowded roofs, with stone spires, bridges, towers, dark crisscrossing streets, and from which a continual bustle rose up to him.

[6]   The need to share in the life of others impelled him to go down into the town. But the beastlike faces, the noise made by the craftsmen, the trivial conversations chilled his heart. On holidays, when the tolling cathedral bells from daybreak on filled the whole community with gladness, he watched the townspeople leave their houses, then the dances on the public squares, the fountains of ale at the crossroads, the damask hangings before the princely mansions and, at nightfall, through ground floor windows, the long family tables with old folks holding little children on their laps; sobs would choke him, and he would go back to the open country.

[7]   He felt pangs of love as he gazed at colts in the pastures, at birds in their nests, at insects on flowers; as he came near, all ran away, hid in fear, flew off in haste.

[8]   He sought out lonely places. But the wind brought to his ears sounds resembling death rattles; the tears of the dew falling on the ground reminded him of other, weightier drops. The sun, every evening, spread blood over the clouds; and each night, in his dreams, he relived his parricide.

[9]   He made himself a hairshirt with iron spikes. He climbed on both knees every hill with a chapel at its top. But the unrelenting thought darkened the splendor of the tabernacles, tortured him amid the penitential mortifications.

[10]   He did not rebel against God who had inflicted this act upon him, and yet despaired that he should have committed it.

[11]   His own person was so repugnant to him that in the hope of freeing himself he risked it in perilous tasks. He rescued paralytics from blazes, children from deep chasms. The abyss rejected him, flames spared him.

[12]   Time did not soothe his suffering. It was becoming intolerable. He resolved to die.

[13]   And one day as he happened to be at the edge of a spring,

while he was stooping over it to judge the water's depth, there appeared before him a very emaciated man, with a white beard and of such piteous aspect that he found it impossible to hold back his tears. The other also wept. Without recognizing his face, Julian had a blurred recollection of features resembling it. He cried out; it was his father; and he gave up all thought of killing himself.

[14]   Thus, burdened with the weight of his memories, he traveled through many countries; and he arrived at a river which was dangerous to cross, due to its violence and because of the great stretch of mud along its banks. No one for ages had ventured to make the passage.

[15]   An old boat, whose stern was buried, showed its bow among the reeds. Julian on examining it found a pair of oars; and he came upon the idea of using his life in the service of others.

[16]   He began by establishing on the bank a kind of ramp which would make it possible to reach the fairway; and he broke his nails lifting the huge stones, pressed them against his belly to move them, slipped on the mud, sank into it, nearly died several times.

[17]   Next, he repaired the boat with driftwood, from shipwrecks, and he built himself a hut out of clay and tree trunks.

[18]   As soon as the passageway was known, the travelers appeared. They hailed him from the opposite side, by waving flags; Julian was most prompt in jumping into his boat. It was very heavy; and it got overloaded with all sorts of bags and freight, not to mention the pack animals which reared with fear, and added to the overcrowding. He asked nothing for his trouble; some gave him leftover food which they took from their sacks, or the worn-out garments they no longer wanted. Some brutish passengers yelled out blasphemies. Julian rebuked them gently; and they replied with insults. He was content to bless them.

[19]   A small table, a stool, a bed of dead leaves, and three earthen bowls, such were his furnishings. Two holes in the wall served as windows. On one side, as far as the eye could see there stretched barren wastes on whose surface were pale pools of water, here and there; and the broad river, in front of him, rolled its greenish masses. In the spring, a putrid odor arose from the damp sod. Then, a fierce wind lifted swirls of dust. It permeated

everything, muddied the water, left grit between one's teeth. A little later, there were swarms of mosquitoes, whose buzzing and stinging did not cease either day or night. Next, came appalling frosts which gave things a stonelike rigidity, and induced a mad craving for meat.

[20]   Months passed by when Julian saw no one. He often closed his eyes, yearning, through memory, to come back to his youth;—and a castle courtyard would appear, with greyhounds on the steps, servants in the armory, and, under a vine-covered arbor, a blond youth between an old man wrapped in furs and a lady with a high cap; suddenly, the two corpses were there. Sprawled on the bed, flat on his belly, he would sob, repeating:

[21]   —"Ah! poor father! poor mother! poor mother!" And would drop into a slumber while the ghastly visions continued.

[22]   One night as he slept, he imagined hearing someone call him. He listened intently and could make out nothing save the roar of the waters.

[23]   But the same voice repeated:

[24]   —"Julian!"

[25]   It proceeded from the opposite shore, which amazed him, considering the breadth of the river.

[26]   There was a third call:

[27]   —"Julian!"

[28]   And the loud voice had the tone of a church bell.

[29]   Having lit his lantern, he stepped out of the hut. A raging storm filled the night. The darkness was deep, and torn here and there by the tumbling white waves.

[30]   After a minute's hesitation, Julian untied the rope. The water, immediately, stilled, the boat glided over to the opposite shore, where a man was waiting.

[31]   He was wrapped in coarse linen rags, his face like a plaster mask and both eyes redder than coals. When he brought the lantern closer to him, Julian found that he was covered with hideous leper's sores; yet, there was in his demeanor something of a king's majesty.

[32]   As soon as he stepped into the boat, it sank wondrously, borne down by his weight; with a jolt it rose again; and Julian began to row.

[33]   With each stroke of the oars, the undertow lifted its bow. The water, blacker than ink, rushed furiously along both sides. Abysses formed, mountains rose, and the boat bobbed on top, then went pitching down and whirled around, buffeted by the wind.

[34]   Julian leaned his body forward, extended his arms, and, bracing his feet, arched himself back, twisting at the waist to apply greater power. Hail lashed at his hands, rain streamed down his back, the violent air made him choke, he stopped. Then the boat was sent drifting away. But, realizing that this was a matter of import, a command not to be disobeyed, he picked up his oars; and the clattering oarlocks cut through the clamor of the storm.

[35]   The small lantern burned before him. Fluttering birds occasionally hid it from view. But always he could see the eyes of the Leper who stood at the rear, motionless as a column.

[36]   And this lasted a long, long time!

[37]   Once they were in the hut, Julian closed the door; and he saw him seated upon the stool. The shroudlike garment had fallen to his hips; and his shoulders, his chest, his thin arms were hidden under blotches of scaly pustules. Huge furrows cut across his forehead. Like a skeleton, he had a hole in place of a nose; and out of his bluish lips came breath thick like a fog, and foul.

[38]   —"I am hungry!" he said.

[39]   Julian gave him what he had, an old scrap of bacon and pieces of stale black bread.

[40]   After gulping them down, the table, the bowl, and the handle of the knife bore the same blotches that were visible on his body.

[41]   Next, he said:—"I am thirsty!"

[42]   Julian fetched his jug; and as he lifted it, he smelled an aroma that gladdened his heart and his nostrils. It was wine; what a boon! but the Leper stretched out his arm, and at one draught emptied the whole jug.

[43]   Then he said:—"I am cold!"

[44]   Julian, with his candle, ignited a bundle of ferns, in the middle of the hut.

[45]   The Leper came over to warm himself; and, squatting on his

heels, he trembled all over, was failing; his eyes shone no more, his sores were running, and, in an almost lifeless voice, he whispered:—"Thy bed!"

[46]   Julian helped him gently to drag himself there, and even laid over him, as a cover, the sail of his boat.

[47]   The Leper groaned. The corners of his mouth were drawn up over his teeth, a quickening death rattle shook his chest, and his belly, each time he breathed in, sank down to his spine.

[48]   Then he closed his eyes.

[49]   —"My bones feel like ice! Come near me!"

[50]   And Julian, pulling the cloth up, lay down on the dead leaves, near him, side by side.

[51]   The Leper turned his head.

[52]   —"Undress, I need the warmth of thy body!"

[53]   Julian took off his clothes; then, naked as on the day he was born, again took his place in the bed; and he could feel against his thigh the Leper's skin, colder than a snake and rough as a file.

[54]   He tried to hearten him; and the other would reply, gasping:

[55]   —"Ah! I am about to die! . . . Come closer, warm me up! Not with the hands! no! thy whole person."

[56]   Julian stretched himself out on top, mouth against mouth, chest upon chest.

[57]   Then the Leper clutched him; and his eyes suddenly began to shine like stars; his hair lengthened like sunbeams; the breath of his nostrils had the sweetness of roses; a cloud of incense rose from the hearth, the waves sang. Meanwhile a fullness of bliss, a superhuman joy flooded down into the soul of the swooning Julian; and he whose arms embraced him still was growing, growing, touching with his head and his feet the two walls of the hut. The roof flew off, the firmament unfolded;—and Julian ascended toward the blue expanses, face to face with Our Lord Jesus, who was carrying him into the heavens.

[58]   So there is the story of saint Julian the Hospitaler, about as it is found on the stained-glass window of a church, in my birth-place.

———

Poetics and Translation

Michel Grimaud

••

Translations of *La Légende*

La Légende de Saint Julien l'Hospitalier has been rendered into
English, along with the two other tales of *Trois contes*, by five
translators: Arthur McDowall in 1923, an anonymous translator
in 1926, Mervyn Savill in 1950, Robert Baldick in 1961, and Walter
Cobb in 1964. Additionally, in his *Great French Short Novels*
(1952), Frederick Dupee offers a free reading of the tale whose
lacy, Pre-Raphaelite elegance is close to Gustave Moreau, or
Huysmans, but not Flaubert.[1] All the translators provide an accurate account of the details of Julian's story; yet they are not
faithful to the most pervasive features of Flaubert's writing prac-

1. McDowall, London, 1923; New York, 1924, 1944, etc.; Anonymous, London, 1926, in the *Complete Works of Flaubert*; Mervyn Savill, London, 1950; Frederick Dupee, *Great French Short Novels*, New York, 1952; Robert Baldick, New
York, 1961; Walter Cobb, New York, 1964.

tice. They disregard the semiotic properties of discourse: punctuation, paragraphing, syntax. Flaubert's text is normalized: the unexpected placement, repetition, or omission of logical connectives like "and" is modified to conform to the rules of freshman composition. Flaubert's often choppy style is naturalized: not only is word order regularized, but the sequencing of clauses is made to conform to the way things ought to be. The text is expanded, difficult passages are clarified or explained. As a result, *Saint Julian* sounds remarkably smooth, banal.

For what has been lost is that vital part of our understanding which depends on prose rhythms, the precise ordering, spacing, and timing of events in a universe of discourse. In English, poets and such prose writers as Hemingway have long practiced this art:

> There were funny parts always and she liked them and also what the Germans call gallows-humor stories.

> Then as I was getting up to the Closerie des Lilas with the light on my old friend, the statue of Marshal Ney with his sword out and the shadows of the trees on the bronze, and he alone there and nobody behind him and what a fiasco he'd made of Waterloo, I thought that all generations were lost by something and always had been and always would be and I stopped at the Lilas to keep the statue company and drank a cold beer before going home to the flat over the sawmill.

Surely, *Saint Julian* deserves to be read as closely as the two sentences from a *Moveable Feast*—and in the same spirit.[2]

Therefore, we believe that the present translation should adhere as strictly as possible to Flaubert's text, and especially to his punctuating and linking practices. As mentioned above, the earlier English translations often paid no attention to Flaubert's paragraphing as it appears in French editions. Because the punctuation of *Saint Julian* generally corresponds to or violates both

---

2. Ernest Hemingway, "Une génération perdue," in a *Moveable Feast* (New York, 1964), pp. 25 and 30. Emile Benveniste points out that most translating problems are related to what he terms the "semiotic" aspects of "semantics" (*Problèmes de linguistique générale*, vol. II [Paris, 1974]). It is paradoxical, therefore, that paragraphing and punctuation should be the major problems in the case of *Saint Julian*.

French and English rules, it is an easy feature to preserve—one that should provide readers with a new experience of Flaubert's text.

Flaubert's Peculiar Style

The new English version of *Saint Julian* often sounds strange; but the reader must bear in mind that *the original French also sounds strange* to a French ear. Witness examples 1 through 8:

> (1a) Le cerf, qui était noir et monstrueux de taille, portait seize andouillers avec une barbe blanche.
> (1b) The stag, which was black and of monstrous size, bore sixteen points with a white beard. [I, 64]

Note the lack of a comma resulting in the unusual pairing of "beard" and "points" in the previous example, and the absence of logical connectives in the next one:

> (2a) La grêle cinglait ses mains, la pluie coulait dans son dos, la violence de l'air l'étouffait, il s'arrêta.
> (2b) Hail lashed at his hands, rain streamed down his back, the violent air made him choke, he stopped. [III, 34]

Placing of adverbs (as well as length and choice of word):

> (3a) Le ciel continuellement était bleu, . . .
> (3b) The sky unceasingly was blue, . . . [II, 15]

Paratactic sequences separated by periods as well as commas:

> (4a) Elle grossit. Il devint fameux. On le recherchait.
> (4b) [His army] grew. He became famous. He was in demand. [II, 6]
> (5a) tous, à son approche, couraient plus loin, se cachaient effarés, s'envolaient bien vite.
> (5b) as he came near, all ran away, hid in fear, flew off in haste. [III, 7]

Tangled clause structure (relation of first clause to others):

> (6a) Un soir du mois d'août qu'ils étaient dans leur chambre, elle venait de se coucher et il s'agenouillait pour sa

prière quand il entendit au loin le jappement d'un re-
nard, puis des pas légers sous la fenêtre; et il entrevit
dans l'ombre comme des apparences d'animaux.

(6b) One evening in the month of August while in their bedroom, she had just gone to bed and he was about to
kneel in prayer when he heard the yelping of a fox, then
light footsteps under the window; and he caught a
glimpse in the dark of some animallike shadows. [II, 27]

Anacoluthon:

(7a) Eclatant d'une colère démesurée, il bondit sur eux à
coups de poignard;. . .

(7b) Bursting into boundless rage, he sprang upon them
thrusting his dagger;. . . [II, 75]

The absence of a comma after "them" adds value to the syntactic
non sequitur that accompanies it in the French text, thus
suggesting a fusion of Julian's bounding and thrusting. Clearly,
then, Flaubert exploits punctuation and the syntactic organization of discourse in order to convey meaning. In fact, the syntactic and psychological mood is set by the very first clause sequence in the story:

(8a) Le père et la mère de Julien habitaient un château, au
milieu des bois, sur la pente d'une colline.

(8b) Julian's father and mother dwelt in a castle, in the midst
of the woods, on the slope of a hill. [I, 1]

Comparing Translations

Because the effect of features such as punctuation is cumulative,
neglecting them radically alters our understanding of *Saint Julian*,
particularly of its affective tone and the narrator's stance. It is in-
structive, in this respect, to compare the various renderings of
the first sentence of I, 66 and of the one-line paragraph in III, 12:

(9a) Le grand cerf l'avait vu, fit un bond.

(9b) The great stag had seen it and made a bound. [1923]

(9c) The great stag had watched everything and suddenly he
sprang forward. [1926]

(9d) The great stag had seen him and gave a bound. [1950]

(9e) Seeing her [the doe] fall the great stag leaped and received Julian's arrow, his last one, between the eyes. [1952]

(9f) The great stag had seen him and bounded forward. [1961]

(9g) The huge stag saw the hunter and jumped. [1964]

(9h) The great stag had seen him, made a leap. [M.G.]

Apart from the difference in interpretation of the direct object pronoun ("it," "him," "her"), the issue is that the French version is quick and to the point: it does not link the first clause to the second but merely juxtaposes the two, without explaining their relationship or the direction of the leap. An unusual phrasing, at such a crucial point, is certainly worth maintaining.

In III, 12 there are three sentences in one short paragraph:

(10a) Le temps n'apaisa pas sa souffrance. Elle devenait intolérable. Il résolut de mourir.

(10b) Time brought no relief to his suffering. It became intolerable, and he resolved to die. [1923]

(10c) Time did not allay his torment, which became so intolerable that he resolved to die. [1926]

(10d) Time did not heal his suffering; it grew intolerable. He made up his mind to die. [1950]

(10e) With the passing of time he suffered not less but more and finally he resolved to die. [1952]

(10f) Time did not ease his sufferings. It became so intolerable that he resolved to die. [1961]

(10g) Time did not allay his suffering. It became intolerable; he resolved to die. [1964]

(10h) Time did not soothe his suffering. It was becoming intolerable. He resolved to die. [M.G.]

Apart from Dupee's fanciful translation (10e), the other versions only mildly rationalize the text with a "which," a "so," and a "that" (10c); with an "and" (10b); or with a "that" (10f). Even those versions (10d and 10g) which do not add words to the text freely modify the punctuation. Yet the original points to a kind of closure, an isolation of thoughts and affects that has its own power and that is typical of Julian throughout the story. Finally, the imperfect tense of the middle verb provides a transition between the first and last simple past verbs, which can and should be kept in English.

The Poetics of Translation

While it seemed appropriate in 10h to use a past progressive, Flaubert's characteristic mix of the simple past with the imperfect tense (indicating recurrent or habitual actions) is an aspect of meaning which can rarely be conveyed in English without considerable artificiality. Like previous translators, we generally simplified Flaubert's text in passages like II, 63, or III, 57, in order not to make those passages sound stilted. That this results in an impoverishment of our text is clear from an example like I, 51, where the imperfect, along with the choice and placing of the adverbs, significantly contributes to the feeling of flippancy created in the last clause:

(11a) Les deux bassets, tout de suite, se précipitèrent sur eux; et, çà et là, vivement, leur *cassaient* l'échine.

(11b) The two bassets, instantly, were upon them; and, at random, quickly, *broke* their backs. [I, 51]

Among other features that were awkward to translate, one might mention the words "puis," "ensuite," and "alors" ("next," "then," "so") and the frequent and characteristic use of the present participle. Both categories allow for a more economical but less precise phrasing in keeping with Flaubert's interest in the syntactic montage of discourse. The use of "avec" ("with") for similar purposes is also noteworthy (see example 1a).

At times English forces one to clarify textual presuppositions that might otherwise have gone unnoticed. It seems that in I, 56 and 59, we are not dealing with deer but only with stags (see "antlers" in I, 59). However, such "clarifications" must usually be considered improper since they change the original's emphasis.

"Vieillards," in II, 4, is rendered as "old men" by all the

translators. This is a likely interpretation, but by no means a necessary one: even though the following sentence uses a masculine pronoun, the reference could still be to "old people." Sartre seems to support the former reading (Chapter 4, p. 182). It is the interpreter's prerogative, not the translator's, to change the story from parricide to patricide. The problem is certainly a crucial one since the whole of II, 4, is puzzling (see Chapter 3, p. 150).

In II, 31, translators attribute surprise to Julian concerning his wife's allegedly illogical reaction. Yet the drift of the scene might imply that Julian is puzzled over his own change of mood: "étonné de son [his/her] inconséquence." After his protracted and stubborn refusals to hunt, mingled as they are with desire (II, 21), Julian finally decides on the spur of the moment to go out hunting at night rather than at daybreak (as in I, 50)—and he lies about his reasons to his wife, pretending that he is merely obeying her orders (II, 29). The problem also occurs in II, 26: in both cases, to avoid a choice, a neutral phrasing was chosen: "this urge," "this change of mood" (see Chapter 3, p. 152).

The different occurrences of "embrasser" pose a different problem, since the French verb is truly ambiguous and, till the end of the nineteenth century, meant usually, though not exclusively, "to embrace" rather than "to kiss." The only occurrence of the term for which it seems likely that the second meaning is the intended one is II, 73. All other uses of it (I, 48; II, 45: III, 57) point to the sensual paradox of the tale. The only time the verb "to kiss" ("baiser") appears, in fact, is when Julian's parents kiss his gentle wife (II, 45). While the leper's kiss of death and eternal life ("mouth against mouth," III, 56) is not named, the use of the verb "étreindre" ("to clasp, embrace") may remind us of the only other occurrence of this root (the participial noun "étreinte"), when Julian, after hunting, received his mother's embrace coldly (I, 48).

The 1923, 1926, and 1964 translators used the "thou" forms for the rare instances of direct speech in the tale. Since this permits one to note, for example, the unexpected use of "you" ("vous") by Julian's wife when she addresses him in II, 23, we felt that the distinction was worth preserving, although Flaubert uses archaic phrasings in only a few cases such as "déduit des chasses" (I, 36) and "occis" (I, 56).

Whenever possible, repeated French words were translated in identical ways, particularly when they occurred in the two hunts or in the final episode. This practice often implied a choice between a thematic repetition and a more idiomatic translation, or even between two thematic patterns. As a translation for "éteintes" ("burnt out," said of the old man's eyes), which is opposed to "scorched" in the parricide scene (II, 79), the word "lifeless" was chosen rather than the more colorful and thematically important "burnt out" because we wished to acknowledge the sole reappearance of this adjective in the final scene (III, 45), where it refers to the voice of the leper and follows a reference to similarly burnt-out eyes ("ses yeux ne brillaient plus"). As the first part of this book has shown, such links between father and stag or leper are vital to an understanding of the story. Similarly, it is through such repetitions that the universe of death and sensual pleasure ("dove" and "lamp" in I, 21) of Julian's childhood becomes associated with a universe of Christian (anti-pagan) heroism and with sudden love for a woman ("lamp" in II, 12). In short, remaining faithful to the text—as translator or as reader—implies being faithful to its letter.

The word "heart," for instance, appears on five significant occasions. First, in the stag's curse ("ferocious heart," I, 68); second, as Julian rushes up the stairs, thinking of his wife—and this "soothed his heart" (II, 71); third, in the paragraph in which the stag's curse is realized and he hears its bellow ("the dead, pierced through their hearts," II, 75); fourth, ironically, when Julian's heart is chilled by the *uneventfulness* of village life (III, 6); finally, in contrast with the preceding earthly events, at the moment when Julian's heart is gladdened by the discovery of a jug of wine—in context, an inescapably, although partly ironic, reference to Holy Communion (III, 42).

The translator's activity naturally fosters a word-oriented analysis. Such an approach to literature and to texts seems conventionally (socially) and psychologically justified by the work of a poetician such as Michael Riffaterre or by that of George Lakoff and Mark Johnson.[3] But our reading is directed, in part,

3. Michael Riffaterre, *The Semiotics of Poetry* (Bloomington, 1978) and *La Production du texte* (Paris, 1979). George Lakoff and Mark Johnson, *Metaphors We Live By* (Chicago, 1980).

independently from such verbal patterns. We have no trouble relating the religious aspects of Julian's experience in III, 42, to the ecstasy he experiences in the last lines of the story. More subtly, perhaps, the recurrent verb "to put together" is only part of what may lead us to reflect humorously on the similarities between Julian's father's putting together a pack of hounds in I, 37, and Julian's putting together an army of outlaws in II, 5. However, it is likely that if we notice the homology at all, it will be because of conceptual rather than verbal similarities.

The Abstractness of French

That French tends to be more abstract than English is one of the stereotypes that teachers use most often; it is accurate. The major difficulty in translating *Saint Julian* was related to differences in what would be considered an optimal degree of abstraction or concreteness. English readers ought not to feel that Flaubert wrote *Saint Julian* using an impoverished or overly abstract vocabulary—since this is not the feeling of a French reader. On the other hand, one of the pleasures in reading a foreign text is the experience of a notably different universe of discourse as well as, simply, a different universe. Nonetheless, like most translations, the present one takes advantage of the greater resources of English whenever it seemed appropriate to do so. Our general criterion was that if Flaubert had a choice, yet selected the more common French word, then we should do the same in English. In the other cases, we tried to imagine Flaubert as a native English writer.

This issue appears mostly in two categories: verbs of movement and nominalizations. Examples 12 through 16 provide typical instances of the differences between French and English. The last example is analyzed in some detail to show how Flaubert exploits the indirect qualities of nominalization. The first two examples concern verbs of movement:

(12a) Julien, d'un revers d'épée, lui faucha les deux pattes, et sans le ramasser *continua sa route.*

(12b) Julian, with a sweep of the sword, cut off both its feet, and without picking [the grouse] up *rode on.* [I, 52]

In French, the added precision of "rode" would have been considered boringly obvious—while, in English, too many instances
of "continuing" and "going on one's way" would seem unduly
repetitive in view of the ease with which one can use postposi-
tions in English. Paragraph II, 33, is a more complex illustration of
the same principle:

> (13a) ... la chaloupe sautait dessus, puis redescendait dans
> des profondeurs où elle tournoyait, ballottée par le
> vent.
> (13b) ... the boat bobbed on top, then went pitching down
> and whirled around, buffeted by the wind. [III, 33]

As illustrated by the next three examples, nominalizations were
not systematically avoided or preserved:

> (14a) Les ténèbres étaient... déchirées par *la blancheur* des
> vagues qui bondissaient.
> (14b) The darkness was... torn... by the tumbling *white*
> waves. [III, 29]
> (15a) ... *le claquement* des tolets coupait *la clameur* de la tem-
> pête.
> (15b) ... the *clattering* oarlocks cut through *the clamor* of the
> storm. [III, 34]

However, the case of II, 12, is special. Through his use of a
double nominalization in the third sentence, Flaubert diminishes the felt impact of the only directly erotic passage in the
whole narrative:

> (16a) Ses grands yeux noirs brillaient comme deux lampes
> très douces. Un sourire charmant écartait ses lèvres.
> Les anneaux de sa chevelure s'accrochaient aux pier-
> reries de sa robe entr'ouverte; et, sous *la transparence*
> de sa tunique, on devinait *la jeunesse* de son corps. Elle
> était toute mignonne et potelée, avec la taille fine.
> (16b) Her big dark eyes shone like two very soft lamps. A
> charming smile parted her lips. The ringlets of her hair
> were caught among the jewels of her half-opened
> bodice; and her *translucid* tunic revealed *the youthful-*

ness of her body. She was so dainty and plump, with a slender waist. [II, 12]

In French, the distance created by the nominalizations fits in well with the childlike "big dark eyes" of the emperor's daughter and with her childlike or maternal plumpness. Yet, despite his naïve tone (she is "*so* dainty . . ."), the narrator does insist on Julian's perception of the adolescent woman's sexual attributes: her smile, the half-opened bodice, the translucid tunic. It is not surprising, therefore, that the next paragraph should contain equally ambivalent notations. Being "dazzled with *love*" may seem spiritual, except that this is followed by a mention of Julian's status as a virgin.[4] And the next paragraph briskly expedites the wedding day itself, insisting only on two details: the dowry and the "endless courtesies" exchanged on the day after (II, 14).

The Value of Details

An analysis of the different translations of paragraph III, 56, and a comment on I, 61, will serve to summarize our main goal: to normalize Flaubert's text as little as possible.

In III, 56, the leper has asked Julian to lie close to him—though not, it should be noted, "on top" of him, as Julian decides to do:

(17a) Julien s'étala dessus complètement, bouche contre bouche, poitrine sur poitrine.

(17b) Julian stretched himself completely over him, mouth to mouth and chest on chest. [1923]

(17c) Julian stretched himself out upon the leper, lay on him, lips to lips, chest to chest. [1926]

(17d) Julian laid himself completely over him, mouth to mouth, breast to breast. [1950]

---

4. A second possibly sexual (though not erotic) notation in the tale concerns Julian's father. The narrator says: "After many adventures he had taken himself a wife of high lineage" (I, 9). The collocation of the French "aventures" with marriage suggests the common meaning "love affairs." But the inference is not required by the context as it was in II, 13.

(17e) Julian laid himself at full length upon him, mouth to mouth, breast to breast. [1952]

(17f) Julian stretched himself out on top of him, mouth to mouth, breast to breast. [1961]

(17g) Julian stretched himself out, mouth to mouth, breast to breast. [1964]

(17h) Julian stretched himself out on top, mouth against mouth, chest upon chest. [M.G.]

The only difference between the last translation and the six preceding ones is that 17h does not needlessly change the text. Flaubert, at this crucial point, does not use a pronoun: he says "on top," not "on top of him." He does not make the obvious choices "mouth *to* mouth" and "breast *to* breast," but rather decides in favor of the less common phrases "mouth *against* mouth, chest *upon* chest."

But, of course, we all know that perfect translations are impossible. How could one translate the famous "nappe de sang" that Julian sees in the sky after his first series of murders:

(18a) . . . le ciel était rouge comme une nappe de sang.

(18b) . . . the sky was red like a sheet of blood. [I, 61]

"Nappe" may further evoke an (altar) cloth (as in I, 10), but it also refers in its technical sense to the (deer's) hide on which the quarry is laid for the hounds. This is a most appropriate image, since it occurs just after the slaughter of the stags and after the direct reference to this technical usage in I, 46—but it is a condensation of meanings to which no single English word could do full justice.

In the case of *Saint Julian*, the remarkable point is that this commonsensical view of the translator's dilemma is quite inappropriate: if one resists the urge to improve on the original, it is easy to preserve a surprisingly large number of the features that make Flaubert's text unique.

PART THREE

A Reader's Guide to Psychoanalysis

An Overview of
Psychoanalytic Theory
and the Psychoanalytic
Approach in Literary Theory
and Practice, with Emphasis
on French Studies

Michel Grimaud

••

The present overview is intended to complement previous surveys of psychoanalysis found in the journal *Sub-Stance*.[1] While the annotated bibliography "Recent Trends in Psychoanalysis"[2] emphasized current English-language psychoanalytic theory and literary criticism, this overview stresses French-language studies.

In many ways psychoanalysis, like literary criticism, has not been cumulative, but rather repetitive and infinitely varied. The fact that psychoanalysis is a hermeneutic art as well as a multimodel system[3] has prevented it from becoming adequately sys-

1. See the yearly "Critical Notes" published in *Sub-Stance*, e.g., nos. 20 (1978) and 28 (1980).

2. Michel Grimaud, "Recent Trends in Psychoanalysis: A Survey, with Emphasis on Psychological Criticism in English Literature and Related Areas [in the Social Sciences]," *Sub-Stance*, no. 13, (1976), pp. 136–162.

3. Pinchas Noy, "Metapsychology as a Multimodel System," *International Review of Psychoanalysis*, 4 (1977), 1–12.

tematized. As a consequence, no comprehensive textbook of psychoanalysis exists. Our goal is to alleviate this problem, in part, by furnishing a relatively focused survey of books and articles on psychoanalytic theory, literary theory, and their practice. Some of the items mentioned here will also be found in "Recent Trends," to which we refer the reader since it is an annotated survey, though more restricted in scope.

The survey is arranged by category:

PSYCHOANALYTIC THEORY

1. Reference Tools
2. Psychoanalytic Journals
3. Methodology
4. Classics Old and New
5. Case Histories
6. Dreams and Other Topics
7. Language and Symbolization
8. French Theorists

APPLIED PSYCHOANALYSIS

9. Literary Theory
10. Literary Applications of Theoretical Interest
11. French Literary Theory
12. Literary Criticism (French authors)
13. French Psychoanalysis, Philosophy, and the Social Sciences

1. Reference Tools

Arieti, Silvano, ed. *American Handbook of Psychiatry*. New York: Basic Books, 1966.

Dufresne, Roger. *Bibliographie des écrits de Freud*. Paris: Payot, 1973. [Lists French translations and their equivalents in English and German.]

Eidelberg, Ludwig. *Encyclopedia of Psychoanalysis*. New York: Free Press, 1968.

*Fenichel, Otto. *The Psychoanalytic Theory of Neurosis*. New York: Norton, 1945. [Outdated, but still the best overview.]

*Freud, Sigmund. *The Standard Edition of the Complete Psychological Works* *of Sigmund Freud*. Translated by James Strachey, Anna Freud, Alix Strachey, and Alan Tyson. Edited by James Strachey. 24 volumes. London: Hogarth Press, 1953–1974.

Greenson, Ralph. *The Technique and Practice of Psychoanalysis*. New York: International Universities Press, 1967.

*Grimaud, Michel. "Recent Trends in Psychoanalysis: A Survey with Emphasis on Psychological Criticism in English Literature and Related Areas." *Sub-Stance*, no. 13 (1976), pp. 136–162.

Grinstein, Alexander, ed. *Index of Psychoanalytic Writings*. 14 volumes. New York: International Universities Press, 1956–1975.

Guttman, Samuel, Randall Jones, and Stephen Parrish. *A Concordance to the Standard Edition of the Complete Psychological Works of Sigmund Freud*. Boston: G. K. Hall, 1980.

Kiell, Norman. *Psychoanalysis, Psychology, and Literature: A Bibliography*. Madison: University of Wisconsin Press, 1963.

Klumpner, George H., and Ernest S. Wolf. " A Pagination Converter Relating the *Gesammelte Werke* to the *Standard Edition of the Complete Psychological Works of Sigmund Freud*." *International Journal of Psychoanalysis*, 52 (1971), 207–224.

*Miller, Joan M. *French Structuralism: An Annotated Bibliography*. New York: Garland Publishing, 1982. [Seven major structuralists are listed: Jacques Lacan, Roland Barthes, Jacques Derrida, Michel Foucault, Lucien Goldmann, and Claude Lévi-Strauss. Reviews and translations as well as author and subject indexes are included.]

Smirnoff, Victor. *The Scope of Child Analysis*. New York: International Universities Press, 1971. [Despite its title, furnishes a good introduction to psychoanalysis in general, from a French point of view.]

Waelder, Robert. *Basic Theory of Psychoanalysis*. New York: International Universities Press, 1960.

2. *Psychoanalytic Journals*

ENGLISH-LANGUAGE JOURNALS

*American Imago: A Psychoanalytic Journal for Culture, Science and the Arts, 1939+.

*Annual of Psychoanalysis: A Publication of the Chicago Institute for Psychoanalysis, 1973+.

Contemporary Psychoanalysis: Journal of the William Alanson White Psychoanalytic Society, 1964+.

Glyph, 1977+ [Literature].

Gradiva, 1976+ [Literature].

*Hartford Studies in Literature, 1969+.

History of Childhood Quarterly: The Journal of Psychohistory, 1973+.

*International Journal of Psychoanalysis, United Kingdom, 1920+.

*International Review of Psychoanalysis, United Kingdom, 1974+.

*Journal of the American Psychoanalytic Association, 1953+.

Journal of the Philadelphia Association for Psychoanalysis, 1974+.
*Literature and Psychology, 1951+.
Modern Psychoanalysis: Journal Dedicated to Extending Psychoanalytic Treatment to the Full Range of Emotional Disorders, 1976+.
*Psychiatry and the Humanities, 1976+ [Psychoanalysis, linguistics, literature].
*Psychoanalysis and Contemporary Science: An Annual of Integrative and Interdisciplinary Studies, 1972–1977 [see next entry].
*Psychoanalysis and Contemporary Thought: A Quarterly of Integrative and Interdisciplinary Studies, 1978+.
Psychoanalytic Forum: Psychiatric Research Foundation, 1966+.
Psychoanalytic Inquiry, 1981+.
*Psychoanalytic Quarterly, 1932+.
*Psychoanalytic Review, 1913+.
*Psychoanalytic Study of Society, 1960+.
*The Psychoanalytic Study of the Child, 1945+ [Title is misleading: range of articles is broad].
Psychocultural Review, 1977+ [Film/Psychology Review, since volume 4, 1980].
Psychohistory: Bulletin of the International Psychohistorical Association, 1976+.
Psychohistory Review, 1972+.
*Psychological Issues, 1959+ [Psychoanalytic Monograph Series].
*Review of Psychoanalytic Books, 1982+.
Samiksa, India, 1947+.
Science and Psychoanalysis, 1958+.
Seminars in Psychiatry, 1969+.

FRENCH-LANGUAGE JOURNALS

(PUBLISHED IN FRANCE EXCEPT WHERE NOTED OTHERWISE)

L'Ane: Le magazine freudien, 1981+.
Bloc-notes de la psychanalyse, Switzerland, 1981+.
Bulletin de l'Association Psychanalytique de France, 1965–1968.
Bulletin du Champ Freudien, 1974+.
*Cahiers Confrontation, 1979+ [Psychoanalysis; also literature].
Le Discours psychanalytique, 1981+.
*Etudes freudiennes, 1969+.
*L'Inconscient, 1967–1968.
Interprétation: Psychiatrie, Pédagogie, Linguistique, Canada, 1967+ [Psychoanalytic, despite title].
*Nouvelle Revue de Psychanalyse, 1970+.
L'Ordinaire du psychanalyste, 1973+ [Politics, case reports].
Ornicar, 1975+.
*Psychanalyse: Recherche et enseignement freudiens de la Société Française de Psychanalyse [Jacques Lacan], 1956–1964.

Psychanalyse à l'université: Revue du Laboratoire de Psychanalyse et de Psychopathologie [Jean Laplanche], 1975+.
*Revue française de psychanalyse, 1927+.
Scilicet: Ecole freudienne de Paris [Jacques Lacan], 1968+.
*Topique: Revue freudienne, 1969+.

OTHER LANGUAGES

Cuadernos de Psicoanálisis: Asociación Psicoanalítica Mexicana, Mexico, 1965+.
Cuadernos Sigmund Freud, Argentina, 1971+.
Dynamische Psychiatrie, Germany, 1968+ [Psychoanalysis].
Estudos de Psicanálise, Brazil, 1969+.
Fortschritte der Psychoanalyse, Germany, 1964+.
*Imago, Austria, 1912–1937.
*Internationale Zeitschrift für (ärtzliche) Psychoanalyse, Austria, 1913–1937.
*Internationale Zeitschrift für Psychoanalyse und Imago, Austria, 1938–1941.
*Jahrbuch der Psychoanalyse, Germany, 1960+.
Jahrbuch für Psychoanalytische und Psychopathologische Forschungen, Germany, 1909–1913.
*Psiche: Bolletino dell' Istituto di Psicanalisi di Roma, Italy, 1964+.
*Psyche: Zeitschrift für Psychologische und Medizinische Menschenkunde, Germany, 1947+.
Psychoanalytische Bewegung, Austria, 1929–1933.
Revista brasileira de Psicanálise, Brazil, 1967+.
Revista de Psicoanálisis, Psiquiatria y Psicologia, Mexico, 1960+.
Revista Uruguaya de Psicoanálisis, Uruguay, 1956+.
Rivista di Psicanalisi, Italy, 1955+.
Sic: Materiali per la Psicanalisi, Italy, 1975+.
Zeitschrift für Psychoanalytische Pädagogik, Austria, 1926–1937.
Zentralblatt für Psychoanalyse und Psychotherapie, Austria, 1910–1914.

3. Methodology

Bowlby, John. *Attachment and Loss.* 3 volumes, New York: Basic Books, 1969, 1973, 1980.
*Crews, Frederick. *Out of My System: Psychoanalysis, Ideology, and Critical Method.* New York: Oxford University Press, 1975.
*Devereux, George. *From Anxiety to Method in the Behavioral Sciences.* New York: Humanities Press, 1967.
*Fisher, Seymour, and Roger Greenberg. *The Scientific Credibility of Freud's Theories and Therapy.* New York: Basic Books, 1977.
Gedo, John, and Arnold Goldberg. *Models of the Mind.* Chicago: University of Chicago Press, 1973.

Laplanche, Jean, and Jean-Baptiste Pontalis. *The Language of Psychoanalysis.* New York: Norton, 1974. [Alphabetized historical and methodological discussion of 288 basic concepts.]

*Peterfreund, Emanuel. *Information, Systems, and Psychoanalysis.* New York: International Universities Press, 1971.

————. "The Need for a New General Theoretical Frame of Reference." *Psychoanalytic Quarterly,* 44 (1975), 534–549.

Ricoeur, Paul. *Freud and Philosophy: An Essay on Interpretation.* New Haven: Yale University Press, 1970.

*Rosenblatt, Allan D., and James T. Thickstun. *Modern Psychoanalytic Concepts in a General Psychology.* New York: International Universities Press, 1977.

*Sherwood, Michael. *The Logic of Explanation in Psychoanalysis.* New York: Academic Press, 1969.

*Wachtel, Paul. *Psychoanalysis and Behavior Therapy.* New York: Basic Books, 1977.

Wilden, Anthony. *System and Structure: Essays in Communication and Exchange.* 2d ed. New York: Methuen, 1980.

4. Classics Old and New

Abraham, Karl. *Selected Papers of Karl Abraham.* London: Hogarth Press, 1942.

Basch, Michael Franz. "Developmental Psychology and Explanatory Theory in Psychoanalysis." *Annual of Psychoanalysis,* 5, 1977, 229–263.

Blos, Peter. "The Epigenesis of the Adult Neurosis." *Psychoanalytic Study of the Child,* 27, 1973, 106–135. [Compare Viderman in Section 8.]

Blum, Harold P., ed. *Female Psychology.* New York: International Universities Press, 1977.

Erikson, Erik. *Childhood and Society.* Rev. ed. New York: Norton, 1963.

Esman, Aaron H. "The Primal Scene: A Review and Reconsideration." *Psychoanalytic Study of the Child,* 28 (1973), 49–81.

————. *The Psychology of Adolescence: Essential Readings.* New York: International Universities Press, 1975.

Fenichel, Otto. *The Psychoanalytic Theory of Neurosis.* New York: Norton, 1945.

————. *Collected Papers of Otto Fenichel.* New York: Norton, 1953–54.

Ferenczi, Sandor. *Further Contributions to the Theory and Technique of Psychoanalysis.* London: Hogarth Press, 1950.

————. *Sex in Psychoanalysis.* New York: Robert Brunner, 1950.

Freud, Anna. *The Writings of Anna Freud.* volumes 1–7. New York: International Universities Press, 1966–1975. [Especially volume 2, *The Ego and the Mechanisms of Defense,* rev. ed. 1966, and volume 6, *Normality and Pathology in Childhood,* 1965.]

Green, André. "Surface Analysis, Deep Analysis." *International Review of Psychoanalysis*, 1 (1974), 415–424.

Greenacre, Phyllis. *Trauma, Growth, and Personality*. New York: Norton, 1952.

_____. *Emotional Growth: Studies of the Gifted and a Great Variety of Other Individuals*. 2 volumes. New York: International Universities Press, 1971. [See especially chapters 22–29.]

Greenfield, Norman S., and William C. Lewis. *Psychoanalysis and Current Biological Thought*. Madison: University of Wisconsin Press, 1965.

Greenspan, Stanley I. "The Oedipal–Pre-Oedipal Dilemma: A Reformulation according to Object Relations Theory." *International Review of Psychoanalysis*, 4 (1977), 381–392.

Jones, Ernest. *Papers on Psychoanalysis*. New York: W. Wood, 1950.

_____. *Essays in Applied Psychoanalysis*. 2 volumes. New York: International Universities Press, 1964.

Khan, M. Masud R. "The Concept of Cumulative Trauma." *Psychoanalytic Study of the Child*, 18 (1963), 286–306.

Klein, George S. *Psychoanalytic Theory: An Exploration of Essentials*. New York: International Universities Press, 1976.

Klein, Melanie. *Contributions to Psychoanalysis, 1921–1945*. London: Hogarth Press, 1948.

_____. *Developments in Psychoanalysis*. London: Hogarth Press, 1952.

Kohut, Heinz. *The Analysis of the Self*. New York: International Universities Press, 1971.

_____. *The Restoration of the Self*. New York: International Universities Press, 1977.

Kris, Ernst. *The Selected Papers of Ernst Kris*. New Haven: Yale University Press, 1975.

Loewenstein, Rudolph M., ed. *Psychoanalysis: A General Psychology*. New York: International Universities Press, 1966.

McDevitt, John B., and Calvin F. Settlage, eds. *Separation-Individuation*. New York: International Universities Press, 1971.

*Noy, Pinchas. "A Revision of the Psychoanalytic Theory of the Primary Process." *International Journal of Psychoanalysis*, 50 (1969), 155–178.

*Ornstein, Paul H. "On Narcissism: Beyond the Introduction." *Annual of Psychoanalysis*, 2 (1974), 127–149.

Rapaport, David, ed. *Organization and Pathology of Thought*. New York: Columbia University Press, 1951.

*Sandler, Anne-Marie. "Comments on the Significance of Piaget's Work for Psychoanalysis." *International Review of Psychoanalysis*, 2 (1975), 365–378.

Waelder, Robert. *Psychoanalysis: Observation, Theory, Application*. New York: International Universities Press, 1975.

Winnicott, Donald W. *Collected Papers (Through Pediatrics to Psychoanalysis)*. Basic Books, 1957. [See especially chapter 18 on transitional phenomena.]

5. Case Histories

Dewald, Paul. *The Psychoanalytic Process: A Case Illustration.* New York: Basic Books, 1972.

Diatkine, René and Simon, Janine. *La Psychanalyse précoce.* Paris: PUF, 1972.

Dolto, Françoise. *Dominique: The Analysis of an Adolescent.* New York: Dutton, 1973.

Gill, Merton M., and Irwin Z. Hoffman. *Analysis of Transference.* Vol. 2: *Studies of Seven Audio-Recorded Psychoanalytic Sessions.* New York: International Universities Press, 1981.

Goldberg, Arnold, ed. *The Psychology of the Self.* New York: International Universities Press, 1978.

Kanzer, Mark, and Jules Glenn, eds. *Freud and His Patients.* New York: Jason Aronson, 1980. [Case summaries, background, and discussions of historical interest.]

Klein, Melanie. *Narrative of a Child Analysis: The Conduct of the Psychoanalysis of Children as Seen in the Treatment of a Ten-Year-Old Boy.* London: Hogarth Press, 1974.

Moore, William Thomas. "The Wish to Steal a Baby in a 15-Year-Old Girl." *Psychoanalytic Study of the Child,* 31 (1976), 349–388.

Rosner, Henry. "Clinical and Prognostic Considerations in the Analysis of a Five-Year-Old Hysteric." *Journal of the American Psychoanalytic Association,* 23 (1975), 507–534.

Shapiro, Vivian, Selma Fraiberg, and Edna Adelson. "Infant-Parent Psychotherapy on Behalf of a Child in a Critical Nutritional State." *Psychoanalytic Study of the Child,* 31 (1976), 461–491.

Tolpin, Marian. "The Infantile Neurosis: A Metapsychological Concept and a Paradigmatic Case History." *Psychoanalytic Study of the Child,* 25 (1970), 273–305. [See also Viderman in section 8.]

6. Dreams and Other Topics

Bell, Anita I. "The Significance of the Scrotal Sac and Testicles for the Prepuberty Male." *Psychoanalytic Quarterly,* 34 (1965), 182–206.

——. "Male Anxiety during Sleep." *International Journal of Psychoanalysis,* 56 (1975), 455–464.

Castle, Peter W. "Contributions of Piaget to a Theory of Dreaming." *Science and Psychoanalysis,* 19 (1971), 98–113.

Chaitin, Gilbert D. "The Representation of Logical Relations in Dreams and the Nature of the Primary Process." *Psychoanalysis and Contemporary Thought,* 1 (1978), 477–502.

Cohen, David B. *Sleep and Dreaming: Origins, Nature, and Functions.* New York: Pergamon Press, 1979. [Biological and psychological overview.]

*Greenberg, Ramon, and C. Pearlman. "If Freud Only Knew: A Reconsideration of Psychoanalytic Dream Theory." *International Review of Psychoanalysis*, 5 (1978), 71–75.

*Izard, Carroll E. *Human Emotions*. New York: Plenum Press, 1977.

Jones, Richard M. *The New Psychology of Dreaming*. New York: Grune and Stratton, 1970.

Kaplan, Linda Joan. "The Concept of the Family Romance." *Psychoanalytic Review*, 61 (1974), 169–202.

Marcus, Irwin M., and John J. Francis. *Masturbation: From Infancy to Senescence*. New York: International Universities Press, 1975.

Mitchell, Juliet. *Psychoanalysis and Feminism: Freud, Reich, Laing, and Women*. New York: Pantheon, 1974.

Palombo, Stanley. "The Adaptive Function of Dreams." *Psychoanalysis and Contemporary Thought*, 1 (1978), 443–476.

Rycroft, Charles. *Imagination and Reality: Psychoanalytic Essays, 1951–1961*. London: Hogarth Press, 1968.

Schafer, Roy. *A New Language for Psychoanalysis*. New Haven: Yale University Press, 1976.

Stoller, Robert. *Sex and Gender: On the Development of Masculinity and Feminity*. London: Hogarth Press, 1969.

7. Language and Symbolization

Anzieu, Didier, Bernard Gibello, et al. *Psychanalyse et langage: Du corps à la parole*. Paris: Dunod, 1977.

Bateson, Gregory. *Steps to an Ecology of Mind*. San Francisco: Chandler Publishing Company, 1972. [See the chapters on the double-bind.]

*Benveniste, Emile. *Problems in General Linguistics*. Translated by Mary E. Meek. Coral Gables, Fla.: University of Miami Press, 1971. [See the translation of his 1956 "Remarques sur la fonction du langage dans la découverte freudienne."]

Edelson, Marshall. *Language and Interpretation in Psychoanalysis*. New Haven: Yale University Press, 1975.

Galenson, Eleanor, and Herbert Roiphe. "Impact of Early Sexual Discovery on Mood, Defensive Organization, and Symbolization." *Psychoanalytic Study of the Child*, 26 (1971), 195–216.

Gear, Maria Carmen, and Ernesto Cesar Liendo. *Sémiologie psychanalytique*. Paris: Editions de Minuit, 1975.

Kubie, Lawrence E. "Body Symbolization and the Development of Language." *Psychoanalytic Quarterly*, 3 (1934), 430–444.

Litowitz, Bonnie E., and Norman S. "The Influence of Linguistic Theory on Psychoanalysis: A Critical Historical Survey." *International Review of Psychoanalysis*, 4 (1977), 419–448.

Major, René. "Notes sur le symbolisme." *Interprétation*, 1 (1967), 21–34.

——. "La Symbolisation et son achoppement." *Revue française de psychanalyse*, 35 (1971), 129–146.

*Martindale, Colin. "The Grammar of Altered States of Consciousness:

A Semiotic Reinterpretation of Aspects of Psychoanalytic Theory."
Psychoanalysis and Contemporary Science, 4 (1975), 331–354.
Matte Blanco, Ignacio. *The Unconscious as Infinite Sets: An Essay in Bi-Logic*. London: Duckworth, 1975. [See Parts I–IV.]
*Noy, Pinchas. "Symbolism and Mental Representation." *Annual of Psychoanalysis*, 1 (1973), 125–158. [See also Chaitin in section 6.]
Palombo, Stanley R. "The Associative Memory Tree." *Psychoanalysis and Contemporary Science*, 2 (1973), 205–219.
Perron-Borelli, Michèle. "L'Investissement de la signification." *Revue française de psychanalyse*, 40 (1976), 681–692.
Phillips, John Hickman. *Psychoanalyse und Symbolik*. Bern: H. Huber, 1962.
*Piaget, Jean. *Play, Dreams, and Imitation in Childhood*. New York: Norton, 1967.
Rogers, Robert. *Metaphor: A Psychoanalytic View*. Berkeley: University of California Press, 1978.
Rubinstein, Benjamin B. "On Metaphor and Related Phenomena." *Psychoanalysis and Contemporary Science*, 1 (1972), 70–108.
Segal, Hanna. "Notes on Symbol Formation." *International Journal of Psychoanalysis*, 38 (1957), 391–397.
Shands, Harley. "Anxiety, Anaclitic Objects, and the Sign Function: Comments on Early Development in the Use of Symbols." *American Journal of Orthopsychiatry*, 24 (1954), 84–97.
*Todorov, Tzvetan. "La Rhétorique de Freud." In *Théories du symbole*. Paris: Editions du Seuil, 1977.

8. French Theorists

Barande, Ilse and Robert. *Histoire de la psychanalyse en France*. Toulouse: Privat, 1974.
Bourguignon, André. "Rêve et folie." *Annales de psychothérapie*, 3, no. 4 (1972), pp. 36–42.
Chasseguet-Smirgel, Janine, *et al*. *Female Sexuality*. Ann Arbor: University of Michigan Press, 1970.
——, ed. *Les Chemins de l'Anti-Oedipe*. Toulouse: Privat, 1974.
Chiland, Colette. "Des Apories de toute réflexion sur la normalité." *Revue française de psychanalyse*, 36 (1972), 411–419.
Deleuze, Gilles, and Félix Guattari. *Anti-Oedipus*. New York: Viking Press, 1977.
Fagès, Jean-Baptiste. *Histoire de la psychanalyse après Freud*. Toulouse: Privat, 1976.
Green, André. "L'Inconscient freudien et la psychanalyse française contemporaine." *Temps modernes*, no. 195 (1962), pp. 365–379.
——. "Sur l'Anti-Oedipe." *Revue française de psychanalyse*, 36 (1972), 491–499.
Lacan, Jacques. *Ecrits: A Selection*. New York: Norton, 1977.

——. *Four Fundamental Concepts of Psychoanalysis*. London: Hogarth Press, 1977. [Translation of volume 11 of a projected 20-volume series entitled *Séminaire*. On Lacan, see Miller (section 1), Wilden (section 3), Mehlman, Muller, Rosolato, and Turkle in this section.]

——. *Speech and Language in Psychoanalysis*. Translated with notes and commentary by Anthony Wilden. Baltimore: Johns Hopkins University Press, 1981. [New title for *The Language of the Self*, 1968.]

Laplanche, Jean. *Life and Death in Psychoanalysis*. Translated by Jeffrey Mehlman. Baltimore: Johns Hopkins University Press, 1976.

——. *Problématiques*. Vol. 4: *L'Inconscient et le Ça*. Paris: Presses Universitaires de France, 1981. [Laplanche's seminars. Preceding volumes were about anxiety, castration, and symbolization and sublimation.]

Lebovici, Serge, and Daniel Widlöcher, eds. *Psychoanalysis in France*. New York: International Universities Press, 1980.

*Leclaire, Serge. *Psychanalyser*. Paris: Editions du Seuil, 1968.

——. *Démasquer le réel*. Paris: Editions du Seuil, 1971.

Le Guen, Claude. *L'Oedipe originaire*. Paris: Payot, 1974.

Mehlman, Jeffrey, ed. *French Freud: Structural Studies in Psychoanalysis*. *Yale French Studies*, no. 48, 1973.

Muller, John P., and William J. Richardson. *Lacan and Language: A Reader's Guide to Ecrits*. New York: International Universities Press, 1981.

Nouvelle revue de psychanalyse:
Lieux du corps, no. 3, 1971.
L'Espace du rêve, no. 5, 1972.

Pontalis, Jean-Baptiste. "La Lecture de Freud." *Temps modernes*, no. 195, (1962), pp. 380–384.

——. *Après Freud*. Paris: René Julliard, 1965.

——. "Les Mots du psychanalyste." *Informations sur les sciences humaines*, 6, no. 2–3 (1967), pp. 39–54.

Rosolato, Guy. *Essais sur le symbolique*. Paris: Gallimard, 1969.

Schneiderman, Stuart, ed. *Returning to Freud: Clinical Psychoanalysis in the School of Lacan*. New Haven: Yale University Press, 1980.

Turkle, Sherry R. *Psychoanalytic Politics: Freud's French Revolution*. New York: Basic Books, 1978.

*Viderman, Serge. *La Construction de l'espace analytique*. Paris: Denoël, 1970.

9. Literary Theory

Beres, David. "Communication in Psychoanalysis and in the Creative Process: A Parallel." *Journal of the American Psychoanalytic Association*, 5 (1957), 408–423.

Bergler, Edmund. "Did Freud Really Advocate a 'Hands off' Policy toward Artistic Creativity?" *American Imago*, 6 (1949), 205–210.

Bergmann, Martin S. "Limitations of Method in Psychoanalytic Biography: A Historical Enquiry." *Journal of the American Psychoanalytic Association*, 21 (1973), 833–850.

Binstock, William A. "Purgation through Pity and Terror." *International Journal of Psychoanalysis*, 54 (1973), 499–504, and 56 (1975), 225–227.

Brantlinger, Patrick, "Romances, Novels, and Psychoanalysis." *Criticism*, 17 (1975), 15–40.

David, Michel. *Letteratura e psicanalisi*. Milan: Mursia, 1967.

Deltmering, Peter. *Dichtung und Psychoanalyse*. Munich: Wilhelm Fink, 1969.

Ehrenzweig, Anton. *The Psychoanalysis of Artistic Vision and Hearing*. New York: George Braziller, 1965.

———. *The Hidden Order of Art*. Berkeley: University of California Press, 1967. 2d ed., 1979.

Eissler, Kurt R. "The Function of Details in the Interpretation of Works of Literature." *Psychoanalytic Quarterly*, 28 (1959), 1–20.

Grimaud, Michel. 'Psychology, Language, Esthetics, Computers: Critical Notes." *Sub-Stance*, no. 25 (1980), pp. 111–117. [Reviews nonpsychoanalytic literary theory.]

Hamilton, James W. "Transitional Fantasies and the Creative Process." *Psychoanalytic Study of Society*, 6 (1975), 53–70.

Havelka, Jaroslav. *The Nature of the Creative Process in Art*. Amsterdam: Martinus Nijhoff, 1968.

*Holland, Norman N. *Psychoanalysis and Shakespeare*. New York: McGraw-Hill, 1964.

*———. *The Dynamics of Literary Response*. New York: Oxford University Press, 1968.

———. *Poems in Persons*. New York: Norton, 1973. [Includes a short bibliographical survey of psychoanalysis and literature.]

———. *5 Readers Reading*. New Haven: Yale University Press, 1975.

*Kaplan, Morton, and Robert Kloss. *The Unspoken Motive: A Guide to Psychoanalytic Literary Criticism*. New York: Free Press, 1973.

*Kris, Ernst. *Psychoanalytic Explorations in Art*. New York: Schocken Books, 1964.

Kubie, Lawrence S. *Neurotic Distortion of the Creative Process*. Lawrence: University of Kansas Press, 1958.

*Lesser, Simon O. *Fiction and the Unconscious*. Boston: Beacon Press, 1957.

Martindale, Colin. *Romantic Progression: The Psychology of Literary History*. Washington D.C.: Hemisphere Publishing Corporation, 1975.

———. "Preface: Psychological Contributions to Poetics." *Poetics*, 7 (1978), 121–133.

Noy, Pinchas. "A Theory of Art and Esthetic Experience." *Psychoanalytic Review*, 55 (1968), 623–645.

———. "About Art and Artistic Talent." *International Journal of Psychoanalysis*, 53 (1972), 243–249.

Peller, Lili E. "Libidinal Phases, Ego Development, and Play." *Psychoanalytic Study of the Child*, 9 (1954), 178–198.

Prescott, Peter. *The Poetic Mind*. Boston: Four Seas, 1912.

Rank, Otto. *The Myth of the Birth of the Hero and Other Essays*. 1909. Reprint. New York: Vintage Books, 1959.

——. *Das Inzest-Motiv in Dichtung und Sage*. 2d ed. 1926. Reprint. Darmstadt: Wissenschaftliche Buchgesellschaft, 1974.

Rogers, Robert. *The Double in Literature*. Detroit: Wayne State University Press, 1970.

*Roland, Alan, ed. *Psychoanalysis, Creativity, and Literature: A French-American Inquiry*. New York: Columbia University Press, 1978. [See Roland's "Towards a Reorientation of Psychoanalytic Literature Criticism."]

*Swan, Jim. "Giving New Depth to the Surface: Psychoanalysis, Literature, and Society." *Psychoanalytic Review*, 62 (1975), 5–28.

Thoma-Herterich, Christa. *Zur Kritik der Psychokritik: Eine literaturwissenschaftliche Auseinandersetzung am Beispiel französischer Arbeiten*. Bern: Herbert Lang, 1976.

Urban, Bernd. *Psychoanalyse und Literatur Wissenschaft*. Tübingen: Max Niemeyer Verlag, 1975.

10. Literary Applications of Theoretical Interest

Bettelheim, Bruno. *The Uses of Enchantment: The Meaning and Importance of Fairy Tales*. New York: Knopf, 1976. [See Howard Gardner, below.]

Eissler, Kurt R. *Leonardo da Vinci: Psychoanalytic Notes on an Enigma*. New York: International Universities Press, 1961.

——. *Discourse on Hamlet and Hamlet*. New York: International Universities Press, 1971.

Fraiberg, Selma. "Tales of Discovery of the Secret Treasure." *Psychoanalytic Study of the Child*, 9 (1954), 220–241.

Gardner, Howard. "Brief on Behalf of Fairy Tales." *Semiotica*, 21 (1977), 363–380. [On Bettelheim's *Uses of Enchantment*.]

Hamilton, James W. "Object Loss, Dreaming, and Creativity: The Poetry of John Keats." *Psychoanalytic Study of the Child*, 24 (1969), 488–531.

Kahn, Coppelia. *Man's Estate: Masculine Identity in Shakespeare*. Berkeley: University of California Press, 1981.

Kiell, Norman. *The Adolescent through Fiction*. New York: International Universities Press, 1959.

——. *Varieties of Sexual Experience: Psychosexuality in Literature*. New York: International Universities Press, 1976.

Kofman, Sarah. *Quatre romans analytiques*. Paris: Galilée, 1974. [On Jensen's *Gradiva*, Hoffmann's *Sandmann*, and Freud.]

Rogers, Robert. *Metaphor: A Psychoanalytic View*. Berkeley: University of California Press, 1978.

11. French Literary Theory

Anzieu, Didier, ed. *Psychanalyse du génie créateur.* Paris: Dunod, 1974.

Baudouin, Charles. *Psychanalyse de l'art.* Paris: PUF, 1929.

Baudry, Jean-Louis. "Freud et la 'Création littéraire.'" In *Théorie d'ensemble,* edited by Tel Quel. Paris: Editions du Seuil, 1968.

Bellemin-Noël, Jean. *Psychanalyse et littérature.* Paris: PUF, 1978.

Berge, André, Anne Clancier, *et al. Entretiens sur l'art et la psychanalyse.* Paris: Mouton, 1968.

Chasseguet-Smirgel, Janine. *Pour une psychanalyse de l'art et de la créativité.* Paris: Payot, 1971.

*Clancier, Anne. *Psychanalyse et critique littéraire.* Toulouse: Privat, 1973.

Dracoulides, Nicolas N. *Psychanalyse de l'artiste et de son oeuvre.* Genève: Editions du Mont Blanc, 1952. [Of historical interest only.]

Fernandez, Dominique. *L'Arbre jusqu'aux racines: Psychanalyse et création.* Paris: Bernard Grasset, 1972.

Fónagy, Ivan. "Les Bases pulsionnelles de la phonation." *Revue française de psychanalyse,* 34 (1970), 101–136, and 35 (1971), 543–591. [Naïve but influential.]

Genette, Gérard. "Psycholectures." In *Figures.* Paris: Editions du Seuil, 1966. [On Charles Mauron.]

Georgin, Robert. *La Structure et le style.* Geneva: L'Age d'homme, 1975.

Gohin, Yves. "Progrès et problèmes de la psychanalyse littéraire." *La Pensée,* no. 215 (1980), pp. 58–81.

Green, André. "Idealization and Catharsis." *Psychoanalytic Study of Society,* 6 (1975), 11–19.

———. *The Tragic Effect: The Oedipus Complex in Tragedy.* New York: Cambridge University Press, 1979. [Racine, Shakespeare, Greek plays.]

Grimaud, Michel. "La Rhétorique du rêve: Swann et la psychanalyse." *Poétique,* no. 33 (1978), pp. 90–106. [A dream in Proust.]

*———. "Psychologie et littérature." In *Théorie de la littérature,* edited by Aron Kibédi Varga, pp. 256–281. Paris: A. et J. Picard, 1981.

*Kofman, Sarah. *L'Enfance de l'art: Une interprétation de l'esthétique freudienne.* Paris: Payot, 1970.

Kristeva, Julia. *Semiotike: Recherches pour une sémanalyse.* Paris: Editions du Seuil, 1969.

Le Galliot, Jean. *Psychanalyse et langages littéraires: Théorie et pratique.* Paris: Nathan, 1977.

Lyotard, Jean-François. *Discours, Figure.* Paris: Klincksieck, 1971.

*Mannoni, Octave. *Clefs pour l'imaginaire ou l'autre scène.* Paris: Editions du Seuil, 1969.

*Mauron, Charles. *Des métaphores obsédantes au mythe personnel.* Paris: José Corti, 1963.

———. *Psychocritique du genre comique.* Paris: José Corti, 1964.

———. "Note Annexe." In *Le Dernier Baudelaire.* Paris: José Corti, 1966. [On his method. A discussion and complete bibliography of Mauron

will be found in Clancier, above; see also Genette, Georgin, and Mehlman in this section and Thoma-Herterich in section 9.]
Mehlman, Jeffrey. "Entre psychanalyse et psychocritique." *Poétique*, no. 3 (1970), pp. 365–383.
Mendel, Gérard. "Le Roman comme fiction et comme ensemble: A propos des 'Souvenirs du Colonel de Maumort' de Roger Martin du Gard." *Revue française de psychanalyse*, 28 (1964), 729–779.
Metz, Christian. *Le Signifiant imaginaire*. Paris: U.G.E., 1977.
Milner, Max. *Freud et l'interprétation de la littérature*. Paris: C.D.U.-SEDES, 1980.
Revue française de psychanalyse:
    La créativité, 36, no. 4 (1972).
    L'humour, 37, no. 4 (1973).
    Esthétiques, 38, no. 1 (1974).
*Robert, Marthe. *The Origins of the Novel*. Translated by Sacha Rabinovitch. Bloomington: Indiana University Press, 1980.
Semiotext(e)
    Ego traps/Theory of literature, 1, no. 3 (1975).
    Anti-Oedipus: From Psychoanalysis to Schizopolitics, 2, no. 3 (1977).
Soriano, Marc. "Le Premier des Contes de Perrault ou la psychanalyse comme méthode d'identification." *Nouvelle revue de psychanalyse*, no. 4 (1971), pp. 179–202.
Wells, Charles Verlin. "Psychoanalysis in French Literary Criticism, 1920–1939." Ph.D. dissertation, University of California, Berkeley, 1960.

12. Literary Criticism (French Authors)

André, Robert. *Ecriture et pulsions dans le roman stendhalien*. Paris: Klincksieck, 1977.
Anzieu, Didier. "Julien Gracq, les figures de la position dépressive et le procès de la symbolisation." *Etudes philosophiques*, no. 3 (1971), 291–303.
———. "Les Traces du corps dans l'écriture: Une étude psychanalytique du style narratif." Chapter 8 of *Psychanalyse et langage*. Paris: Dunod, 1977. [On Alain Robbe-Grillet.]
Baudouin, Charles. *Psychanalyse de Victor Hugo*. Paris: Armand Colin, 1972.
Bellemin-Noël, Jean. *Vers l'inconscient du texte*. Paris: PUF, 1979. [Jules Verne, Proust, Gautier, Verlaine, Mérimée.]
Bem, Jeanne. "Psychanalyse et poétique baudelairienne." *Poétique*, no. 25 (1976), pp. 31–35.
*Chaitin, Gilbert D. *The Unhappy Few: The Psychological Novels of Stendhal*. Bloomington: Indiana University Press, 1972.
———. "The Voices of the Dead: Love, Death, and Politics in Zola's

Fortune des Rougon.'' Literature and Psychology, 26 (1976), 131–144, 148–158.

_____. "De l'autobiographie au roman: Quelques remarques sur la création chez Stendhal." *Stendhal Club*, 21 (1979), 99–108. [*The Red and the Black.*]

_____. "Châtiment et scène primitive: Le contre-sens de l' 'Expiation.' " *Revue des lettres modernes: Série Victor Hugo*, 1 (1982).

Costes, Alain. *Albert Camus ou la parole manquante.* Paris: Payot, 1973.

de Mijolla, Alain. "La Désertion du capitaine Rimbaud." *Revue française de psychanalyse*, 39 (1975), 427–458.

Doubrovsky, Serge. *La Place de la Madeleine.* Paris: Mercure de France, 1974. [On Marcel Proust.]

*_____. " 'The Nine of Hearts': Fragment of a Psychoreading of [Sartre's] *La Nausée.*" In *Psychoanalysis, Creativity, and Literature*, edited by Alan Roland. New York: Columbia University Press, 1978.

*_____. *Parcours critique.* Paris: Editions Galilée, 1980. [On Claude Simon, Racine, Proust, La Rochefoucauld.]

Enriquez, Eugène. "Le Gardien des clés: Système et volupté chez Sade." *Topique*, no. 19 (1977), pp. 117–162.

Felman, Shoshana. *La Folie et la chose littéraire.* Paris: Seuil, 1978. [On Nerval, Rimbaud, Balzac, Flaubert.]

Fitch, Brian T. *L'Etranger d'Albert Camus.* Paris: Larousse, 1972.

Grimaud, Michel. "Petite psychanalyse du *Cid.*" *Sub-Stance*, no. 3 (1972), pp. 77–84. [On Pierre Corneille.]

_____. "Les Mystères du *Ptyx*: Hypothèses sur la remotivation psychopoétique à partir de Mallarmé et Hugo." *Michigan Romance Studies*, 1 (1980), 98–162.

Hofling, Charles K. "On Camus's *L'Etranger.*" In *The Human Mind Revisited*, edited by Sydney Smith, pp. 159–203. New York: International Universities Press, 1978.

Leites, Nathan. "Trends in Affectlessless." In *Art and Psychoanalysis*, edited by William Phillips, pp. 247–267. New York: Meridian Books, 1963. [On Camus' *L'Etranger.*]

Lejeune, Philippe. "Ecriture et sexualité." *Europe*, no. 502–503 (1971), pp. 113–143. [On the "madeleine" episode in Proust.]

Lesser, Simon O. "The Role of Unconscious Understanding in Flaubert and Doestoevsky." *Daedalus*, 92 (1963), 363–382.

*Mauron, Charles. *Manon Lescaut et le mélange des genres.* Actes du colloque d'Aix sur l'Abbé Prévost. Annales de la Faculté no. 50. Aix: Editions Ophrys, 1965.

_____. *L'Inconscient dans l'oeuvre et la vie de Jean Racine.* Paris: José Corti, 1969.

Mauron, Claude. *Le Jeu de la feuillée: Etude psychocritique.* Paris: José Corti, 1973.

*Meares, Russell. "Beckett, Sarraute, and the Perceptual Experience of Schizophrenia." *Psychiatry*, 36 (1973), 61–69.

Nelson, Benjamin. "Sartre, Genet, Freud." *Psychoanalytic Review*, 50 (1963), 505–521.

——. "Avant-garde Dramatists from Ibsen to Ionesco." *Psychoanalytic Review*, 55 (1968), 505–512.

Porter, Laurence M. *The Literary Dream in French Romanticism: A Psychoanalytic Interpretation*. Detroit: Wayne State University Press, 1979. [Nerval, Lautréamont, Flaubert, Nodier.]

*Ragland-Sullivan, Mary Eloise. "Julien's Quest for 'Self': *Qui Suis-je?*" *Nineteenth-Century French Studies*, 8 (1979), 1–13. [On Stendhal's *The Red and the Black*.]

——. "The Psychology of Narcissism: Jean Genet's *The Maids*." *Gradiva*, 2 (1979), 19–40.

Richard, Jean-Pierre. "Feu rué, feu scintillé." In *Microlectures*. Paris: Editions du Seuil, 1979. [On Mallarmé.]

Speziale-Bagliacca, Roberto. "Monsieur Bovary, c'est moi: Portrait psychanalytique de Charles Bovary, masochiste moral." *Revue française de psychanalyse*, 38 (1974), 669–705.

*Starobinski, Jean. "L'Interprète et son cercle." *Nouvelle revue de psychanalyse*, no. 1 (1970), pp. 7–23. [On Book III of J.-J. Rousseau's *Confessions*.]

Sterba, Editha. "The Schoolboy Suicide in André Gide's novel *The Counterfeiters*." *American Imago*, 8 (1951), 307–320.

*Tolpin, Marian. "Eugène Ionesco's *The Chairs* and the Theater of the Absurd." *American Imago*, 25 (1968), 119–139.

Valeros, J. A. "On Masturbation: A Study of Jean Genet's *Our Lady of the Flowers*." *Psychiatric Quarterly*, 42 (1968), 252–262.

Verhoeff, Han. "Les Comédies de Corneille: Problématique du genre à la lumière de la psychanalyse." *Littérature*, no. 31 (1978), pp. 77–89.

Viderman, Serge. "La Plaie et le couteau: L'Ecriture ambiguë de Jean Genet." *Revue française de psychanalyse*, 38 (1974), 137–151.

13. French Psychoanalysis, Philosophy, and the Social Sciences

Assour, Paul-Laurent. *Freud et Nietzsche*. Paris: PUF, 1980.

Besançon, Alain. *Histoire et expérience du moi*. Paris: Flammarion, 1971.

*——, ed. *L'Histoire psychanalytique: Une anthologie*. Paris: Mouton, 1974.

Dadoun, Roger. *Géza Roheim et l'essor de l'anthropologie psychanalytique*. Paris: Payot, 1972.

Irigaray, Luce. *Speculum: De l'autre femme*. Paris: Editions de Minuit, 1974. [Freud, philosophy, and feminism.]

Kaufmann, Pierre. *Psychanalyse et théorie de la culture*. Paris: Denoël, 1974.

Kofman, Sarah. *L'Enigme de la femme*. Paris: Editions Galilée, 1980. [Freud and women by a philosopher. See also Juliet Mitchell in section 6.]

Mauco, Georges. "Origine et fonction de la culture par Géza Roheim." *Revue française de psychanalyse,* 36 (1972), 524–528.

———. "L'Expression des pulsions dans une société indienne." *Revue française de psychanalyse,* 37 (1973), 269–279.

*Mendel, Gérard. *Anthropologie différentielle: Vers une anthropologie socio-psychanalytique.* Paris: Payot, 1972.

*———. *La Révolte contre le père: Une introduction à la sociopsychanalyse.* Paris: Payot, 1972.

Moscovici, Serge. *La Psychanalyse, son image, son public.* Paris: PUF, 1976.

Nacht, Sacha, René Diatkine, and Pierre Racamier. "Psychanalyse et sociologie." *Revue française de psychanalyse,* 21 (1957), 244–282.

Valabrega, Jean-Pierre. "L'Anthropologie psychanalytique." *La Psychanalyse,* 3 (1957), 221–246.

Bibliography of Works Cited

Adler, Alfred. *The Neurotic Constitution*. Translated by Barbara Glueck and John Lind. New York: Dodd, Mead, 1926.

Baddeley, Alan D. *The Psychology of Memory*. New York: Basic Books, 1976.

Bart, Benjamin F. "Flaubert and Hunting: *La Légende de Saint Julien l'Hospitalier*." *Nineteenth-Century French Studies*, 4 (1975–1976), 31–52.

———. "Psyche into Myth: Humanity and Animality in Flaubert's *Saint-Julien*." *Kentucky Romance Quarterly*, 20 (1973), 317–342.

———, and Robert F. Cook. *The Legendary Sources of Flaubert's "Saint Julien."* Toronto: University of Toronto Press, 1977.

Bart, Heidi Culbertson, and Benjamin F. Bart. "Space, Time, and Reality in Flaubert's *Saint Julien*." *Romanic Review*, 59 (1968), 30–39.

Barthes, Roland. *Le Degré zéro de l'écriture*. Utrecht, Holland: Gonthier, 1968.

———. *S/Z*. Paris: Editions du Seuil, 1970.

Basch, Michael Franz. "Developmental Psychology and Explanatory Theory in Psychoanalysis." *Annual of Psychoanalysis*, 15 (1977), 229–263.

Bateson, Gregory. "Towards a Theory of Schizophrenia." In *Steps to an Ecology of Mind*. San Francisco: Chandler, 1972.

Beaugrande, Robert de. *Text, Discourse, and Process*. Norwood, N.J.: Ablex, 1980.

———, and Benjamin Colby. "Narrative Models of Action and Interaction." *Cognitive Science*, 3 (1979), 43–66.

Bellemin-Noël, Jean. " 'Psychanalyser' le rêve de Swann?" *Poétique*, no. 8 (1971), pp. 447–469.

Benveniste, Emile. *Problèmes de linguistique générale*. 2 volumes. Paris: Editions de Minuit, 1974.

———. *Problems in General Linguistics*. Translated by Mary E. Meek. Coral Gables, Fla.: Miami University Press, 1971.

Berg, William. "Cryptographie et communication dans *La Chartreuse de Parme*." *Stendhal Club*, 78 (1978), 170–182.

Bergeret, Jean. *La Personnalité normale et pathologique*. Paris: Dunod, 1974.

Bertrand, Marc. "Parole et silence dans les 'Trois contes' de Flaubert." *Stanford French Review*, 1 (1977), 191–204.

Bettelheim, Bruno. *The Uses of Enchantment: The Meaning and Importance of Fairy Tales*. New York: Knopf, 1976.

Bowlby, John. *Attachment and Loss*. 3 volumes. New York: Basic Books, 1969–1980.

Brombert, Victor. *The Novels of Flaubert: A Study of Themes and Techniques*. Princeton: Princeton University Press, 1966.

Caldwell, Richard. "The Blindness of Oedipus." *International Review of Psychoanalysis*, 1 (1974), 207–218.

Carlut, Charles. *Concordance to Flaubert's "Trois contes."* New York: Garland, 1980.

———, ed. *Essais sur Flaubert: En l'honneur du professeur Don Demorest*. Paris: Nizet, 1979.

Chaitin, Gilbert D. *The Unhappy Few: The Psychological Novels of Stendhal*. Bloomington: Indiana University Press, 1972.

Cohen, Gillian. "The Psychology of Reading." *New Literary History*, 4 (1972), 75–90.

Costes, Alain. *Albert Camus ou la parole manquante*. Paris: Payot, 1973.

Debray-Genette, Raymonde. "Du mode narratif dans les *Trois contes*." *Littérature*, no. 2 (1971), pp. 39–62.

Dewald, Paul. *The Psychoanalytic Process: A Case Illustration*. New York: Basic Books, 1972.

Diatkine, René, and Janine Simon. *La Psychanalyse précoce: Le processus psychanalytique chez l'enfant*. Rev. ed. Paris: Presses Universitaires de France, 1973.

Dijk, Teun van. *Macrostructures: An Interdisciplinary Study of Global Structures in Discourse, Interaction, and Cognition*. Hillsdale, N.J.: Lawrence Erlbaum, 1980.

Dubois, Jacques. "Code, texte, métatexte." *Littérature*, no. 12 (1973), pp. 3–11.

———, et al. *Rhétorique générale*. Paris: Larousse, 1970.

Duckworth, Colin, ed. *Trois contes*. London: Harrap, 1959.

Edinger, Edward F. *Ego and Archetype: Individuation and the Religious Function of the Psyche*. 1972. Reprint. Baltimore: Penguin Books, 1973.

Eidelberg, Ludwig. *Encyclopedia of Psychoanalysis*. New York: Free Press, 1968.

Eissler, Kurt R. *Goethe: A Psychoanalytic Study (1775–1786)*. Detroit: Wayne State University Press, 1963.

Ellis, John M. *The Theory of Literary Criticism: A Logical Analysis*. Berkeley: University of California Press, 1974.

Esman, Aaron H. "The Primal Scene: A Review and Reconsideration." *Psychoanalytic Study of the Child*, 28 (1973), 49–81.

Ferguson, George. *Signs and Symbols in Christian Art*. New York: Oxford University Press, 1966.

Flaubert, Gustave. *Correspondance*. Edited by Jean Bruneau. 2 volumes. Paris: Gallimard, 1973–1980.

———. *Correspondance*. 9 volumes. Paris: L. Conard, 1926–1933.

———. *La Légende de Saint Julien l'Hospitalier*. In *Trois contes*. Paris: G. Charpentier, 1877.

Translations of *La Légende de Saint Julien l'Hospitalier*:

Arthur McDowall. London: Chatto & Windus, 1923; New York: Knopf and New Directions, 1924, 1944, etc.

Anonymous. In *Complete Works of Flaubert*. London: Privately printed, 1926.

Mervyn Savill. London: Arthur Baker, 1950.

Frederick Dupee. In *Great French Short Novels*. New York: Dial Press, 1952.

Robert Baldick. New York: Penguin, 1961.

Walter Cobb. New York: New American Library, 1964.

Michel Grimaud. Included here. In our references, the roman numeral (I, II, or III) designates the section of the story, the arabic numeral the paragraph, where the quotation can be found.

———. *Oeuvres*. Edited by Albert Thibaudet and René Dumesnil. 2 volumes. Paris: Pléiade, 1952.

———. *Oeuvres de jeunesse inédites*. 3 volumes. Paris: L. Conard, 1910.

———. *Salammbô*. Edited by Edouard Maynial. Paris: Garnier, 1961.

———. *Trois contes*. Edited by Edouard Maynial. Paris: Garnier, 1961.

Freud, Anna. *The Ego and the Mechanisms of Defense*. 1936. Rev. ed. New York: International Universities Press, 1966.

Freud, Sigmund. *The Standard Edition of the Complete Psychological Works of Sigmund Freud*. Translated by James Strachey, Anna Freud, and Alan Tyson. Edited by James Strachey. 24 volumes. London: Hogarth Press, 1953–1974.

Fromm, Erich. *Man for Himself*. New York: Fawcett World Library, 1947.

Gediman, Helen K. "Narcissistic Trauma, Object Loss, and the Family Romance." *Psychoanalytic Review*, 61 (1974), 169–202.

Genette, Gérard. *Figures III*. Paris: Editions du Seuil, 1972.

Giraud, Jean. "La Genèse d'un chef-d'oeuvre: 'La Légende de Saint Julien l'Hospitalier.'" *Revue d'histoire littéraire de la France*, Jan.–March 1919, pp. 87–93.

Green, André. *Un oeil en trop*. Paris: Minuit, 1969.

———. "Surface Analysis, Deep Analysis." *International Review of Psychoanalysis*, 1 (1974), 415–424.

Greenson, Ralph. *The Technique and Practice of Psychoanalysis.* New York: International Universities Press, 1967.

Greenspan, Stanley I. "The Oedipal–Pre-Oedipal Dilemma: A Reformulation according to Object Relations Theory." *International Review of Psychoanalysis,* 4 (1977), 381–392.

Greimas, Algirdas J. *Essais de sémiotique poétique.* Paris: Larousse, 1972.

———. *Maupassant: La sémiotique du texte: Exercices pratiques.* Paris: Editions du Seuil, 1976.

———. *Sémantique structurale.* Paris: Larousse, 1966.

Grimaud, Michel. "The Framework for a Science of Texts: The Compleat Semiotician." *Semiotica,* 1981–82.

———. "Préliminaires pour une psycholinguistique des discours: Le Champ de la poétique." *Langue française,* no. 49 (1981), pp. 14–29.

———. "Prosopopée de Sainte Sophie, patronne des poéticiennes (Vers une science des textes)." *Poétique,* no. 43 (1980), pp. 372–392.

———. "Psychoanalysis, Contemporary Science, and the Quandaries of Psychocriticism." *Literature and Psychology,* 27 (1977), 183–189.

———. "Psychologie et littérature." In *Théorie de la littérature,* edited by Aron Kibédi Varga, pp. 256–281. Paris: A. et J. Picard, 1981.

———. "La Rhétorique du rêve: Swann et la psychanalyse." *Poétique,* no. 33 (1978), pp. 90–106.

Hamon, Philippe. "Clausales." *Poétique,* no. 24 (1975), pp. 495–526.

Hanouelle, Marie-Julie. "Quelques manifestations du discours dans *Trois contes.*" *Poétique,* no. 9 (1972), pp. 41–49.

Hansen, Kirsten Lund. "*St. Julien l'Hospitalier* ou l'Oedipe de Flaubert, ou encore: Le Bestiaire de 'Trois contes.'" *(Pré)Publications* (Aarhus), no. 1 (1973), pp. 7–18.

Holland, Norman N. *The Dynamics of Literary Response.* New York: Oxford University Press, 1968. Reprint. New York: Norton, 1973.

———. *5 Readers Reading.* New Haven: Yale University Press, 1975.

———. "Shakespearean Tragedy and the Three Ways of Psychoanalytic Criticism." In *Psychoanalysis and Literature,* edited by Hendrik Ruitenbeek. New York: Dutton, 1964.

Issacharoff, Michael. " 'Trois contes' et le problème de la non-linéarité." *Littérature,* no. 15 (1974), pp. 27–40.

Izard, Carroll. *Human Emotions.* New York: Plenum Press, 1977.

Jacobson, Roman. "Linguistics and Poetics." In *Style in Language,* edited by Thomas A. Sebeok, pp. 350–377. Cambridge, Mass.: M.I.T. Press, 1960.

Jasinski, René. "Sur le 'Saint Julien l'Hospitalier' de Flaubert." *Revue d'histoire de la philosophie,* April 15, 1935, pp. 156–172.

Jean, Raymond. "Ouvertures, phrases-seuils." *Critique,* no. 288 (1971), pp. 421–431.

Jung, C. G. *The Collected Works of C. G. Jung.* Edited by Sir Herbert Read, Michael Fordham, and Gerhard Adler. Bollingen Series 20. 20 volumes. New York: Pantheon Books, 1953–1979. [This edition of the *Collected Works* was reprinted, with the same pagination, by Princeton University Press, beginning in 1967.]

———. *Contributions to Analytical Psychology*. New York: Harcourt, Brace and Co., 1928.

Kaplan, Linda Joan. "The Concept of the Family Romance." *Psychoanalytic Review*, 61 (1974), 203–216.

Kaplan, Morton, and Robert Kloss. *The Unconscious Motive: A Guide to Psycho-Analytic Literary Criticism*. New York: Free Press, 1973.

Kellman, Steven. "Grand Openings and Plain: The Poetics of First Lines." *Sub-Stance*, no. 17 (1977), pp. 139–148.

Keppler, Carl Francis. *The Literature of the Second Self*. Tucson: Arizona University Press, 1972.

Kohut, Heinz. *The Analysis of the Self*. New York: International Universities Press, 1971.

———. *The Restoration of the Self*. New York: International Universities Press, 1977.

Lacan, Jacques. *Ecrits: A Selection*. Translated by Alan Sheridan. New York: Norton, 1977.

———. "Fonction et champ de la parole et du langage en psychanalyse." In *Ecrits I*. Paris: Editions du Seuil, Collection Points, 1971.

———. "L'Instance de la lettre dans l'inconscient." In *Ecrits*. Paris: Editions du Seuil, 1966.

———. *Le Séminaire: Livre II*. Paris: Editions du Seuil, 1978.

———. "Seminar on [Poe's] 'Purloined Letter.'" *Yale French Studies*, no. 48 (1972), pp. 38–72.

Lakoff, George, and Mark Johnson. *Metaphors We Live By*. Chicago: University of Chicago Press, 1980.

Leach, Edmund. "Virgin Birth." In *Genesis and Other Myths*. New York: Grossman, 1969.

Lecointre-Dupont, G. F. G. "La Légende de Saint Julien le Pauvre, d'après un manuscrit de la Bibliothèque d'Alençon." *Mémoires de la Société des Antiquaires de l'Ouest* (Poitiers) for the year 1838, pp. 190–210.

Lesser, Simon O. *Fiction and the Unconscious*. Boston: Beacon Press, 1957.

Levin, Samuel R. *Linguistic Structures in Poetry*. New York: Mouton, 1962.

Lindsay, Peter, and Donald Norman. *Human Information Processing*. New York: Academic Press, 1977.

McDevitt, John B., and Calvin F. Settlage, eds. *Separation-Individuation: Essays in Honor of Margaret S. Mahler*. New York: International Universities Press, 1971.

Margolis, Marvin. "Preliminary Report of a Case of Consummated Mother-Son Incest." *Annual of Psychoanalysis*, 5 (1977), 267–293.

Martindale, Colin. "Preface: Psychological Contributions to Poetics." *Poetics*, no. 7 (1978), pp. 121–133.

———. *Romantic Progression: The Psychology of Literary History*. New York: Halsted Press, 1975.

Mauron, Charles. *Des Métaphores obsédantes au mythe personel*. Paris: José Corti, 1963.

——. "Les Personnages de Victor Hugo: Etude psychocritique." In *Victor Hugo: Oeuvres complètes,* Vol. II. Paris: Le Club français du livre, 1967.

——. "Psychocriticism." Translated by Barbara Blackbourn. *Sub-Stance,* no. 3 (1972), pp. 53–59.

Mullahy, Patrick. *Oedipus/Myth and Complex.* New York: Grove Press, 1948.

Neisser, Ulric. *Cognitive Psychology.* New York: Appleton-Century-Crofts, 1967.

Neumann, Erich. *The Child: Structure and Dynamics of the Nascent Personality.* New York: G. P. Putnam's Sons, 1973.

——. "Creative Man and Transformation." In *Art and the Creative Unconscious.* Bollingen Series 61. Princeton: Princeton University Press, 1971.

——. *The Origins and History of Consciousness.* Bollingen Series 42. Princeton: Princeton University Press, 1970.

Noy, Pinchas. "About Art and Artistic Talent." *International Journal of Psychoanalysis,* 53 (1972), 243–249.

——. "A Revision of the Psychoanalytic Theory of the Primary Process." *International Journal of Psychoanalysis,* 50 (1969), 155–178.

——. "Symbolism and Mental Representation." *Annual of Psychoanalysis,* 1 (1973), 125–158.

——. "A Theory of Art and Esthetic Experience." *Psychoanalytic Review,* 55 (1968), 623–645.

Nykrog, Per. "Les 'Trois contes' dans l'évolution de la structure thématique chez Flaubert." *Romantisme,* no. 6 (1973), pp. 55–66.

Ornstein, Paul. "On Narcissism: Beyond the Introduction." *Annual of Psychoanalysis,* 2 (1974), 127–149.

Peterfreund, Emanuel. *Information, Systems, and Psychoanalysis. Psychological Issues,* monograph 25/26, 1971.

Pratt, Mary-Louise. *Toward A Speech-Act Theory of Literary Discourse.* Bloomington: Indiana University Press, 1977.

Raitt, Alan W. "The Composition of Flaubert's 'Saint Julien l'Hospitalier.'" *French Studies,* 19 (1965), 358–372.

Rank, Otto. *Das Inzest-Motiv in Dichtung und Sage.* 2d ed. 1926. Reprint. Darmstadt: Wissenschaftliche Buchgesellschaft, 1974.

——. *"Will Therapy"* and *"Truth and Reality."* Translated by Jessie Taft. New York: Knopf, 1968.

Rengstorf, Michael. "Les 'Trois contes' de Flaubert: Essai de sémiotique narrative." Ph.D. dissertation, State University of New York at Buffalo, 1976.

Richards, Ivor A. *The Philosophy of Rhetoric.* New York: Oxford University Press, 1965.

Riffaterre, Michael. "The Poetic Functions of Intertextual Humor." *Romanic Review,* 65 (1974), 78–93.

——. *La Production du texte.* Paris: Editions du Seuil, 1979.

———. *The Semiotics of Poetry.* Bloomington: Indiana University Press, 1978.

———. "The Stylistic Approach to Literary History." *New Literary History,* 2 (1970), 39–55.

Robert, Marthe. *The Origins of the Novel.* Translated by Sacha Rabinovitch. Bloomington: Indiana University Press, 1980.

———. *Roman des origines et origines du roman.* Paris: Grasset, 1972.

Rogers, Robert. *The Double in Literature.* Detroit: Wayne State University Press, 1970.

Rosenblatt, Alan, and James Thickstun. *Modern Psychoanalytic Concepts in a General Psychology. Psychological Issues,* monograph 42/43, 1977.

Ruitenbeek, Hendrik, ed. *Psychoanalysis and Literature.* New York: Dutton, 1964.

Sandler, Anne-Marie. "Comments on the Significance of Piaget's Work for Psychoanalysis." *International Review of Psychoanalysis,* 2 (1975), 365–378.

Sartre, Jean-Paul. *Being and Nothingness.* Translated by Hazel E. Barnes. New York: Washington Square Press, 1966.

———. *L'Idiot de la famille: Gustave Flaubert de 1821 à 1857.* 3 volumes. Paris: Gallimard, 1971–1972.

———. *Qu'est-ce que la littérature?* Paris: Idées, 1970.

Shepler, Frederic. "La Mort et la rédemption dans les *Trois contes* de Flaubert." *Neophilologus,* 56 (1972), 407–417.

Sherzer, Dina. "Narrative Figures in *La Légende de Saint Julien l'Hospitalier.*" *Genre,* 7 (1974), 54–70.

Smith, Barbara Herrnstein. *Poetic Closure: A Study of How Poems End.* Chicago: University of Chicago Press, 1968.

Smith, Sheila M. "Les Sources de 'La Légende de Saint Julien l'Hospitalier' de Gustave Flaubert." M.A. thesis, Manchester University, 1944.

Starobinski, Jean. Preface to *Hamlet et Oedipe,* by Ernest Jones. Paris: Gallimard, 1967. (*Hamlet and Oedipus.* Garden City, N.Y.: Doubleday, 1954.)

Sussmann, George D. "The Wet-Nursing Business in Nineteenth-Century France." *French Historical Studies,* 9 (1975), 304–328.

Swan, Jim. "Giving New Depth to the Surface: Psychoanalysis, Literature, and Society." *Psychoanalytic Review,* 62 (1975), 5–28.

Terman, David M. "Aggression and Narcissistic Rage: A Clinical Elaboration." *Annual of Psychoanalysis,* 3 (1975), 239–255.

Todorov, Tzvetan. "La Quête du récit." In *Poétique de la prose.* Paris: Editions du Seuil, 1972. (*The Poetics of Prose.* Translated by Richard Howard. Ithaca: Cornell University Press, 1977.)

Tolpin, Marian. "The Daedalus Experience." *Annual of Psychoanalysis,* 2 (1974), 213–228.

Vinaver, Eugène. "Flaubert and the Legend of Saint Julian." *Bulletin of the John Rylands Library* (Manchester), 36 (1953), 228–244.

Vinay, Jean-Paul, and John Darbelnet. *Stylistique comparée du français et de l'anglais.* Paris: Didier, 1958.

Wachtel, Paul. *Psychoanalysis and Behavior Theory.* New York: Basic Books, 1977.

———. "Structure or Transaction? A Critique of the Historical and Intrapsychic Emphasis in Psychoanalytic Thought." *Psychoanalysis and Contemporary Science,* 5 (1976), 101–137.

Wilden, Anthony. *The Language of the Self.* 1968. Reprint. New York: Delta Books, 1975.

Index

In this index we have emphasized concepts (from literary criticism and psychoanalysis) and scenes (from *Saint Julian the Hospitaler*) rather than persons (except for those mentioned at least twice and/or discussed in detail).

SAINT / OEDIPUS

Designed by G. T. Whipple, Jr.
Composed by The Composing Room of Michigan
in 10 point VIP Palatino, 2 points leaded,
with display lines in Palatino.
Printed offset by Thomson-Shore, Inc.
on Warren's Number 66 Text, 50 pound basis.
Bound by John H. Dekker & Sons
in Holliston book cloth
and stamped in Kurz-Hastings foil.

Library of Congress Cataloging in Publication Data

BERG, WILLIAM J.
    Saint/Oedipus: psychocritical approaches to
Flaubert's art.

      Bibliography: p.
      Includes index.
      1. Flaubert, Gustave, 1821–1880. Légende de Saint-
Julien l'hospitalier. I. Grimaud, Michel, 1945–
II. Moskos, George, 1948–   . III. Flaubert, Gustave,
1821–1880. Legende de Saint-Julien l'hospitalier.
English. 1982. IV. Title.
PQ2246.L5B47   843'.8   81-17441
ISBN 0-8014-1383-4   AACR2